American Feasts
Cheese Straws 84
Corn Chowder 104
Conch Salad 142
Carrot Cake 230

FUTURES REHAB®
Napa 707-254-7175
Santa Rosa 707-568-0123

American Feasts

★ The Best of American Regional Cooking ★

American Feasts

★ The Best of American Regional Cooking ★

Sallie Y. Williams

William Morrow and Company, Inc.

New York

◄ *Trout Crepes*

created by Media Projects Incorporated

Design: Blackbirch Graphics
Project Editor: Ellen Coffey
Executive Editor: Carter Smith

Library of Congress Catalog Card Number: 85-61578

ISBN: 0-688-05707-1

Printed in Hong Kong by South China Printing Co.
First U.S. Edition

1   2   3   4   5   6   7   8   9   10

Contents

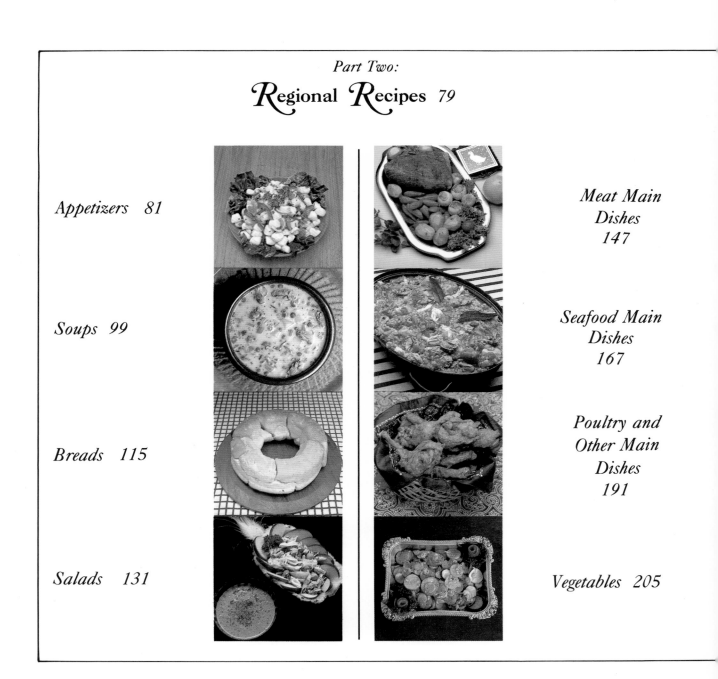

Part Two:
Regional Recipes 79

Introduction to AMERICAN FEASTS

by Sallie Y. Williams

When people ask me about American food, I find that it is much harder to define than Italian or German or Indian food. American cooking is all of these and many more. There are, of course, dishes that are common to the whole country—hamburgers, for example, French fries, spaghetti, fried chicken, and steak, to name a few—but each region has its own very distinct specialties.

Sometimes these regional favorites are the result of one ethnic group's having settled in a small area—the Germans and Swiss who became the "Pennsylvania Dutch" (Deutsch), the Spanish in the Southwest, the French in Louisiana—but often there were other reasons, too, for the development of regional cuisines. Settlers, often low on supplies, food, and equipment, were forced to make the most of whatever native foods were available. They applied their own familiar methods of cooking to these new foods and often produced dishes so good that they have become traditional American foods.

The Thanksgiving Dinner is a classic American feast. This charming representation is Norman Rockwell's "Freedom from Want," one of a series of inspirational "Freedom" posters created during the Second World War.

The inset above shows part of the preparation for a Hawaiian Luau.

A Rhode Island Clambake is quite an undertaking, but the results are well worth the effort.

With each wave of immigration, from the first settlers to the latest arrivals from the Orient, America has welcomed people from all over the world. Not only did each nationality bring with it a culinary heritage; even the first settlers found a flourishing American Indian cuisine when they arrived. In fact, without the Indians' knowledge of how to use the native plants and wildlife for food, the first English-speaking settlers might never have survived to prepare New World foods using Old World methods. And throughout the country, as settlements spread across our continent, new Americans created our cuisines in the various regions of our country.

As a child growing up in the South, I learned to eat soul food practically before I could walk. Even today, nothing is so tempting to me as ham biscuits and grits, which we had for breakfast at my grandmother's house. My father was a career officer in the navy, and our family spent most of my childhood either settling into one new place or moving to another. We crisscrossed the United States by car long before one could travel on a dual-laned concrete ribbon from coast to coast. Fast food then was the blue-plate special in a local diner. Motels were few and far between, but there were small local hotels and guest houses—boardinghouses—whose proprietors often prided themselves on the variety of dishes, including regional specialties, served "family style" at every meal. I don't think there could be a better way to learn about local specialties, and I have fond memories of favorite dishes encountered along the way in our trips across America.

Both my parents loved to cook, and my mother was accomplished at finding the best of local products everyplace we lived, seemingly before the moving van had even pulled away. We never shopped at the local commissary but sought out new eating experiences and new foods in each new region to which we were posted.

This book is intended to introduce these regions of America, along with some of the best-loved dishes of each: crispy fried clams from Rhode Island; foods from the groaning tables of Lancaster County, home of the Pennsylvania Dutch; the fiery dishes and salsas of Tex-Mex concoction. I have tried to include as many as I can of those that I remember with affection, foods I have incorporated in the repertoire of dishes I serve to my family as well as those that are reserved for festive occasions.

Some of these American feasts are feasts in the true sense of the word and are intended for very large groups. Somehow a Rhode Island clambake just isn't the same unless it is intended to feed at least a hundred people. Obviously anything that big must be a joint effort on the part of many, but I have never known people to refuse to help if they knew they would share the bounty when the work was done. Children especially love to pitch in and can often do a great deal to make a party successful. No matter how exotic it may seem, a Hawaiian luau is as

American a feast as a Texas-size barbecue, and just as much fun to create. Though we haven't given instructions for pit-roasting a whole pig, as they do in the islands, there are recipes for making several authentic luau specialties.

If some ingredients for dishes from other regions are not available in your area, you can probably purchase them from mail-order sources. I have included a resource guide at the end of the recipe section that will help you locate some of these special ingredients as well as equipment or other supplies that might help to make your preparation and presentation of these regional menus festive occasions.

I have tried to make it possible for the home cook to travel—tasting and savoring many new flavors along the way—from the coast of New England to the wine country of California and beyond, all without moving from a kitchen stool. The menus I have chosen are intended to create a whole meal with the flavor of one specific region. As the recipe section contains many more than just the recipes included in the menus, you can substitute other regional specialties for one or several menu dishes, or cross from one region to another. The color-coding of recipes by region makes this easy to do. Full-color photographs illustrating many of these menus will provide ideas for presentation and serving, and the recipes are straightforward and easy to follow.

Popular American cuisine is constantly changing, affected by styles and fads from all over the world. But the delicious heritage of traditional local foods is too exciting not to explore and to keep. That is what this book is intended to do. I hope it brings exciting ideas for new foods and festive occasions that will provide many pleasant hours for you, and for your family and friends.

Sallie Y. Williams

Part One

Regional Menus

The Northeast

In New England—a stark, cold region—our forebears developed a cuisine that not only made use of everything available for consumption but created wholesome, unforgettable dishes in the process.

From a very unpromising beginning, when the Pilgrims nearly starved to death before they learned from the American Indians to fish and to grow native crops, the New Englanders became the self-sufficient, well-fed, prosperous group they are to this day.

As in many parts of Colonial North America, the kitchen was the center of the New England household. Corn was the dominant food, first provided by the Indians, who later taught the colonists how to plant it with pumpkins between the rows in order to have two life-sustaining crops growing in the space of one. Fish, clams, and other shellfish were staple foods. And salt fish took such an important place in the New England diet that it was called "Cape Cod turkey."

Pork, brought from England, was the principal meat. Native turkey and other game birds followed close behind. Root vegetables were mainstays, and until molasses and sugar were imported, maple syrup was the only sweetener. The Indians had added the sweet syrup to their dishes long before the Europeans arrived.

The abundance of preserved meats and fish did not mean that meals were dull. Most cooks grew a profusion of herbs, and spices were often used when they were available. New England cooks were imaginative and clever, and devised dozens of ways to vary the standard fare. They developed substantial dishes, foods that prepared them for the rigors of a very demanding life.

These hearty dishes trace their heritage to both sides of the Atlantic. Once the Pilgrims had settled in, they began to return to the recipes and practices of their homeland. Only the raw ingredients were different. Innovative cooks served Yorkshire pudding with roast venison rather than beef, and hearty bannocks made from cornmeal instead of from oats. Improvisation and make-do—the bywords of the stalwart New England spirit—were alive and well in the Colonial kitchen. Many of these recipes are just as practical today as they were three hundred years ago—and just as delicious, too.

Roast Turkey ►

*T*he boiled dinner is classic
New England winter fare. When
snow starts to fly, nothing satis-
fies so well as corned beef and
cabbage. Serve it with a sharp
horseradish and cream sauce for
added zest. If, by chance, you
have corned beef left over, Red
Flannel Hash is a natural for a
next-night family supper.

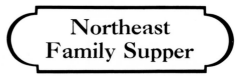

New England Boiled Dinner

Corn Chowder
Corned Beef with
Horseradish Sauce
Onions
Potatoes
Carrots
Cabbage
Cider Baked Apples

Northeast Family Supper

Fried Clams
Red Flannel Hash
Green Beans Supreme
Indian Pudding

*W*arm summer sun, salt sea air, and the feel of sand beneath bare feet mean clambake time. Whether it is a cook-at-home feast for two or four or a steaming pit on the beach for a hundred, the result is superb. Clam Chowder and Fisherman's Pie is a hearty, less rustic alternative to a clambake, and Cob Pie—or Apple Pan Dowdy—is the perfect ending.

Rhode Island Clambake

Steamed Clams
Fish Fillets
Sausages
Potatoes (Sweet and White)
Corn
Watermelon

Fisherman's Dinner

Clam Chowder
Fisherman's Pie
Scalloped Cheese Tomatoes
Cob Pie

*B*aked Beans is a delicious legacy from the early New England settlers. The Indians of the region sweetened the beans with maple syrup. The settlers added salt pork and molasses to the Indians' recipe and then steamed brown bread over the pot for a simple but nourishing treat—an American feast for more than three hundred years. A hearty soup, broiled fish, interesting accompaniments, and a hearty dessert are also longtime New England favorites.

New England Bean Dinner

Baked Beans
Brown Bread and
Parker House Rolls
Green Salad
Assorted Relishes
Lemon Sponge Pudding

Hearty New England Dinner

Sausage and Vegetable Soup
Broiled Scrod
Harvard Beets
Anadama Bread
Strawberry Rhubarb Pie

New England Bean Dinner ➤

Simple and simply delicious, this very New England menu combines the salt sea taste of clams with the homey goodness of Yankee Pot Roast. Johnny-cakes, the "journey cakes" of long ago, are substantial corn-meal pancakes that can be eaten hot with butter and maple syrup or cold in place of bread. Scalloped Fish and Aunt Fanny's Baked Squash are the key elements in a do-ahead dinner perfect for relaxed entertaining after a hard day's work any day of the week.

New England Simple Supper

Deviled Clams
Yankee Pot Roast
Corn Pudding
Johnnycakes
Cranberry Apple Pie

Another Simple Supper

Three Green Salad with Warm Brie
Scalloped Fish
Aunt Fanny's Baked Squash
Maple Syrup Pie

The Middle Atlantic

Middle-Atlantic America can truly be called a melting pot. People from many nations—the Netherlands, Britain, Italy, Ireland, Poland, and many others—have contributed to the growth and success of the states of this region.

As each new group of immigrants settled on these shores, they brought with them centuries of culinary tradition. Faced with a new country, a new language, and new customs, each group looked to their familiar foods for comfort and support. Somehow it was easier to face the New World with an Old World dinner waiting at home.

New York has always been known for fine food, from the days of the stalwart Dutch who first settled on the tip of Manhattan Island to those of the newly arrived Korean greengrocers who today provide New Yorkers with the freshest of fruits and vegetables from all over the world. Great restaurants such as Fraunces Tavern and Delmonico's flourished through the years, and great eaters like Lucius Beebe and Diamond Jim Brady set world records for personal consumption. Today the emphasis is on light and healthy food, and even the most elegant Manhattan restaurants offer dishes to help diners keep waistlines under control while still satisfying body and soul.

The German descendants known as the "Pennsylvania Dutch" came to America in search of religious freedom. They brought with them their love for agriculture and raising livestock, along with a passion for good things to eat. Lancaster County is the center of Pennsylvania Dutch country, and it is still possible to find family-style restaurants where strangers sit together at tables that groan under the burden of meats, vegetables, salads, and desserts and of the traditional seven sweet-and-sour relishes or condiments.

When it comes to seafood, Maryland ranks among the best. The "watermen" who make their living from the Chesapeake Bay have a longstanding love affair with the bay, the sea, and the fish and shellfish they provide for the tables of homes and restaurants all over the East Coast. Maryland crab is a state treasure and finds its way into many local specialty dishes: simply steamed with fragrant hot spices; fried whole when their shells are still soft from moulting; or the meat stirred into cakes, soups, and casseroles.

Those who settled in the Middle-Atlantic region of the United States have made enormous contributions to American cooking. And as they moved westward during the nineteenth century, the pioneers took many of their favorite Eastern recipes with them.

Spicy Crab Soup ►

*H*ere is a hearty cold-weather menu with a decidedly German air. Pennsylvania Dutch (really *Deutsch*, or "German") means good, old-fashioned food with few frills but fabulous taste. This no-crust chicken pot pie is made with *bot boi*—fat, wide noodles. Shoo-fly pie is full of spice and molasses and richly deserves its name. The Lancaster County Dinner has a German accent, too. Schnitz, or dried apples, make a pie unlike any other in the world. Home-dried apples make it even better.

Pennsylvania Dutch Dinner

Yellow Pea Soup
Chicken Pot Pie
Cut Green Beans with Spaetzle
Shaker Bread
Shoo-Fly Pie

Lancaster County Dinner

Snapper Soup
Sauerbraten
*Red Cabbage and Apples
with Port*
Schnitz Pie

Maryland and the Chesapeake Bay seem to be synonymous, for when it comes to seafood, Maryland ranks among the best. Crab is a state treasure, whether steamed with robust spices, tossed into salad, or stirred into a soup. Bluefish, another gift from the bay, can be elegantly delicious when prepared with crabmeat and white wine or richly simple when baked.

Maryland Bluefish Rollups

Dijon Crab Salad
Bluefish Rollups
Carrots
Peas and Onions
Raisin Pie

Eastern Specialties

Asparagus and Crab Soup
Baked Bluefish
Stuffed Baked Tomatoes
Delmonico Potatoes
Strawberries and Meringues

Maryland Bluefish Rollups ▶

$\mathcal{W}$ith so much emphasis today on health and weight control, eating well can sometimes seem difficult. One of these menus was suggested by Jack's, a popular New York restaurant that regularly offers "spa food"— elegant fare that is limited only in calories. Tiny, boned quail halves liven up crunchy salad greens. A charcoal-grilled duck breast tastes more like steak than poultry, with many fewer calories. And fresh oranges topped with beaten egg and just a touch of cream are broiled to puffy perfection. Light City Fare, though simpler, is also a menu for eating wisely and well.

Manhattan Spa Dinner

Quail with Nasturtium Flowers

Grilled Duck Breast

Steamed Baby Vegetables

Gratinéed Oranges à la Monte Carlo

Light City Fare

Vegetables with Caviar Dipping Sauce

Steamed Shrimp

Steamed Baby Vegetables

Zabaglione with Fruit

$\mathcal{S}$unday can be the perfect day
for busy people to entertain.
For a Sunday lunch, some
dishes—such as this menu's
Chicken Hash—can be
prepared ahead of time and
refrigerated. Tiny Philadelphia
Sticky Buns are legendary, and
totally irresistible—the perfect
accompaniment for fresh fruit.
The Mainline Spring Dinner
combines an elegant entrée and
accompaniments with a smooth
and simple dessert.

Philadelphia Sunday Lunch

Chicken Hash
Spinach with Herbs
Fresh Fruit Salad
Sticky Buns

Mainline Spring Dinner

Oysters Casino
Duckling with Orange Sauce
Spinach Soufflé
Popovers
Rice Pudding

The South

In the Deep South, food has always been central to the way of life. No matter how simple the meal had to be, it was an occasion for the whole family to be together, looked upon as a high point in the day. It still is today.

The South has always been blessed with great sources of food. Fish and shellfish abound in the waters of the Atlantic Ocean, the Gulf of Mexico, and in the hundreds of lakes and rivers that meander through the countryside. These last are home to the catfish, a Southern staple that has been gaining in popularity across the country. Game abounds in the forests, and crops are usually plentiful. Any fruit that grows anywhere in the United States grows well somewhere in the South, and Mississippi and Louisiana grow enough rice to satisfy the needs of our own markets and yield surpluses to export to other countries.

Thomas Jefferson—statesman, philosopher, horticulturalist, and farmer—left an indelible mark on Southern cuisine. Besides bringing new fruits and vegetables to America, he developed better methods of raising crops and animals, and he brought the techniques and skills of European cooks to the favorite foods of the New World.

Pork is an essential ingredient in Southern cooking. Lard is the shortening of choice, and many old-time cooks insist that only lard can make the flakiest pastry, the lightest biscuits and the tastiest fried food. Bacon and salt pork figure in many recipes, including most authentic seafood dishes. Pork roasts, pork chops, and, of course, spareribs are local specialties. But the most important contribution pork makes to the Southern diet is ham. Just the thought of an authentic "country ham" makes the mouth water. Ham is sliced paper thin and enjoyed by itself, with greens of any kind, or layered in Baking Powder or Beaten Biscuits, or folded into omelets, or fried with Red-Eye Gravy and served with Grits.

"Soul food"—substantial fare designed to nourish an agrarian society—is the heart of Southern home cooking. Though simple and basic, it incorporates not only the English heritage of some Southerners but the African influences of the many black cooks who developed it, prepared it, and handed it down through generations. Who among us, from anywhere, could resist a plate of Fried Chicken with Cream Gravy, and a dish of Spoon Bread—truly food for the soul.

The South encompasses many distinct areas within its regional boundaries: the Tidewater of Virginia, with its incredible seafood; the Florida Keys, with its Conch Chowder and Key Lime Pie; the Deep South with its Barbecued Pork and Fried Fish. It is a region unified in its love of good food.

Catfish Bake

*S*mithfield Ham is to a Virginian what caviar is to a Russian: unbeatable. These peanut-fed hams are salt-cured and smoked to perfection. Soaking removes some of the salt, but once cooked, the ham should be sliced paper thin, to bring out its uniquely delicate taste. Baking Powder Biscuits are a must, and they can be buttered hot and filled with thin slices of ham or enjoyed with homemade preserves. This is a menu worthy of any celebration. Conch Chowder is a Florida classic. The accompanying elements carry out the Southern theme.

Virginia Ham Dinner

Smithfield Ham with
Baking Powder Biscuits
Sweet Potato Flans on
a Bed of Spinach
Southern Stir Fry
Pecan Tarts
Ambrosia

Florida Favorites

Conch Chowder
Arroz con Pollo
Black-Eyed Peas
Piña Colada Ice Cream

Virginia Ham Dinner ▸

The mountains of North Carolina are ruggedly beautiful, and a long morning walk will bring on an appetite that calls for a substantial meal. Here is a buffet that will fill up even the hungriest guest. Local trout are succulent when baked in parchment, and stuffed cabbage has never been tastier. The nutty flavor of Louisiana pecan rice adds just the right touch to this casserole with chicken and shrimp. And Apple Cider Sherbet is spiked with "white lightning" for additional zip.

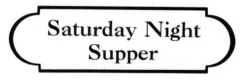

Smoky Mountain Luncheon

*Rainbow Trout with
Blue Crab Stuffing
Country Stuffed Cabbage Leaves
Louisiana Pecan Rice Casserole
Broiled Herbed Tomatoes
String Beans in Dilled Vinaigrette
Apple Cider Sherbet with Raspberry
Sauce*

Saturday Night Supper

*Charleston Okra Soup
Ham and Red-Eye Gravy
Candied Sweet Potatoes
Buttermilk Sherbet*

*B*oth of these menus are perfect for Derby Day. The brunch prepares everyone for the rigors of awaiting the big event and enables guests to take day-long rounds of mint juleps in their stride. The Burgoo is a hearty soup or stew whose ingredients traditionally include what is on hand, be it rabbit, squirrel, or any other game available, along with the freshest of vegetables. It can revive flagging spirits or put overwhelmed revelers back on their feet.

Kentucky Derby Brunch

Pecan Waffles
Strawberry Sauce
Cream Scones
Creamed Chicken with Rice
Sausages
Fried Apples
Scrambled Eggs with Bacon and Cheese

Kentucky Country Fare

Kentucky Burgoo
Rice
Wilted Lettuce
Sweet Potato Pie

Kentucky Derby Brunch ►

In the South there are almost as many ways to fry chicken as there are people. Often, however, the simplest method produces the most delicious result. Hominy grits are wonderful all by themselves, with a well of sweet butter melting in the middle, or you can stir them into the stewed tomatoes for a fine alternative. The Peanut Soup in the Southern Farm Supper is hearty and nourishing, and Hoppin' John, a mixture of black-eyed peas and rice, is simple country cooking at its best. Soul food is not simply a type of cuisine; it is a state of mind.

Down Home Chicken Dinner

Fried Chicken
Grits
Stewed Tomatoes
Strawberry Shortcake
Iced Tea

Southern Farm Supper

Peanut Soup
Broiled Doves
Hoppin' John
Kale
Cracklin' Bread
Chess Pie

Creole and Acadian

If any region of the United States raises the practices of cooking and eating from simple requirements for survival to almost religious experiences, it is the Creole and Cajun country of southern Louisiana.

The same linguistic quirk that turned Indian into "Injun" turned Acadian into "Cajun." Today, descendants of the beleaguered French settlers who fled from old Acadia (Nova Scotia) still spend many hours discussing, planning, and preparing food that will make a strong man weep. Using whatever fresh ingredients are available, usually including local rice, onions, garlic, and, of course, hot peppers, these very skilled cooks create dishes that are truly memorable.

The heart of any Cajun recipe is the *roux*, a combination of fat and flour that is stirred over low heat until, if a dark *roux*, it is nearly the color of bitter chocolate but is never allowed to burn and spoil the taste of the final dish. A patiently prepared *roux* adds both body and flavor, and is essential for a Cajun culinary success.

There is something very satisfying about these substantial dishes. Even in the most humble home along the steaming bayous of coastal Louisiana, these meals are served with great warmth and hospitality. Guests are always welcome, and meals quickly become celebrations.

Creole dishes, less rib-sticking than Cajun specialties but equally flavorful and sometimes just as hot, are modern renditions of the fine foods that appeared on eighteenth-century New Orleans tables. New Orleans has always been the one place in the United States where a weary traveler, tired of overcooked, underimaginative food, could be sure of one of the finest meals of his life.

The most popular restaurants in New Orleans serve many Cajun and Creole combinations, sometimes modified or refined, sometimes as hot as they were generations ago. Restaurateur Paul Prudhomme has elevated many of these dishes to the level of an extraordinary American cuisine.

Seafood is at the heart of much of the local cuisine. Many of the original French- and Spanish-speaking immigrants were fishermen and have passed on their deep respect for the might and abundance of the sea. Freshwater streams and creeks yield massive quantities of crayfish, without which there would be no Crayfish *Étouffée*, no Crayfish Pie, no Crayfish Gumbo, and no old-fashioned Jambalaya—mainstays in the repertoires of local cooks.

From beginning to end, a Cajun or Creole meal will delight every diner. Desserts are rich and satisfying, flaming *Café Brûlot* dark and delicious.

Seafood Gumbo on the deck of a Louisiana Shrimp boat. ▶

*C*ajun and Creole make up one of the most distinctive of America's regional cuisines. Spanish, French, and American Indian influences were wedded into a uniquely different style of cooking. Cajun dishes, sometimes fiery hot and always served in abundance, are rustic and very comforting. Creole cuisine, on the other hand, is more refined, although sometimes equally spicy.

Classic Cajun Lunch

Peacemaker
Seafood Gumbo
Red Beans and Rice
Green Beans Creole
Bread Pudding with Whiskey Sauce

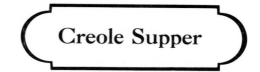

Creole Supper

Shrimp Rémoulade
Redfish Court Bouillion
Rice
Calas

*C*ajun cooking wastes nothing, and everything is prepared with loving attention. Here eggplant is stuffed with a mixture of crab, okra, tomatoes, and green pepper with rice— a meal in itself. Dinner at Antoine's—an elegant menu—is patterned after meals served at the famous New Orleans restaurant. Pompano fillets are baked to perfection in envelopes of parchment. Bananas Foster are simmered in a sugar syrup and then flamed in rum or cognac. The other menu elements are also regional classics.

Stuffed Eggplant Supper

Oyster Artichoke Soup
Eggplant Stuffed with Crabmeat
Tomato, Green Pepper,
and Onion Salad
Fig Ice Cream

Dinner at Antoine's

Crayfish Bisque
Pompano en Papillote
Stewed Okra
Peas with Lettuce
Bananas Foster

Stuffed Eggplant ►

*T*hese wonderful recipes from Commander's Palace restaurant reflect almost one hundred years of New Orleans' tradition. Oysters and shellfish are an integral part of Creole and Cajun cuisine, and these Oysters Marinières are an excellent example. The other dishes on this menu are truly elegant and worthy of New Orleans' reputation for some of the worlds finest foods. And if crabs are delicious, crabs stuffed with crabmeat are even better. Ground Creole pralines provide crunch in vanilla ice cream parfaits for a perfect ending to another real New Orleans dinner.

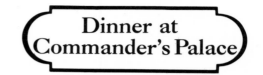

Dinner at Commander's Palace

Garlic Bread
Oysters Marinières
Black Forest Escargot Soup
Trout in Leek Sauce
Creole Mixed Green Salad
White Mousse with
Raspberry Sauce

Creole Seafood Dinner

Cold Shrimp and Tomato Bisque
Crabe avec Crabe
Peas with Lettuce
Praline Parfait

The Midwest

Once the wild frontier border of the United States, the Midwest has become the bread-basket of the country, if not of the world.

Homesteaders and fur hunters led the way. Then came the railroads and mines and the sturdy workers who made this area so strong. Each ethnic group brought with them their traditions and recipes. They treasured their remembered foods and festivals. They were German, Dutch, Swedish, Polish, Hungarian, Greek, Armenian. These and other influences are still strong today, and whole communities frequently share a common heritage. The old recipes are still very much alive and brighten meals all year long. Food is the center of many celebrations and holidays. It was in the Midwest that box suppers and Fourth of July picnics reached a peak of perfection not seen elsewhere. Church suppers and high-school football games are also central to the festivities.

This part of the country produces wild rice, the only native American grain. It isn't really a rice but a grass that grows in water, much as rice does, and it is distantly related to wheat. The Ojibwa Indians of Minnesota, under protection of state law, still harvest the grain in the old way. Though wild rice is now cultivated off the Indian reservations in great commercial paddies, the Indians continue to control the native stands of grain. This rare grain has found its way into every major cuisine in the Western World, and its inclusion in any menu makes a meal truly a festive affair.

The dairy industry is alive and well here, too. Beautiful herds of milch cows are raised in the Midwest, and millions of gallons of milk are produced each year, to be turned into cream, butter, cheese, ice cream, and other dairy products, not only for local tables but for homes and restaurants throughout the country. In addition, the beef of the Great Plains and the ranches of the Great West has been served in abundance on Midwest farm tables for more than a hundred years.

Standing Beef Rib Roast ▶

*T*he Midwest, with its legacy of Old Country cooking, is the heartland of America. Here are two menus of handed-down recipes filled with old-time goodness. Wine Soup is thickened with barley and sparkles with raisins and wine. Dutch Apple Cake is made of layers of bread crumbs and homemade applesauce. *Hutspot,* the origin of our word "hodgepodge," is a one-dish stew with a twist—the vegetables are mashed before serving. *Schnecken* are the antecedents of Sticky Buns, full of nuts, raisins, and caramel.

Old Country Supper

Wine Soup
Pork Roast with Dill Sauce
Mashed Potatoes
Gron Kaal (Kale)
Dutch Apple Cake

Pot Luck Supper

Armenian Appetizers
Hutspot
Schnecken

This fish dinner can be served at home, or under the stars, where the main course will depend on the fisherman's ability or luck. If camping is on the agenda, prepare the other dishes ahead of time and carry them along. Have everything ready to serve, so the trout can be cooked as soon as they are caught. This is one time where freshness definitely makes the difference. If you must stay at home, this hearty supper menu, with its tangy dessert, will warm the coldest winter evening.

Wisconsin Fish Dinner

Baked Trout
Wilted Salad
Glazed Rutabaga
Graham Bread
Fancy Cherry Pie

Tip o' the Mitten Supper

Shrimp Balls
Dilled Beef
Squaw Corn
Cranberry Pudding

*T*he Great Plains buffalo once ran in herds so vast it would take all day for the herd to pass a given point. Plainsmen soon discovered that the meat of the buffalo is very like beef, only leaner. If buffalo is available in your market, this stew will be an authentic rendition of a dish that kept our forebears going during the bitingly cold pioneer winters. Ozark Pudding, an apple-nut pudding cake, adds the right sweet touch. The Mountain Menu is another meal reminiscent of the days of the pioneers.

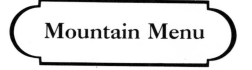

Buffalo Stew Lunch

Buffalo Stew
Sourdough Biscuits
Baked Asparagus
Ozark Pudding

Mountain Menu

Batter Fried Mushrooms
Swiss Steak
Stewed Potatoes
Stuffed Acorn Squash
Peach Crisp

The Great West

The Great West is the dream that still draws people from all countries to states such as Texas, with its wealth, and California, with its promise of golden days and spectacular nights.

The Great West is a diverse area, incorporating the vast, open countryside of Texas and New Mexico as well as the crowded beaches of Los Angeles and the majestic mountains of Colorado. The cuisine is just as varied as the landscape, though a common thread does run through the food of the Southwest: that is, the influence of the Spanish explorers and the Mexican Indians.

This part of the West, like many warm regions of the world, likes its food hot, sometimes so hot it will take your breath away. Capsicum peppers enliven everything from sauces to eggs. Tex-Mex, a combination of Spanish, Mexican, Indian, and local Texan tastes, is on the upswing: Guacamole, Tacos, and Refried Beans are cropping up all over the United States. But usually these transplanted versions are only mild reproductions of the incendiary originals.

The Great West is also the land of the cowboy and the chuck wagon. Open-fire cook-

ing is still dear to the hearts of local citizens, and barbecues play a large part in any outdoor celebration. Like many things Texan, barbecues here are almost larger than life. Enormous quantities of food are prepared, in some cases whole sides of beef and hundreds of pounds of ribs, chicken, and hot sausages (*chorizos*).

California, the land of milk and honey, is a culinary paradise. Fresh produce and poultry, grown the old-fashioned way by people who care, are available everywhere. California cooking, straightforward and often very imaginative, is taking the country by storm. Light, attractive dishes with new tastes and ingredients are being tried everywhere. An emphasis on physical fitness makes some of the innovations just right for the calorie conscious. Here is where the *nouvelle cuisine* of France has been interpreted with skill, where practitioners have applied the principals of *nouvelle* to local foods rather than simply imitating the original dishes.

The Great West offers something for everyone. From the simplest bowl of fiery chili to the most sophisticated San Francisco Chinese dinners, there are great dishes to be tried.

Barbecued Ribs ▶

The Spanish influence on the food of Texas and New Mexico is very strong and has resulted in a unique regional cuisine. Red and green hot peppers play a leading role in many dishes, and local renditions can be blazing. These are milder renderings but can be spiced up to suit personal taste. Molé Poblano marries poultry to a deliciously hot sauce that has unsweetened chocolate as a prime ingredient. Though named for the ingredient that gives the dish its dominant flavor, Green Chili Stew is made with beef and is hearty fare. A refreshingly creamy Flan cools the fires that linger after a Tex-Mex feast.

Tex-Mex Celebration

Guacamole
Tortilla Chips
Chilies con Queso
Green Chili Stew
Flour Tortillas
Refried Beans
Flan

Rio Grande Round-Up

Chicken Molé Poblano
Colachi
Corn Tortillas
Navajo Fry Bread
Avocado Mousse

$\mathcal{S}$un, surf, and sand may be most people's image of California, but it is also a mecca of fresh produce and fine food. And California cooking has begun to move east. The availability of locally grown produce and an eye toward fitness and health have given rise to a cuisine that is light and lean. Trends toward grilled meats and seafood as well as salads and vegetables with a decidedly Oriental flavor give California menus a unique flair and appeal.

California Summer Supper

Scallop Ceviche
Caesar Salad
Chicken Gismonda
Sesame Asparagus
Monkey Bread
Carrot Cake

Wine Country Dinner

Artichoke Bisque
Mesquite-Grilled Scallops
Sweet and Sour Squash
Baked Avocado
Orange Shortcake

$\mathcal{C}$ontrary to general opinion, barbecue did not originate in Texas. But Texans have taken this ancient cooking method and elevated it to new heights. A real Texas barbecue can often feed hundreds; this modified version can feed a dozen or more very hungry folk and leave them satisfied indeed. The real trick to barbecuing is slow-cooking the meats over gentle coals until they are tender and juicy. The sauce should be fiery hot, so plenty of beer, soft drinks, and freshly brewed coffee are a must. The Sunday Supper also features classic dishes of this uniquely American cuisine.

Texas Barbecue

Barbecued Brisket
Barbecued Chicken
Barbecued Ribs
Barbecued Chorizos
Barbecued Beans
Cole Slaw
Salsas
Fresh Fruit

Texas Sunday Supper

Chicken-Fried Steak
Stuffed Chayote
Guava Shells with Cream Cheese

Texas Barbecue ➤

*T*his decidedly different kind of barbecue has long been a traditional Hawaiian celebration. Women prepare the food, but men do all the cooking. Whole pigs are pit-roasted, along with other local specialty foods, such as Laulau, and sweet potatoes, that are steamed alongside. Poi, a paste produced from taro root, is a traditional accompaniment. A fresh salmon appetizer similar to ceviche starts things off, and an assortment of fruit finishes this informal summer party. The accompanying menu features dishes for which California and Hawaii are noted, but they can be re-created anywhere.

Hawaiian Luau

Lomi-lomi Salmon
Pit-roasted Pork
Kahlua Pig
Poi
Fresh Fruit

Oriental Feast

Oriental Shrimp Toast
Szechuan Chicken
Stir-Fry Asparagus
Sweet and Sour Squash
Chinese Chews

The Northwest

This is the land of the last frontier. Alaska, the northwesternmost of all American states, today brings out the same indomitable frontier spirit our forefathers had when they moved west into the unknown. The same strength of character and body is still a prerequisite for surviving outside the Alaskan urban centers.

Ingenuity is a must in the wilds, and old recipes are given new meaning when they incorporate unusual ingredients. *Boeuf Bourguignon* becomes something special when it is Venison Bourguignon instead.

Here we find wild game at its finest and fresh fish from rivers and streams, including some of the finest salmon in the world. Washington and Oregon claim many fine salmon dishes, from Salmon Soufflé to Salmon Mousse to Baked Stuffed Salmon. And there is no finer eating anywhere than the traditional Indian dish of salmon skewered on sticks of alderwood and roasted over a blazing fire. The Indians of this region relied on salmon to sustain them throughout the year and devised excellent methods of salting and smoking it to retard spoilage. Many of the same methods are still used today.

The bounty of this country is astounding. Not only is the sea nearby, with its harvest of shellfish and seafood, but the fertile valleys and plains produce an infinite variety of fruits and vegetables. Cherries are a specialty and appear in many dishes, including a delicious, citrus-flavored Cold Cherry Soup. Some of the most wonderful pears in America are grown here and shipped all over the country, but some are kept for favorite local dishes, such as Pear Pie.

Part of this region is sheep country. Shepherds of Greek and Basque origin tend huge flocks in the high pastures of the Rockies. Though most of the lamb they produce is shipped to Eastern markets, local festivals feature spit-roasted lamb with crisp, browned Basque Potatoes.

Oregon is the birthplace of the late James Beard, one of America's most renowned food experts, and it was in his mother's kitchen that he learned to appreciate the best and freshest foods available. What was true sixty years ago is still true today: The Northwest offers a treasure trove of the finest foods, both wild and cultivated, to be found.

*I*daho and Oregon—with their snow-covered mountains, racing streams, and cool, shady forests —provide the inspiration for this great at-home dinner. Cushion Roast Lamb is an old-fashioned cut—two square-boned shoulders stuffed and sewn together. Serve the roast with a Basque Potato Cake; then sit back and wait for the compliments. Alaska provides the crab, the quail, and the wild mushrooms for the accompanying menu's wonderful saute. Fresh Northwestern plums make the dessert cake something special.

Northwestern Sunday Supper

Pacific Oyster Stew
Cushion Roast Lamb
Basque Potato Cake
Stuffed Onions
Field Salad
Sourdough Bread
Pear Upside-Down Cake

Wild Country Company Dinner

Alaskan King Crab
Roast Quail
Wild Mushroom Saute
Green Beans with Almonds
Plum Cake

Northwestern Sunday Supper ►

No light city meals will satisfy the hunger that comes from working out of doors ten hours a day. Vast quantities of food disappear quickly, and good cooks have a very appreciative audience at least three times a day. The big meal is often at midday, but supper must be substantial, even if simple. Mounds of Barbecued Ribs, deep pots of Nevada Beans, and piles of biscuits are a must. Farther north, cold weather demands the same hearty fare. And wild game often fills in when snow interferes with regular marketing.

Wyoming Ranch Supper

Marinated Mushrooms
Barbecued Ribs Northwestern
Nevada Beans
Sourdough Biscuits
Stack Cake

Tall Timber Treats

Bulgur Salad
Venison Bourguignon
Noodles
Pear Pie

Summers in Washington State and Alaska are short and precious, and time spent out of doors is savored like fine wine. Even meals cooked in the kitchen are likely to be enjoyed on the porch or in the yard or garden. Local fresh produce is incorporated into nearly every summer meal. Salmon from the rivers are stuffed and baked. Fragrant baked potatoes are filled with a mixture of fresh mushrooms (wild, if possible), scallions, sprouts—anything available. Green beans are accented with almonds, and luscious cheesecake is studded with ground hazelnuts. The accompanying menu features a classic dessert made with one of the best of the Northwest's bounty of fruits—the near-legendary blackberry.

Pacific Summer Fare

Cold Cherry Soup
Stuffed Salmon
Stuffed Potatoes
Green Beans with Almonds
Sourdough Bread
Hazelnut Cheesecake

Northwest Specials

Salmon Mousse
Boiled Beef with Horseradish
Tomato Cheese Pie
Blackberry Tarts with Lemon Curd

Pacific Summer Fare ►

Part Two

Regional Recipes

$\mathcal{A}$ppetizers

◄ *Scallop Ceviche*

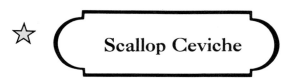

Scallop Ceviche

(6 servings)

½–¾ pound tiny scallops (if not available,
     use large scallops cut into small pieces)
½ cup or more fresh lime juice
1 tomato, peeled, seeded, and finely
     chopped
1 jalapeño chili (or small, red-hot chili)
     washed, seeded, and cut into thin strips
2 tablespoons finely chopped cilantro
½ red onion, very thinly sliced
     Salt and freshly ground pepper
⅓ cup oil
     Whole cilantro leaves

In a glass bowl cover the scallops with lime juice and marinate for 2 hours. Add the remaining ingredients except the whole cilantro leaves and toss lightly. Transfer to serving platter or individual plates and garnish with whole cilantro leaves.

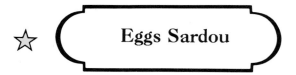

Eggs Sardou

(8 servings)

8 artichoke bottoms
8–10 anchovy fillets, chopped
8 eggs, poached and trimmed
1–1½ cups Hollandaise sauce
⅔ cup ground smoked ham
1 small truffle, slivered

Preheat the oven to 450°.

Fill each artichoke bottom with chopped anchovy. Arrange the artichokes on a baking sheet and heat for 5 minutes. Set aside and keep warm. Set a poached egg on top of each artichoke and sauce with Hollandaise. Sprinkle each egg with chopped ham and top with slivers of truffle. Serve at once.

Note: *If truffles are unavailable, slivers of black olives can be substituted.*

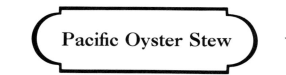

Pacific Oyster Stew

(6 servings)

3 tablespoons butter
1 tablespoon chopped onion
½ pint shucked oysters (Olympia if possible)
1 quart milk
½ cup heavy cream
     Salt and freshly ground white pepper

Melt the butter in a heavy saucepan. Add the onions and saute until soft and transparent, but not browned. Add the oysters and saute 2 minutes. Pour in the milk and cream and season with salt and pepper. Simmer 5 minutes. Serve very hot.

Note: *Olympia are large oysters found off the Pacific Northwest Coast.*

Armenian Appetizer

(8 servings)

2 tablespoons oil
1 cup chopped onions
¼ cup pignoli (pine) nuts
1 cup uncooked white rice
¼ cup fresh parsley, stems removed
¼ cup (or less) currants
½ cup fresh dill
   Salt and freshly ground black pepper
   Juice of 1 lemon
¼ cup tomato paste
2 cups water
1 pound or more grape leaves, rinsed and
   drained, stem end removed or 1 jar preserved grape leaves
½ cup oil
1 tablespoon lemon juice
   Lemon wedges

In a large skillet heat the oil and saute the onions and pine nuts. Add the rice, parsley, currants, dill, salt and pepper to taste, lemon juice, and tomato paste. Cook 5 minutes, stirring. Add 1 cup water and cook 15 minutes. Line a small kettle with a few grape leaves. On a wooden board lay the remaining grape leaves one at a time, dull side up. Place some of the onion-pine nut mixture near the stem end. Fold the stem end up to cover the mixture. Fold in the sides, then roll up. Place the packets in the leaf-lined kettle. Pour the ½ cup oil, 1 tablespoon lemon juice, and 1 cup water over the rolled leaves. Weight the leaves with a small plate. Cover and simmer 30 to 40 minutes. Cool in the kettle. Chill. Serve cold with lemon wedges.

Note: *See the Resource Guide for information on ordering grape leaves.*

Shrimp Rémoulade

(6 servings)

2 cups mayonnaise, preferably homemade
2 cups sour cream
2 cloves garlic, finely minced
2 tablespoons chopped onion
2 tablespoons chopped dill pickle
2 tablespoons capers, chopped
3 hard-cooked eggs, chopped
2 tablespoons lemon juice
2 tablespoons chopped parsley
1 teaspoon paprika
   Salt and freshly ground white pepper to
   taste
   Red pepper sauce to taste
3 pounds medium shrimp, boiled, peeled, and
   deveined

In a bowl mix together all the ingredients except the shrimp. Place the shrimp in a bowl and pour the sauce over them. Marinate in the refrigerator for several hours or overnight.

Cheese Straws

¼ pound (1 stick) butter, softened
1¼ pounds extra sharp cheese, grated
1¾ cups flour
⅓ teaspoon salt
¼ teaspoon red pepper
  Pinch of cayenne

In a bowl cream together the butter and cheese. Add the remaining ingredients and mix thoroughly. Form into logs and chill. Preheat the oven to 350°.

Slice chilled dough ⅛-inch thick with a sharp knife. Bake until brown, about 30 minutes.

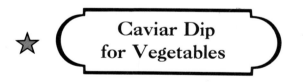

Caviar Dip for Vegetables

(2 cups)

  1 cup homemade mayonnaise
  1 cup sour cream
10 drops red pepper sauce
¼ cup lemon juice
  Freshly ground white pepper
  2 tablespoons freshly chopped dill
¼ cup finely chopped scallions
  2 ounces American golden caviar

In a bowl beat together all the ingredients except the caviar. Stir in the caviar. Chill. Serve with raw or steamed vegetables.

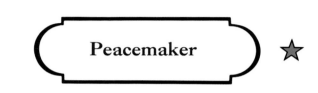

Peacemaker

(8–10 servings)

1 loaf French bread, about 18″
  Butter
2 dozen fresh oysters
  Lard for frying
  Corn flour
  Leaf lettuce (optional)
1 large tomato, sliced (optional)
  Mayonnaise, preferably homemade (optional)
  Pickled peppers

Split the loaf of bread lengthwise. Spread the top and bottom pieces with butter and toast lightly under the broiler.

Heat some lard in a heavy skillet. Roll the oysters in the corn flour, fry in the hot lard, and drain on absorbent paper. Pile the oysters on the bottom half of the loaf. If you like, you can cover with a layer of leaf lettuce, tomatoes, and a touch of homemade mayonnaise. Place the lid in position over the filled bottom section. Cut in pieces. Serve with pickled peppers.

Oysters Bienville

(8 servings)

Rock salt
24 oysters on the half shell
¼ pound (1 stick) butter
½ cup chopped shallots
2 tablespoons flour
2 cups chicken broth
1 pound cooked shrimp, finely chopped
¼ pound mushrooms, finely chopped
3 egg yolks
⅓ cup dry white wine
½ cup half and half
Salt and freshly ground black pepper
Red pepper sauce
¼ cup bread crumbs
¼ cup parmesan cheese

Preheat the oven to 400°.
Make a bed of rock salt on a cooking sheet and place the oysters on the half shell on top. Roast for 5 minutes. Remove from the oven and set aside. Melt the butter in a heavy skillet. Add the shallots and cook until they are golden. Stir in the flour. Cook, stirring until brown, but not burned. Add the chicken broth and stir until smooth. Add the shrimp and mushrooms. Simmer until thick. Cool slightly.
In a bowl beat the egg yolks, wine, and half and half until smooth. Pour the shrimp mixture into the eggs, beating well. Add any liquid from the oysters and season with salt, pepper, and red pepper sauce to taste. Simmer, stirring, over low heat until very thick. In a small bowl mix together the bread crumbs and cheese. Spoon the shrimp sauce over the oysters and sprinkle with the crumb mixture. Place in a hot oven (450°) until the tops turn golden. Serve immediately.

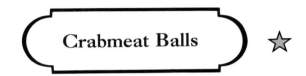

Crabmeat Balls

(24 balls)

1 tablespoon butter
¼ cup finely minced celery
1 small onion, minced
1 tablespoon flour
Salt and freshly ground white pepper
½ cup heavy cream
1 tablespoon chopped parsley
8 ounces crabmeat
½ cup dry bread crumbs
Fat for deep frying

In a small saucepan melt the butter and saute the celery and onion until transparent. Stir in the flour, salt, and pepper. Cook for 1 minute. Stir in the cream and cook until very thick. Stir in the parsley, crabmeat, and bread crumbs. Cool. Form the mixture into 1-inch balls. Fry in hot deep fat (375°) until golden. Drain and serve hot with dipping sauce.

Devilled Clams

(4 servings)

12 large quahog or 25 smaller clams,
   scrubbed
½ cup water
¾ cup dried bread crumbs
   Salt and freshly ground black pepper
2 slices bacon, diced
1 clove garlic, minced
1 tablespoon minced green pepper
1 tablespoon finely minced onion
3 tablespoons dry white wine
⅓ cup or more clam juice (cooking liquid)
3 tablespoons chopped parsley
1–2 tablespoons butter

Preheat the oven to 450°.
Steam the clams in the ½ cup of water for 5 minutes or until the shells open. Cool. Reserve the liquid. Remove the clams from their shells and save the shells. Finely chop the clams or put them through a meat grinder. Stir in the crumbs and salt and pepper to taste. In a skillet saute the bacon until crisp. Remove with a slotted spoon and drain. Saute the garlic, green pepper, and onion in remaining bacon fat until transparent. Drain. Combine the vegetables with the clam mixture. Stir in the wine and enough clam juice to moisten. Stir in 2 tablespoons chopped parsley. Stuff the mixture into the clam shells. Top with the reserved bacon and remaining chopped parsley and dot lightly with butter. Bake for 3 to 5 minutes depending on the size of the clam shells.

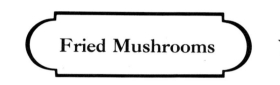

Fried Mushrooms

(4–6 servings)

   Oil or fat for deep frying
2 eggs, beaten
½ cup buttermilk
   Salt and freshly ground pepper
   Pinch of cayenne
1 pound small mushrooms, rinsed well and
   patted dry
   Flour

Heat the oil or fat in a heavy pot or deep fryer.
In a mixing bowl beat together the eggs, buttermilk, salt and pepper to taste, and a pinch of cayenne. Drop the mushrooms in the batter; shake off the excess. Dredge lightly in flour. Fry in the deep fat until golden brown. Drain on absorbent paper. Dust lightly with salt and serve hot.

Variation: *¼ cup parmesan cheese can be added to the dredging flour before frying the mushrooms.*

Eggs Hussarde

(4–8 servings)

8 round slices of ham, preferably good
  smoked ham
2 large tomatoes, sliced
4 whole English muffins, split and toasted
1 cup Marchand de Vin Sauce
8 eggs, poached, trimmed, and kept warm
1 cup Hollandaise sauce
  Paprika

In a large skillet grill the ham slices and
tomatoes until very hot. On each English
muffin half, place a round of ham and sliced
tomato. Spoon a little Marchand de Vin
sauce over all. Top with a hot, poached egg.
Spoon Hollandaise over the egg and garnish
with paprika.

Oysters Marinières

(6 servings)

36 oysters (reserve ½ cup of the liquor)
 1 cup white wine
 1 cup minced shallots
½ cup minced parsley
½ teaspoon black pepper

Salt to taste (you may not need any if you
  use salty oysters)
¼ pound (1 stick) butter, softened and
  creamed with ⅓ cup flour

In a shallow pan poach the oysters in the
reserved oyster liquor to which has been
added the wine, shallots, parsley, pepper,
and salt. Bring the mixture to a boil and
cook for 1 minute. Add the butter-flour
mixture and stir gently until thoroughly
blended. Continue cooking until the floury
taste is gone. Serve as an appetizer or entree
with French bread.

Lobster Rolls

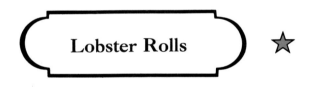

(4 servings)

4 hot dog rolls
2 tablespoons butter, melted
2 cups freshly cooked lobster meat, diced
⅓ cup diced celery
1 teaspoon minced onion
½ cup homemade mayonnaise
  Salt and freshly ground white pepper

Split the hot dog rolls and toast lightly.
Brush with melted butter. In a bowl toss the
lobster, celery, and onion with the mayonnaise. Season to taste. Fill the warm rolls
with the lobster meat salad. Serve at once.

★ Swedish Meatballs and Gravy

(6 servings)

1 pound ground beef
½ pound ground veal
¼ pound pork sausage
1½ cups white bread, cut into cubes
⅔ cup half and half
2 medium onions, chopped
3 tablespoons butter
1 whole egg
4 tablespoons chopped parsley
    Salt and freshly ground black pepper
½ teaspoon ground ginger

Gravy:
2 tablespoons flour
2 cups well-seasoned beef broth
¼ cup strong coffee

Process the beef, veal and sausage in a food processor for 1 minute. Soak the bread in the cream and then add to the meat. In a skillet melt 1 tablespoon butter. Saute the onion until transparent. Add to the meat in the processor. Turn on the processor and add the egg, parsley and seasonings. Process for 2 minutes. Form the mixture into 1-inch balls. Melt the remaining butter in the skillet and fry the meatballs until brown on all sides. Remove and set aside.

To make the gravy stir the flour into the butter remaining in the skillet. Brown well. Add the broth and coffee. Add the meatballs, cover and simmer 30 minutes. Serve the meatballs in the gravy.

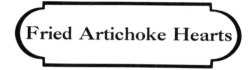

Fried Artichoke Hearts ☆

(6 servings)

8 artichoke hearts, boiled until tender if fresh, rinsed if canned
    Flour for dredging
12 ounces beer
1 cup flour
    Salt and pepper to taste
    Fat for deep frying
    Lemon wedges

Cut the artichoke hearts into quarters. Dredge in flour. Whisk together beer, flour, salt, and pepper. Dip flour-covered pieces of artichoke in batter. Drop at once into hot fat and fry until golden brown. Drain well and serve very hot with lemon wedges.

Note: *The late Albert Stockli taught me this beer batter recipe. It has been a favorite for many years.*

Fried Clams

(4 servings)

    Oil for frying
 2 eggs, well beaten
½ cup milk
    Salt and freshly ground white pepper
 1 pint shucked clams, washed
 1 cup white cornmeal
    Vinegar (optional)

In a heavy pot or deep frying pan heat enough oil for deep frying.

In a bowl beat the eggs and milk with salt and pepper to taste. Dip the clams in the egg mixture and then dredge in the cornmeal. Fry in deep hot fat (375°) until crisp and golden. Drain on absorbent paper. Dust with salt. If desired, sprinkle with vinegar.

Stuffed Crabs

(6 servings)

 6 whole live crabs
 3 tablespoons crab boil spices
 3 tablespoons butter
 1 small onion, minced
½ green pepper, minced
12 ounces crabmeat

 1 tablespoon bread crumbs
 3 tablespoons chopped parsley
 3 tablespoons heavy cream
    Butter
    Lemon wedges

In a large pot steam the crabs with the crab boil spices for 20 minutes. Cool. Pick out the crabmeat, being careful not to break the shells. Wash the shells and set them aside.

Melt the butter in a heavy skillet. Saute the onion and pepper until transparent. Stir in the canned and fresh crabmeat, bread crumbs, and parsley. Stir and cook over low heat for about 10 minutes. Remove from the heat, stir in the cream and let cool. Preheat the oven to 400°.

Stuff the crab shells with the filling. Dot with butter and bake for about 10 minutes, or until golden brown. Serve with lemon wedges.

Notes: *Some fans of stuffed crabs like to add red pepper sauce to the filling. Start with 6 drops and add more to suit your taste.*

Old Bay is the crab boil most often used; see the Resource Guide for information on ordering by mail.

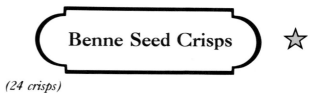

Benne Seed Crisps

(24 crisps)

 1 cup yellow cornmeal
½ cup sifted all-purpose flour

½ teaspoon salt
¼ teaspoon baking soda
 2 tablespoons butter, melted
⅓ cup milk or cream
   Sesame seeds

Preheat the oven to 350°.

In a bowl sift together the cornmeal, flour, salt, and baking soda. Mix in the butter and milk or cream. On a lightly floured board, knead the dough 6 to 8 times or until it holds together. Roll dough by teaspoonfuls on the board and sprinkle with sesame seeds. Roll into very thin 4-inch rounds, leaving edges ragged. Bake on an ungreased cookie sheet for 15 minutes, or until golden. Sprinkle with salt while still barely warm. Store in a tightly closed container. Serve with cocktails or seafood soups.

Mushrooms Stuffed with Crabmeat

(6–8 servings)

 1 pound large mushrooms
⅓ cup dry bread crumbs
¼ teaspoon thyme
   Salt and freshly ground pepper
 2 tablespoons chopped parsley
½ cup crabmeat
 2 tablespoons butter
 1 tablespoon minced onion
   Red pepper sauce to taste
¼ cup mayonnaise

Preheat the oven to 400°.

Twist the stems out of the mushrooms. Finely dice the stems. Wash, dry, and oil the mushroom caps. In a bowl mix together the crumbs, thyme, seasonings, parsley, and crabmeat. In a small saucepan melt the butter and saute the onion and diced mushroom. Stir into the crumb mixture. Stir in the mayonnaise and season with red pepper sauce. Fill the caps with the crabmeat mixture. Bake until lightly brown, about 8 minutes.

Po'Boys (Creole Sandwiches)

(8–10 servings)

1 long loaf of French bread
   Mayonnaise or softened butter
   Hot mustard
   Fillings: any type of meat, shrimp, crabmeat, fried fish fillets, or seafood or meat salads—in fact, anything at all.
   Red pepper sauce
   Tomatoes, sliced
   Leaf lettuce, washed, dried, and chilled
   Vinaigrette, bottled or homemade

Split the loaf in half lengthwise. Spread with mayonnaise or butter. Spread one half with hot mustard. Arrange choice of filling on the bottom half of the loaf. Season well with red pepper sauce. Top with tomato and lettuce. Drizzle with a little vinaigrette. Cut into pieces.

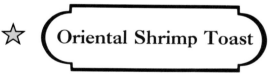

Grilled Alaskan King Crab

(3–4 servings)

4 tablespoons (½ stick) butter, melted
2 tablespoons lemon juice
    Red pepper sauce to taste
6–8 pieces of King Crab leg

In a bowl mix together the butter, lemon juice, and red pepper sauce. Split the crab legs on one side, open and brush the meat with the sauce. Grill the legs over charcoal, split side up, until shells begin to brown. Serve with the remaining sauce on the side.

Oriental Shrimp Toast

(10–12 servings)

1 pound fresh shrimp, shelled, deveined, and finely chopped
¼ pound pork sausage meat
1 tablespoon sherry
1 tablespoon soy sauce
    Freshly ground black pepper
2 bunches scallions, finely chopped
½ cup cornstarch
1 egg
14 slices white bread
2 eggs, beaten
1 cup oil

In a bowl mix together the shrimp, sausage, sherry, soy sauce, black pepper to taste, scallions, and ½ tablespoon cornstarch. Beat in one egg. Dredge the bread in the remaining cornstarch and knock off the excess. Spread shrimp mixture generously on each slice. Cut each slice diagonally in quarters. Brush with beaten egg. In a heavy skillet heat the oil and fry the bread upside down. Turn to brown the underside. Drain on absorbent paper. Serve very hot.

Rice Cakes

(6 servings)

4 slices bacon, cut in 1-inch pieces
¼ small onion, finely chopped
¼ small green pepper, finely chopped
½ teaspoon salt
    Freshly ground pepper
3 cups cooked rice
¾ cup flour
1 teaspoon baking powder
¼ cup grated cheese
2 ripe tomatoes, peeled, seeded, and finely chopped
    Tomato wedges

In a skillet fry the bacon until crisp. Drain on absorbent paper. In a bowl toss together the other ingredients except the tomato wedges. Stir in the bacon. Fry by spoonfuls in a greased skillet. Turn once. Keep warm. Serve hot, garnished with fresh tomato wedges.

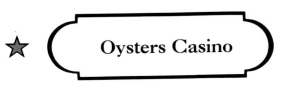

Oysters Casino

(4 servings)

3 slices bacon, cut up
1 small onion, chopped
2 tablespoons celery, chopped
1 teaspoon lemon juice
  Salt and freshly ground pepper
  Red pepper sauce
1 teaspoon thyme
1 pint shucked oysters

Preheat the oven to 400°.

In a skillet saute the bacon until limp. Add the onion and celery, and saute until vegetables are transparent. Add the seasonings. Divide the oysters among four gratin dishes and spread the mixture over the oysters. Bake for 10 minutes, until the edges of the oysters curl. Serve warm.

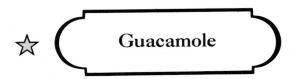

Guacamole

(2–4 servings)

2 large ripe avocados
1 teaspoon lemon juice
3 teaspoons minced onion
1 large tomato, peeled, seeded, and chopped
1 tablespoon chopped green chilies
Salt
Pinch of chili pepper
Fresh coriander

Peel the avocados and mash the flesh with a fork. Stir in the lemon juice, onion, tomato, and chilies. Season with salt and chili powder. Garnish with fresh coriander.

Note: *If guacamole is not to be eaten immediately, bury the pits in the mixture, cover with plastic wrap and refrigerate.*

Welsh Rabbit

(4 servings)

2 teaspoons Worcestershire sauce
½ teaspoon dry mustard
  Salt
  Pinch of cayenne pepper
½ cup beer
2 cups grated cheddar cheese
1 egg
4 slices toast, cut in half diagonally
  Paprika

In a bowl blend together the Worcestershire sauce, mustard, salt, cayenne, and beer. Heat in a large saucepan until the beer is very hot. Add the cheese and stir until melted. Beat the egg in a bowl. Turn the hot cheese mixture into the bowl, beating until egg is fully combined. Serve hot over toast and garnish with paprika.

Chilies Con Queso

(4–6 servings)

12 green chilies (poblano if available), peeled,
   stemmed, seeded, and chopped
 3 ripe tomatoes, peeled, seeded, chopped,
   and mashed
   Salt to taste
 2 cloves garlic, minced
 2 medium onions, finely chopped
 2 tablespoons butter
¾ pound shredded Monterey Jack cheese

Preheat the oven to 375°.

In a bowl mix together the chilies and tomato. Add the salt and half the garlic and
onion. In a saucepan melt the butter and
saute the remaining onion and garlic until
transparent. Stir in the chili mixture. Turn
into an oven-proof dish. Top with cheese
and bake until cheese is bubbly. Serve with
tortilla chips.

Marinated Mushrooms

(3–4 servings)

 1 cup olive oil
½ cup lemon juice
 1 small onion, minced
 2 cloves garlic, minced

 1 tomato, peeled, seeded, and chopped
   Salt and freshly ground pepper
½ teaspoon dry mustard
½ pound button mushrooms

In a large saucepan heat the oil, lemon
juice, onion, garlic, and tomato. Stir in salt
and pepper to taste and the dry mustard.
Wipe the mushrooms, cutting off any dried
stem ends. Add to the oil mixture. Simmer
20 minutes. Remove from heat. Allow mushrooms to cool in the liquid. Refrigerate
overnight.

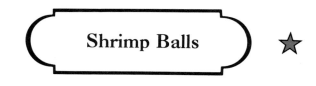

Shrimp Balls

(8 servings)

½ cup fresh soft bread crumbs
 1 tablespoon butter, melted
 1 egg, beaten
 3 cups cooked, peeled shrimp, minced
   Salt and freshly ground pepper
   Red pepper sauce
   Cracker crumbs
 1 egg, beaten
   Fat for deep frying

Mix together bread crumbs, butter, 1
beaten egg, cooked shrimp, and seasonings.

Add red pepper sauce to taste. Shape into 1-inch balls.

Roll balls in cracker crumbs, then in beaten egg, then again in cracker crumbs. Let dry at least 15 minutes. Fry in deep fat until golden brown.

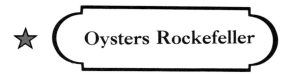

Oysters Rockefeller

(6–8 servings)

Coarse salt (Kosher will do well)
24 oysters, shucked and one shell reserved for each
4 slices bacon, cooked until crisp
1 cup spinach, steamed, drained, and finely chopped
4 tablespoons finely chopped parsley
3 tablespoons finely chopped celery leaves
2 scallions, finely chopped
3 tablespoons cracker crumbs
4 tablespoons (½ stick) butter
1 teaspoon lemon juice
Salt to taste
Red pepper sauce

Preheat the oven to 450°.

Make a layer of coarse salt in the bottom of each of 4 cake tins. Arrange 6 oysters in their half shells in each tin. Chop together the bacon, spinach, parsley, celery leaves, scallions, and cracker crumbs. In a small skillet melt the butter and add the bacon mixture, lemon juice, salt, and red pepper sauce to taste. Cook over low heat for about 4 minutes. Divide the stuffing among the oysters, mounding it on the shell. Bake just until the edges of the oysters begin to curl, about 5 to 8 minutes. Serve very hot.

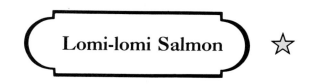

Lomi-lomi Salmon

(6 servings)

3 large tomatoes, peeled, seeded, and chopped
1 pound fresh salmon, boned and cut in small cubes
1 large onion, finely chopped
½–¾ cup lime juice
Pinch of sugar
Salt and freshly ground white pepper to taste
Red pepper sauce to taste

In a glass bowl gently toss tomato, salmon and onion. Stir in lime juice. Add sugar, salt, pepper, and red pepper sauce. Marinate 4 to 6 hours, tossing from time to time. Serve on lettuce leaves or vine leaves.

Oysters Annapolis

(6–8 servings)

24 oysters, shucked and one shell reserved for each
 2 egg yolks
½ cup chopped green pepper
 1 clove garlic, chopped
 1 teaspoon dry mustard
⅓ cup mayonnaise
 3 teaspoons Worcestershire sauce
   Salt and freshly ground pepper
12 ounces crabmeat, well picked over
 3 tablespoons cracker crumbs

Preheat the oven to 350°.

Cut the oysters in several pieces and place in half-shells arranged on a baking sheet. In a small mixing bowl combine the remaining ingredients, tossing gently. Pile the mixture on top of the oysters and bake for 20 to 25 minutes. Serve hot.

Liptauer Cheese

(10 servings)

½ pound (2 sticks) butter, softened
 2 8-ounce packages cream cheese, softened
 1 tablespoon sweet Hungarian paprika
 2 teaspoons caraway seed
 1 teaspoon dry mustard
 1 tablespoon finely minced onion
   Freshly ground pepper to taste
½ cup sour cream
   Chopped chives

In the bowl of a food processor or using an electric mixer beat together the butter and cream cheese until smooth. Beat in the paprika. Stir in the remaining ingredients except chives and beat until very light. Pack into a crock or bowl and garnish with chopped chives. Refrigerate until firm.

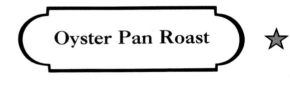

Oyster Pan Roast

(2–4 servings)

 4 tablespoons butter
⅓ cup chopped scallion
⅓ cup finely chopped green pepper
 2 tablespoons chopped parsley
 2 tablespoons ketchup
 1 teaspoon lemon juice
 1 pint freshly shucked oysters, drained
⅓ cup heavy cream
   Salt and freshly ground white pepper
   Toast points

In a heavy skillet melt the butter, add the scallion and pepper and saute gently until transparent. Add the parsley, ketchup, lemon juice, oysters, and cream. Cook just until oysters plump and edges begin to curl. Season with salt and pepper. Serve at once on toast points.

Codfish Balls

(6 servings)

2 cups shredded salt cod
Milk
6 medium-sized potatoes, boiled
2 eggs
¼ teaspoon pepper
⅛ cup milk
Fat for deep frying

Soak the salt cod in milk overnight to soften.

Drain the cod well and dry. Shred with two forks. Peel and mash the potatoes. Add the codfish and eggs and mix thoroughly. Add the pepper and milk. Beat until fluffy. Drop by spoonfuls into deep, hot fat (375°) and fry until brown, about 10 minutes. Drain on absorbent paper.

Note: *This mixture may also be baked as a loaf in a greased baking dish in a moderate oven (350°); or, it may be molded into patties and sauteed in a little fat in a frying pan.*

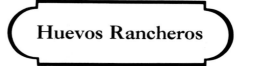

Huevos Rancheros

(6 servings)

¼ cup oil
2 large onions, minced
1 green pepper, seeded and minced
2 cloves garlic, minced
1 large can (28 ounces) Italian-style tomatoes
1 can green chilies, drained, seeded, and minced
Salt and freshly ground pepper
12 tortillas
12 eggs
1 cup Monterey Jack cheese
Freshly chopped coriander

In a heavy skillet heat 3 tablespoons oil and saute the onions and green pepper in oil until just transparent. Add the garlic and saute for 1 minute. Stir in the tomatoes, chilie peppers, and salt and pepper to taste. Simmer 30 minutes. Warm the tortillas in a napkin in the oven. Break 2 eggs for each diner into the sauce. Simmer until the whites are cooked, but the yolks are still runny. Arrange 2 tortillas on each plate. Top with 2 eggs and spoon extra sauce around them. Sprinkle cheese over all and garnish with fresh coriander.

Soups

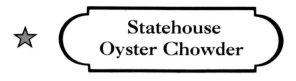

Statehouse Oyster Chowder

(6 servings)

4 strips bacon
2 cups water
1 cup potatoes, diced
1 cup carrots, chopped
½ cup onions, diced
1½ cups kernel corn
1½ cups green peas
1 cup celery, chopped
2 cups milk
½ cup fresh parsley, finely chopped
1 teaspoon oregano
1½ teaspoons salt
¼ teaspoon freshly ground pepper
2 tablespoons Worcestershire sauce
¼ cup cornstarch
1 quart Maryland standard oysters, cut into thirds

In a large skillet cook the bacon over medium heat until half-cooked. Transfer to absorbent paper; crumble when cool. Wipe out skillet and pour in water. Add the vegetables and bacon. Cover and simmer until almost done. Add 1 cup milk, parsley, spices, and Worcestershire sauce. Pour the remaining cup of milk into a small bowl, gradually blend in cornstarch and mix well. Pour the cornstarch mixture into the skillet and stir until well blended. Add the oysters, cover and simmer for 15 more minutes or until oysters curl.

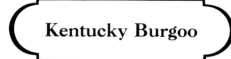

Kentucky Burgoo

(12 servings)

1 pound boneless pork
2 pounds boneless beef chuck
1 pound breast of veal
1 small frying chicken
   Water
1 large potato, peeled and diced
1 onion, chopped
2 carrots, scraped and chopped
½ green pepper, diced
¼ head of cabbage, chopped
3 large tomatoes, peeled, seeded, and chopped
1 cup corn (fresh if possible)
3 tablespoons chopped parsley
1 tablespoon Worcestershire sauce
   Salt and freshly ground black pepper
   Cayenne

Place the meats in a heavy kettle and cover with water. Boil until tender. Drain and reserve the liquid. Cut the meat into cubes. Return the meat to the cooking liquid. Add the vegetables, parsley, Worcestershire, and seasonings to taste. Simmer the mixture until thick. Serve.

Note: *This hearty soup/stew is often served as a main dish, in deep bowls, accompanied by a hearty bread.*

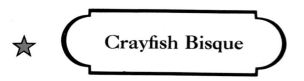

Crayfish Bisque

(6–8 servings)

3 dozen crayfish
¼ cup minced shallots
3 tablespoons lard or butter
3 tablespoons minced parsley
⅓ cup minced scallions
6 slices fresh bread, soaked in water
   Salt and freshly ground pepper
   Cayenne pepper to taste

Bisque:

2 tablespoons flour
1 tablespoon lard or bacon grease
½ onion, minced
½ green pepper, minced
2 tablespoons tomato paste
6–8 cups crayfish cooking water
   Juice from the crayfish heads
   Salt, pepper, and red pepper sauce to taste

Boil the crayfish, in water just to cover, until they turn red. Drain and save the cooking water. Separate the heads from the tails. Clean the heads, saving the juice. Chop up the tail meat.

Preheat the oven to 400°.

In a skillet melt the lard or butter and saute the tail meat for one minute. Add the parsley, scallions, and shallots. Cook two minutes. Squeeze out the bread slices and stir them into the mixture. Season with salt, pepper, and cayenne. Stuff the mixture into the crayfish heads. Arrange the heads on a baking sheet and bake for 5 to 6 minutes, to brown.

To make the bisque, melt the lard in a heavy pot. Add the onion and green pepper. Saute until the onion is transparent. Stir in the flour. Cook until brown. Stir in the tomato paste, juice from the crayfish heads, and cooking water. Simmer at least one hour. Season with salt, pepper, and red pepper sauce. Add the stuffed heads and heat thoroughly. Serve at once over freshly cooked rice.

Note: *See the Resource Guide for information on ordering crayfish.*

Lobster Stew

(6 servings)

3 small lobsters, steamed, cooled, and shelled
2 tablespoons butter
4 cups milk
   Salt and freshly ground white pepper

Cut the lobster meat into 1-inch chunks. In a heavy skillet melt the butter and brown the lobster meat gently. Heat the milk in a saucepan. Season with salt and pepper. Add the lobster meat and heat through. Serve with water crackers.

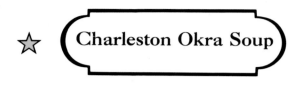

Charleston Okra Soup

(8 servings)

1 hambone with some meat still clinging to it
3 cups okra, thinly sliced
6 large tomatoes, peeled, seeded, and diced
½ cup diced green pepper
1 tablespoon butter
1 small onion, diced
  Salt and freshly ground black pepper
  Cooked rice

In water to cover bring the hambone to a boil. Simmer at least 1 hour. Add the okra, tomatoes, and green pepper. In a small pan melt the butter and saute the onion until golden. Add to the soup. Simmer 2 hours, until soup is thick. Remove the ham bone and shred the meat into the soup. Serve over rice in bowls.

Sauerkraut Soup

(8 servings)

2 pounds smoked pork shanks or knuckles
1 quart water
1 onion, chopped and sauteed until well browned
1 quart sauerkraut juice
¼ cup sugar
¼ cup cream
1 egg
1 tablespoon flour
¾ cup milk

In a large, heavy pot simmer the pork in the water until very tender, about 3 hours. Add the onion, sauerkraut juice, and sugar. In a mixing bowl beat the egg, and add the flour, milk, and cream. Add to the soup and bring just to the boiling point. Serve with Potato Dumplings.

Wine Soup

(6 servings)

½ cup pearl barley, soaked overnight in 2 quarts water
½ cup seedless raisins
⅓ cup dried apricots, cut into small bits
3 tablespoons red currant jelly
3 tablespoons lemon juice
1 cinnamon stick, broken in half
1 cup sweet sherry

In a large pot simmer the barley in its soaking water for one hour. Add the raisins, apricots, jelly, lemon juice, and cinnamon stick. Simmer for 30 minutes. Add the sherry and simmer another 15 minutes. Serve with Betterwheat biscuits or other sweet crackers.

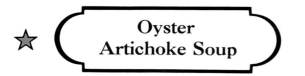

Oyster Artichoke Soup

(6 servings)

- 4 large artichokes
- 4 tablespoons butter
- 2 tablespoons cornstarch
- 2 tablespoons chopped parsley
- 2 scallions with 2 inches of their green tops, finely sliced
- 1 clove garlic, minced
- ¼ teaspoon basil
- ¼ teaspoon thyme
  Dash of red pepper sauce
- 4 cups chicken stock
- 4 dozen shucked oysters and their liquor
- 1 cup heavy cream
- ⅓ cup sherry
  Salt and freshly ground black pepper
- 1 tablespoon butter

Boil the artichokes in a pot of salted water until soft and tender. Remove from the pot, drain, and cool. Scrape the artichoke leaves, saving the pulp. Chop the artichoke hearts into ¼-inch cubes, and set aside. In a heavy pot melt the butter, add the cornstarch, and make a light roux by stirring 15 minutes over a low flame. Add the parsley, scallions, and garlic, and cook until soft. Stir in the artichoke pulp, basil, thyme, and red pepper sauce. Add the chicken stock and simmer 10 minutes. Add the oysters and their liquor (if the oysters are large, cut them in half). Cook until the edges of the oysters curl. Add the cream and the sherry. Simmer 5 minutes. Add salt and pepper to taste. Finish by stirring in the butter.

Polish Beet Soup

(8 servings)

- ¼ cup navy beans
- 2 tablespoons butter
- 4 large tomatoes, peeled, seeded, and chopped
- 6 medium beets, peeled, sliced, and boiled
- 1 head cabbage, quartered and scalded in hot water
- 1 sour apple, chopped
- 1 quart beef stock
  Sour rye bread crust
  Salt and freshly ground black pepper
  Sour cream

Soak the beans overnight in water to cover.

Simmer the beans in their soaking liquid until tender. In a heavy pot melt the butter and simmer the tomatoes for 5 minutes. Add the beets, cabbage, beans, apple, and stock and cook for 30 minutes. Put the rye bread crust into the soup and simmer until it becomes very soft, but lift it out before it falls apart. Pour the hot soup into bowls and stir a tablespoon of sour cream into each serving.

Pepper Pot Soup

(6 servings)

⅓ pound tripe, cut into ¼-inch pieces
2 cups water
2 tablespoons chicken fat
¼ cup chopped onion
¼ cup chopped celery
3 tablespoons finely chopped green pepper
1 cup well-flavored chicken stock
2 cups beef stock
　Salt and freshly ground black pepper
1 teaspoon fresh thyme
½ cup diced raw potato
3 tablespoons flour
3 tablespoons water
¼ cup milk

　In a heavy pot simmer the tripe in water over low heat until tender—as long as 2 hours. In a heavy saucepan melt the chicken fat and add the vegetables. Cook until very tender and transparent. Add ¾ cup of the tripe broth and the chicken and beef stocks to the vegetables. Simmer. Add the salt and pepper, thyme, potatoes, and drained tripe. Cook until the potatoes are tender, about 30 minutes. In a cup combine the flour and water to make a paste. Add to the soup, stirring constantly. Cook for 10 minutes. Remove from heat and add the milk. Season with freshly ground pepper.

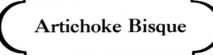

Artichoke Bisque

(6 servings)

8 large artichoke hearts
1 large onion, chopped
2 potatoes, chopped
4 cups well-seasoned chicken stock
　Salt and freshly ground pepper
1 cup heavy cream
　Red pepper sauce

　In a large kettle simmer the artichoke hearts, onion, and potatoes in chicken stock until tender. Puree the vegetables in a blender or food processor. Season with salt and pepper and stir in the heavy cream. Add red pepper sauce to taste. Serve very hot.

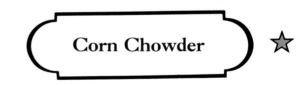

Corn Chowder

(6 servings)

¼ pound salt pork, cut into cubes
1 large onion, sliced thin
4–5 medium potatoes (with or without skin), cubed
2 cups well-seasoned chicken stock
1 cup half and half
2 cups cooked corn
2 teaspoons salt
¼ teaspoon paprika

Brown the salt pork in a heavy saucepan. Add the onion and brown. Pour off the fat. Add the potatoes and broth and simmer until the potatoes are tender. Stir in the half and half, corn, salt, and paprika. Simmer 10 minutes longer and serve very hot, sprinkled with the paprika.

Note: *Traditionally this soup is accompanied by oyster crackers.*

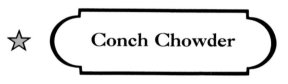

★ Conch Chowder

(6 servings)

6 slices bacon, diced
½ cup chopped onion
¼ cup diced sweet red pepper
2 tomatoes, peeled, seeded, and diced
3 cups water
2 carrots, diced
3 potatoes, washed and diced
2 tablespoons Worcestershire sauce
2 tablespoons butter
1 pound conch, ground
2 tablespoons bread crumbs
2 cups half and half or milk
    Salt and freshly ground pepper
½ teaspoon allspice
    Red pepper sauce to taste

In a heavy pot fry the bacon, onion and red pepper until transparent. Add the tomatoes, water, carrots, potatoes, Worcestershire, butter, and conch. Simmer for 45 minutes. Add the bread crumbs, half and half, and seasonings. Simmer 15 minutes longer. Retaste and add more red pepper sauce if desired.

Notes: *Conch is a large snail-like shellfish found in warm Southern waters. It is available fresh in fine fish shops. There are perhaps hundreds of local variations on this basic recipe.*

Snapper Soup ★

(8–10 servings)

4 tablespoons butter
4 tablespoons flour
1½ quarts well-seasoned veal stock
1 12-ounce can of tomatoes
1 cup canned turtle meat
2 tablespoons lemon juice
    Salt and freshly ground pepper
¼ cup sherry

In a large kettle melt the butter, stir in the flour, and cook gently for 10 minutes until browned but not burned. Add 2 cups of stock and simmer until the mixture thickens. Add the remaining ingredients, except the sherry, and simmer 15 minutes. Stir in the sherry and serve hot with more sherry on the side.

Note: *Traditionally the stock was made from the turtle carcass. Since they are somewhat rare these days, veal stock is a fine substitute.*

New Mexico Chili Soup

(4 servings)

2 tablespoons oil
1 pound ground beef
1 onion, chopped
1 tablespoon flour
1 16-ounce can of tomatoes
½ teaspoon minced garlic
4 green chilies, peeled, seeded, and chopped
1 tablespoon chili powder
  Pinch of cumin
  Salt
  Water

In a skillet heat the oil and brown the meat and onion. Stir in the flour. Add the tomatoes and break them up with a fork. Stir in the garlic, chilies, chili powder, and cumin. Season with salt. Add enough water to moisten the mixture. Simmer for several hours.

Sausage and Vegetable Soup

(12 servings)

½ medium cabbage, shredded
4 medium carrots, peeled and sliced
3 medium potatoes, peeled and cubed
3 stalks celery with leaves, chopped
1 turnip, cubed (optional)
1 large onion, peeled and thinly sliced
2 quarts beef stock
4 tablespoons tomato paste
2 tablespoons vinegar
1 teaspoon salt
½ teaspoon dried thyme, crushed
¼ teaspoon black pepper
1 pound kielbasa, cut in ¼-inch slices

In a large kettle or Dutch oven combine the cabbage, carrots, potatoes, celery, turnip and onion. Add the stock, tomato paste, vinegar and seasonings. Bring to a boil. Reduce the heat and stir in the sausage. Simmer, covered, for 35 to 45 minutes or until vegetables are tender.

New England Fish Chowder

(6 servings)

2 pounds haddock or cod in a solid piece
3 cups boiling water
2 ounces fat salt pork, diced
2 medium sized onions, peeled and sliced
3 medium sized potatoes, peeled and sliced
3 cups milk, scalded
1 tablespoon salt
¼ teaspoon freshly ground white pepper

In a pot simmer the fish in 2 cups of water until tender, about 15 minutes. Strain, reserving the liquid. Discard the bones, skin, etc. In a deep saucepan brown the salt pork lightly. Add the onions, potatoes, and the rest of the water; cook until the potatoes are tender. Combine with the fish and fish broth. Add the scalded milk, salt, and pepper. Heat thoroughly and serve at once.

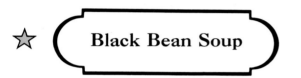

★ Black Bean Soup

(10 servings)

1 pound black beans
¼ pound bacon, diced
2 cups finely chopped onion
1 tablespoon minced garlic
2 cups diced green pepper
8 cups water (including the bean-soaking water)
1½ pounds smoked ham bones or knuckles
1 teaspoon dried oregano
½ teaspoon red pepper sauce
½ cup dry sherry
Lemon slices

Soak the beans in water to cover overnight.

Drain the beans, reserving the liquid. Cook the bacon in a large soup pot until most of the fat is extracted. Discard all but 2 tablespoons of the fat and saute the onion, garlic, and green pepper until transparent. Add the beans and all the other ingredients except the sherry and lemon slices. Bring to

a boil, reduce the heat and simmer gently for 2 hours, stirring occasionally. Remove from the heat and cool slightly. Remove the ham hocks, dice the meat and reserve. Discard the bones. Degrease the soup. Puree half the soup in a food processor. Combine the puree, diced meat, and sherry with the remaining soup, and adjust the seasonings. Reheat and serve immediately, garnished with lemon slices.

Cream of Sorrel Soup ★

(6 servings)

1 pound fresh sorrel, washed and stems removed
3 tablespoons butter
4 cups well-seasoned chicken stock
1 bunch scallions, finely sliced
1 slice white bread, cut into pieces
1 cup heavy cream
Salt and freshly ground white pepper

In a large pot melt the butter and wilt the sorrel. Pour in the stock and add the scallions. Simmer 30 to 35 minutes. Add the bread. Stir until the bread falls apart. Remove the soup from the pot and puree in a food processor until smooth. Return the puree to the pot. Season with salt and pepper. Stir in the cream and heat thoroughly. Finish the soup by beating in one tablespoon butter, if desired.

Peanut Soup

(6–8 servings)

4 tablespoons butter
3 tablespoons minced onion
1 clove garlic, minced
1 tablespoon flour
1 cup peanut butter
4 cups well-seasoned chicken stock
   Salt and freshly ground black pepper
1 cup heavy cream
½ cup finely chopped or ground peanuts

In a heavy kettle melt the butter and add the onion, garlic, flour, and peanut butter and stir until smooth. Beat in the stock. Simmer over very low heat for 20 minutes or until thick. Add the cream, heat through and serve with ground peanuts.

Clam Chowder

(6–8 servings)

1 quart shucked clams and their liquor
¼ pound salt pork, diced
2 medium onions, chopped
4 potatoes, chopped
   Salt and freshly ground white pepper
4 cups milk
2 tablespoons butter

Chop the clams. Strain the liquor and set aside. Fry the salt pork in a skillet until crisp. Remove with a slotted spoon and drain on absorbent paper. Add the onions and saute until golden. Add the potatoes. Season with salt and pepper and add the clam liquor. Simmer 10 minutes. Add the milk and salt pork. Heat well. Stir in the butter and serve at once.

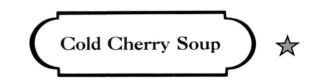

Cold Cherry Soup

(6 servings)

4 cups fresh pitted cherries, pureed in food processor or blender
⅓ cup sugar
1 lemon, halved lengthwise and sliced thin
2 cups water
1 cinnamon stick
1 cup dry red wine
1 cup heavy cream, whipped

In a saucepan gently simmer the cherry puree, sugar, lemon slices, water, and cinnamon for 25 minutes, stirring frequently. Remove from the heat. Cool. Remove the cinnamon stick. Stir in the wine and chill at least 4 hours. Stir well. Serve topped with whipped cream.

Cold Cherry Soup ▶

Black Forest Escargot Soup

(6 servings)

4 tablespoons butter
¼ cup minced French shallots
1½ tablespoons minced garlic
½ pound mushrooms, cleaned and finely chopped
1 cup white wine
1 cup beef broth
1 cup chicken broth
1 cup heavy cream
3½ ounces minced escargots
1 tablespoon minced green onion
3 tablespoons minced parsley
½ teaspoon salt or to taste
¼ teaspoon white pepper or to taste
4 tablespoons butter, softened and creamed with 3 tablespoons flour
2 teaspoons Pernod
3½ ounces whole escargots

In a heavy saucepan heat the butter over a low flame. Add the shallots, garlic and mushrooms. Saute for 2 minutes or until tender. Pour in the wine and the broths and simmer for 15 minutes. Add the cream, chopped escargots, green onion, parsley, salt, and pepper. Blend in the butter-flour mixture. Add the Pernod. Simmer over low heat 1 to 2 minutes. Do not boil. Add the whole escargots and serve.

Note: *Pernod is one of the most popular brand names for the French liqueur anisette.*

Spicy Crab Soup

(8 servings)

1 quart water
3 chicken necks or wings
3 pounds canned tomatoes, quartered
1 cup fresh corn kernels
1 cup fresh peas
1 cup diced potatoes
¾ cup chopped celery
¾ cup diced onion
¾ tablespoon seafood seasoning
1 teaspoon salt
¼ teaspoon lemon pepper
1 pound Maryland crabmeat, cartilage removed

Place water and chicken parts in a 6-quart soup pot. Cover and simmer over low heat for at least 1 hour. Add vegetables and seasonings and simmer, covered, over medium low heat for about 45 minutes, or until vegetables are almost tender. Add crabmeat, cover, and simmer for 15 minutes more or until hot.

Note: *For a milder soup, decrease the amount of seafood seasoning to 1–1½ teaspoons.*

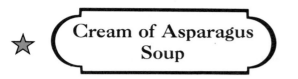

Cream of Asparagus Soup

(6 servings)

1 pound fresh asparagus
4 cups well-seasoned chicken stock
1 onion, chopped
  Salt and freshly ground white pepper
1 cup heavy cream
1 tablespoon butter

Cut off the asparagus tips and steam over hot water until tender. Reserve. Chop the remaining asparagus stems. Place in a small kettle. Add the stock, onion and salt and pepper to taste. Simmer 30 to 35 minutes. Puree the mixture in a blender until smooth. Return the soup to the kettle and stir in the cream. Heat thoroughly and whisk in the butter. Serve in a tureen with asparagus tips floated on top.

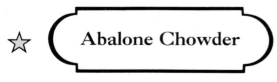

Abalone Chowder

(4–6 servings)

¼ pound salt pork, diced
½ cup diced potato
½ cup diced onion
 6 slices abalone, pounded thin and diced
1 clove garlic, minced
2 cups hot water
2 cups cream
  Salt and freshly ground pepper to taste

In a kettle fry the salt pork until golden. Remove all but 3 tablespoons of the drippings. Brown the potato, onion, abalone, and garlic. Add the 2 cups water. Simmer until tender. Add the cream and salt and pepper. Serve hot.

Lima Bean Soup

(6 servings)

½ pound dried lima beans, soaked overnight
3 cups well-seasoned chicken stock
1 carrot, diced
1 onion, diced
1 stalk celery, diced
1 tablespoon freshly chopped parsley
1 cup cream
  Salt and freshly ground pepper

In a large kettle simmer the beans in the stock along with the carrot, onion, and celery until beans are very tender, 2 to 3 hours. Puree half of the mixture and return puree to the soup. Stir in the parsley, cream, and salt and pepper to taste. Simmer 5 minutes and serve hot.

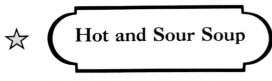

Hot and Sour Soup

(6–8 servings)

⅓ cup shredded seaweed
⅓ cup shredded wood ear mushrooms, softened
⅓ cup shredded bean curd
¼ pound shredded cooked pork loin
1 teaspoon and 2 tablespoons soy sauce
4 tablespoons cornstarch
1½ teaspoons sesame oil
6 cups water
2 teaspoons salt
1 teaspoon sugar
3 tablespoons vinegar
1 teaspoon pepper
1 tablespoon chopped coriander
2 tablespoons shredded scallions
2 tablespoons shredded ginger root
3 tablespoons water
2 eggs, beaten

In a kettle of boiling water blanch the seaweed, wood ears, and bean curd for 30 seconds. Drain. Mix the pork loin with 1 teaspoon soy sauce, 1 tablespoon cornstarch and ½ teaspoon sesame oil. In another kettle heat the water, salt, and sugar to boiling. Add the seaweed, wood ears, and bean curd. When the water boils again, add the pork loin. Stir well.

Place the remaining soy sauce, vinegar, remaining sesame oil, pepper, chopped coriander, scallions, and ginger root in a bowl, mix and set aside. Dissolve the remaining 3 tablespoons cornstarch in 3 tablespoons water and add to the soup. Turn off the heat and add the beaten egg to the soup in a thin stream, stirring all the time. Stir in the scallion mixture. Ladle the soup into bowls.

Note: *Wood ear mushrooms—Black Tree Fungus—are sometimes called Cloud ear mushrooms. See the Resource Guide for information on ordering ingredients not generally available in your area.*

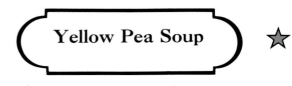

Yellow Pea Soup

(8 servings)

2 cups dried yellow split peas
1 ham bone (smoked ham or packers ham)
1 clove garlic, minced
1 large onion, minced
½ cup celery, minced
2½ quarts water
1 tablespoon butter
1 tablespoon flour
Salt and freshly ground pepper
½ cup milk

Soak the peas overnight.

Drain the peas. Add the ham bone, garlic, onion, and celery with 2½ quarts water and cook until the peas are very tender. Remove and discard the ham bone. In the bowl of a food processor, or in a blender, puree the peas with some of the cooking liquid. Return the puree to the remaining cooking liquid. Melt the butter in a saucepan. Add the flour and cook about 5 minutes over low heat. Do not allow it to brown. Add salt and pepper, if necessary. Stir in the milk and cook until it begins to thicken. Pour into the soup and simmer for 10 minutes. Serve with buttered toast or croutons.

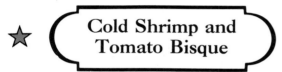

Cold Shrimp and Tomato Bisque

(8 servings)

1 pound shrimp
1 quart water
1 stalk celery, cut up
1 onion, chopped
2 cloves garlic, crushed
10 peppercorns
    Salt
½ cup white wine
2 cups peeled, seeded, and chopped tomatoes
½ cup sherry
½ cup heavy cream
    Chopped fresh parsley

In a large kettle boil the shrimp in the water with the celery, onion, garlic, peppercorns, and salt to taste for 5 minutes. Cool the shrimp in the liquid. Shell the shrimp and return the shells to the cooking liquid. Set the shrimp aside. Add the wine to the liquid and boil for 20 minutes. Strain the cooking liquid into another saucepan, press-

ing down on the shells and vegetables to obtain as much pulp and flavor as possible. Add the tomatoes and sherry. Simmer 20 minutes. Add all but 8 shrimp to the tomato mixture. Heat thoroughly. Puree the soup in a blender or food processor. Return to the kettle, add the cream and check for seasonings. Simmer 5 minutes. Refrigerate at least four hours. Garnish with the reserved whole shrimp and chopped parsley.

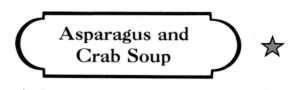

Asparagus and Crab Soup

(6 servings)

1 pound fresh asparagus, cleaned and cut into 1-inch lengths
1 quart well-seasoned chicken broth
1 onion, chopped
1 cup heavy cream
12 ounces crabmeat, well picked over
    Salt and freshly ground pepper

Steam just the asparagus tips until just tender and then set aside. Bring the chicken broth to a boil in a kettle. Add the rest of the asparagus along with the onion. Boil gently until the asparagus is very tender. Puree the mixture in a blender or food processor. Return the puree to the kettle. Stir in the cream and bring to a simmer. Stir in the crabmeat and reserved asparagus tips. Season with salt and pepper and heat thoroughly. Serve very hot.

$\mathcal{B}$reads

◄ *Swedish Rye Bread*

Graham Bread

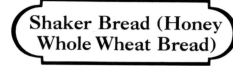

Shaker Bread (Honey Whole Wheat Bread)

(Makes 1 loaf)

- 1 cup milk
- 2 tablespoons butter
- 4 tablespoons sugar
- 1 teaspoon salt
- 1 package dry yeast
- 2 tablespoons lukewarm water
- 2 cups flour (unbleached is best)
- 1 cup chopped walnuts
- ½ cup plumped raisins, dredged in flour
- 2 tablespoons brown sugar
- 2 cups or more whole wheat flour

In a saucepan heat the milk, add the butter, sugar, and salt and stir until melted. Soften the yeast in warm water. Add to the milk. Stir in the white flour, walnuts, raisins, and brown sugar. Set aside and allow to rise until double in bulk.

Punch down the dough, add the whole wheat flour and knead until shiny and elastic—at least 10 to 15 minutes. Allow to rise again.

Punch down. Shape into a loaf and place in greased loaf pan. Let rise until doubled in bulk. Preheat the oven to 350°.

Bake for 50 to 60 minutes.

(2 loaves)

- 2 envelopes dry yeast
- 2¾ cups warm water
- ½ cup honey
- ¼ cup shortening (butter, margarine, or solid vegetable shortening)
- 1 tablespoon salt
- 2 cups unbleached white flour
- 5 cups whole wheat flour (approximately)

Soften the yeast in ½ cup of warm water. Add 3 tablespoons honey and let stand for five minutes. Stir in remaining honey, shortening, salt, and remaining water. Add white flour and enough whole wheat flour to make a soft dough.

Knead until smooth and shiny, about 10 minutes or more. Cover and let rise 2 hours or until doubled in bulk. Punch down and let rise 30 minutes. Punch down and shape dough into two loaves. Lightly oil two loaf pans. Place loaves in pans, cover and let rise until doubled. Preheat the oven to 375°.

Bake 35 to 40 minutes, or until a loaf sounds hollow when tapped on the bottom.

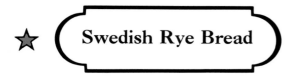

Swedish Rye Bread

(4 loaves)

    4 cups milk
    3 tablespoons margarine
 3½ ounces yeast (3 cakes or 3 envelopes)
    ½ tablespoon salt
    ¾ cup corn syrup or molasses
    3 teaspoons fennel seeds (optional)
    3 teaspoons caraway seeds (optional)
 1¾ pounds rye flour
 1½ cups bran or wheat germ
 2¼ pounds all-purpose unbleached flour

In a small saucepan warm the margarine and milk. Pour into a large bowl and add the yeast, salt, syrup, seasonings and half the rye flour. Add the bran and the rest of the flour. Knead thoroughly and set aside for raising, about 40 minutes. Form dough into 4 loaves and place on buttered baking sheets. Let rise until double in bulk. Preheat the oven to 400°.

Make a couple of incisions in each loaf and bake for 35 to 40 minutes. Brush several times during baking with warm water mixed with 1 teaspoon corn syrup.

Note: *The Swedish settlers of the Midwest would have called this "Plain Bread."*

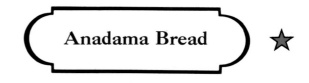

Anadama Bread

(2 loaves)

 1½ cups boiling water
    1 cup yellow cornmeal
    4 tablespoons (½ stick) butter, melted
    ½ cup molasses
    2 tablespoons salt
    1 package dry yeast
    ¼ cup milk, scalded and cooled slightly
 4–5 cups flour

In a mixing bowl beat together the water, cornmeal, butter, molasses, and salt. Cool to lukewarm. Dissolve the yeast in the scalded milk. Stir into the cornmeal mixture. Stir in 2 cups of flour. Add more flour until dough is fairly stiff. Knead until shiny and elastic, working in more flour, at least 10 to 15 minutes. Gather the dough into a ball. Grease lightly and let rise until doubled in bulk. Punch down. Shape into loaves and place in greased bread pans. Let rise until doubled in bulk. Preheat the oven to 400°.

Bake for 20 minutes. Reduce heat to 325° and bake 30 to 40 minutes longer, until the loaf pulls away from the sides of the pan. Turn out onto racks and cool.

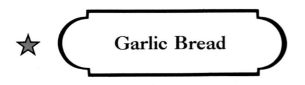

Garlic Bread

(6 servings)

1 loaf French bread, about 14 inches long
¼ pound (1 stick) butter
1 teaspoon garlic powder
¼ cup finely chopped parsley
¼ cup freshly grated parmesan cheese

Preheat the oven to 375°.

Slice the French bread lengthwise. In a small skillet melt the butter and add the garlic powder. Heat for 2 minutes. Brush the butter-garlic mixture on the cut side of the French bread halves. Sprinkle the bread with the parsley and parmesan cheese. Cut each half crosswise into 1-inch slices. Heat the bread for 5 to 8 minutes. Serve immediately.

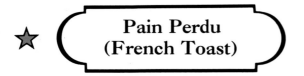

Pain Perdu (French Toast)

(3–4 servings)

3 tablespoons sugar
½ teaspoon cinnamon
1 teaspoon brandy
2 eggs, well beaten
¾ cup milk

6 thick slices day-old French bread
2–3 tablespoons butter

In a shallow pan beat the sugar, cinnamon, brandy, and eggs together well. Beat in the milk. Soak the bread slices in the mixture, turning once. In a heavy skillet melt the butter. When the bubbling stops, fry the bread until brown on both sides, turning once. Serve at once with cane syrup, cinnamon sugar, or powdered sugar.

Muffins

(12 muffins)

1 cup milk
1 egg, beaten
4 tablespoons (½ stick) butter, melted
2 cups flour
2 teaspoons baking powder
3 tablespoons sugar
  Pinch of salt

Preheat the oven to 425°.

In a mixing bowl beat together the milk, egg, and butter. In a separate bowl sift together the flour, baking powder, sugar, and salt. Stir the flour mixture into the milk just until moistened. Do not beat. Fill greased muffin tins ⅔ full. Bake for 20 to 25 minutes.

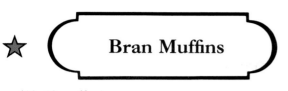

Bran Muffins

(10–12 muffins)

1 cup shredded bran cereal
1 cup milk
2 tablespoons butter
1 egg
1 cup flour
3 teaspoons baking powder
Pinch of salt

Preheat the oven to 375°.

Soak the bran in the milk until soft. In another bowl beat the butter and egg until smooth. Stir into the bran mixture. Stir in the flour, baking powder and salt. Do not over-mix. Spoon the mixture into greased muffin tins, filling each tin two-thirds full. Bake for 25 to 30 minutes.

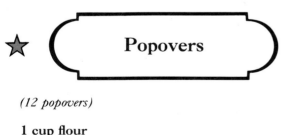

Popovers

(12 popovers)

1 cup flour
Pinch of salt
1 cup milk
2 eggs
1 tablespoon butter, melted

Preheat the oven to 400°.

Put all the ingredients in a food processor or blender. Process until smooth, stopping occasionally to scrape down the sides. Grease muffin tins or Pyrex cups generously and heat in the oven. Pour the batter into the hot tins. Bake for 30 minutes. Reduce heat to 300° and dry out the popovers for 15 minutes. Serve with butter and homemade jelly.

Southern Spoon Bread

(8 servings)

2 cups sweet milk
½ cup white cornmeal
½ teaspoon baking powder
1 teaspoon salt
3 eggs, separated, yolks well beaten, whites beaten until stiff peaks form
3 tablespoons butter, melted

Preheat the oven to 275°.

In a saucepan scald the milk and slowly stir in the cornmeal. Cook over low heat until the consistency of soft grits. Add the baking powder, salt, and well-beaten egg yolks. Add the melted butter. Fold in the stiffly beaten egg whites. Bake in a well-greased casserole for 30 minutes. Serve immediately.

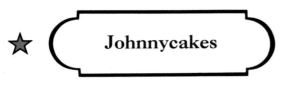

Johnnycakes

(6 servings)

2 cups yellow cornmeal
¼ cup sugar
½ teaspoon salt
1 cup or more boiling water
2 tablespoons bacon drippings

In a mixing bowl stir together the corn-meal, sugar, salt, and boiling water to make a thick, smooth batter. Lightly grease a griddle with bacon fat and preheat. Drop the batter by spoonfuls onto the hot griddle. When cakes are crisp and beginning to brown on one side, turn and cook on the other. Continue until all the batter is used.

Note: *Johnnycakes are often served accompanied by butter and maple syrup.*

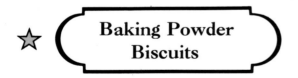

Baking Powder Biscuits

(12 2½-inch biscuits)

2 cups flour
2½ teaspoons baking powder
¼ teaspoon baking soda
3 tablespoons butter
1 cup buttermilk
⅛ teaspoon salt

Sift the flour, baking powder, and baking soda into a bowl. Cut in the butter until the mixture resembles coarse meal. Stir in the buttermilk and salt. Cover the dough and refrigerate for 30 minutes. Preheat the oven to 375°.

Turn the dough out on a lightly floured board. Pat, but do not roll, to ½-inch thickness. Cut with a biscuit cutter. Bake on an ungreased cookie sheet for 20 minutes or until lightly browned.

Variation: *Increase baking powder to 3 teaspoons and substitute cream for the buttermilk.*

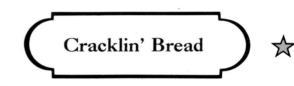

Cracklin' Bread

(14–16 pones)

2 cups cornmeal
1 teaspoon salt
1 cup Cracklin's, broken into pieces
1 cup boiling water, approximately

Preheat the oven to 350°.

In a bowl mix together the cornmeal and salt. Add the cracklin's. Add sufficient boiling water to make a stiff dough. Shape the dough into pones and bake on a greased cookie sheet for about 45 minutes.

Notes: *Pones are small, elongated bread shapes, molded by hand, each containing about 3 tablespoons of dough. Cracklin's are the small pieces of meat left in the pan after rendering lard.*

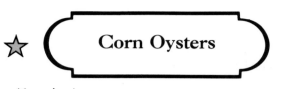

Corn Oysters

(6 servings)

2 cups corn, freshly cut from cob
2 eggs, beaten
   Salt and freshly ground white pepper
2 tablespoons flour
   Fat or oil for deep frying

In the bowl of a food processor chop the corn coarsely. Do not drain. Set aside until the corn mixture resembles a thick custard. Beat in eggs, salt and pepper, and flour. Drop by tablespoonfuls into hot deep fat. Drain on absorbent paper and salt lightly. Serve very hot.

Navajo Fry Bread

(8 servings)

3 cups flour (all white or half whole wheat)
1½ teaspoons baking powder
½ teaspoon salt
1⅓ cups warm water
   Shortening for deep frying

In a large bowl, stir together the flour, baking powder, and salt. Add the warm water and mix (the dough should be soft but not sticky). Knead the dough until it is smooth.

In a large, heavy skillet heat enough shortening for deep frying. (Lard is the traditional shortening, but you might prefer to use vegetable oil.)

Tear off a piece of dough about the size of a peach. Pat and stretch it until it is thin. Poke a hole through the middle, and drop into the sizzling-hot deep fat. Brown on both sides. Drain and serve hot with honey or jam.

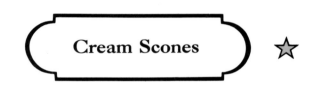

Cream Scones

(12 scones)

2 cups flour
⅔ teaspoon baking powder
   Pinch of salt
3 tablespoons sugar
4 tablespoons (½ stick) butter
¾ cup cream, soured with 2 teaspoons vinegar
1 egg, beaten with a pinch of salt

Preheat the oven to 475°.

In a bowl combine the flour, baking powder, salt, and sugar. Cut in the butter until the mixture resembles coarse meal. Add the soured cream to the flour mixture. Knead two or three times on a floured board. Do not overwork. Roll out ¼- to ⅜-inch thick. Cut in rounds, squares or diamonds. Brush with egg and bake for 10 to 12 minutes.

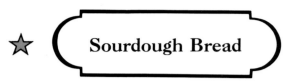

Sourdough Bread

(1 loaf)

Sourdough starter:
1 package dry yeast
2 cups warm water
3 teaspoons sugar
2 cups unbleached flour

Bread dough:
   1 cup starter
   ½ cup warm milk
   3 tablespoons butter, melted
   3 tablespoons sugar
2½–3 cups unbleached flour

To make the starter dissolve the yeast in the warm water. Stir in the sugar and flour. Let stand, lightly covered, at room temperature at least 24 hours, or until mixture begins to bubble and work.

In a bowl combine the starter, milk, and butter. Stir in the sugar and half the flour. Add remaining flour, or enough to make a soft ball.

Turn out the dough on a well-floured board. Knead for 10 minutes until smooth and shiny. Cover and let rise until double in bulk. Punch down and let rise again. Punch down, turn out on a floured board, and knead out the air bubbles, about 5 minutes. Shape into a loaf and place in a greased loaf pan. Let rise until doubled again. Preheat the oven to 400°.

Bake for 35 to 40 minutes. Cool on a rack.

Variation: To make Sourdough Biscuits, roll out the dough to a thickness of ¼ inch and cut with a 1½-inch biscuit cutter. Let rise 15 minutes, then bake at 400° for 15 to 20 minutes or until golden brown. Serve hot, with lots of butter.

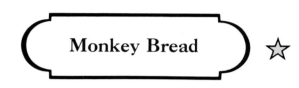

Monkey Bread

(1 loaf)

   1 cup milk, scalded
1½ tablespoons sugar
   1 teaspoon salt
   1 tablespoon butter
   1 package dry yeast
   ¼ cup warm water
3–4 cups flour
   ½ cup butter, melted

In a mixing bowl add the sugar, salt, and butter to the hot milk. Dissolve the yeast in the warm water. Cool the milk and stir in the yeast. Add the flour to the milk, stirring in enough to make an easily handled dough. Knead until smooth and shiny, at least 5 minutes. Form into a long, narrow loaf. Cover and let rise until double in bulk. Cut the loaf into 2-inch pieces. Dip the pieces in the melted butter and arrange in layers in a 9-inch tube pan. Let rise again until doubled again. Preheat the oven to 350°.

Bake for 50 minutes. Turn out of mold and cool, or serve hot.

Monkey Bread ▶

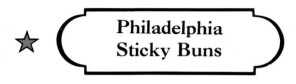

Philadelphia Sticky Buns

(8 servings)

> 1 package dry yeast
> 1 cup warm water
> 5 tablespoons sugar
> 2 cups milk
> 2 eggs, beaten
> ½ cup melted butter
> 4½–5½ cups flour
> 4 tablespoons butter
> 1 cup chopped raisins
> ¼ cup plumped currants
> ¼ cup chopped pecans
> 2 teaspoons cinnamon
> ¼ cup sugar

Syrup:

> 4 tablespoons butter
> ½ cup brown sugar

In a mixing bowl soften the yeast in the warm water. Add the sugar, milk, beaten egg, melted butter, and flour to make a soft dough. Knead lightly. Let rise until double in bulk. Punch down and roll out into a rectangle. In a bowl mix together the 4 tablespoons butter, the raisins, currants, pecans, cinnamon, and sugar. Spread the filling on the dough and roll up from the long side like a jelly roll. Cut into 1-inch pieces.

To make the syrup, melt the butter and sugar in the bottom of a baking pan. Arrange the rolls in the syrup, cut side down. Let rise until double in bulk. Preheat the oven to 400°.

Bake for 15 to 20 minutes.

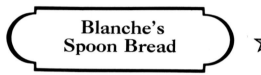

Blanche's Spoon Bread

(8 servings)

> 1 cup self-rising cornmeal
> 3 cups milk
> 2 tablespoons shortening
> 3 eggs
> Salt to taste
> 2 tablespoons sugar or more to taste

Preheat the oven to 400°.

In a heavy saucepan, mix the cornmeal with 2 cups of the milk, reserving the remaining cup of milk. Place over medium heat; add the shortening and stir until the mixture is smooth. Increase the heat and bring to a boil.

In a large bowl beat together the eggs, salt, sugar, and the remaining cup milk. Add to the cornmeal mixture. Pour into a 1½-quart casserole or baking pan. Bake for 30 to 35 minutes or until spoonbread feels firm in the center and top is richly browned.

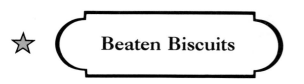

Beaten Biscuits

(About 3 dozen biscuits)

6 cups all-purpose flour
1 tablespoon salt
2 tablespoons sugar
1 cup lard
1½ cups milk

Sift together dry ingredients and cut in lard to a consistency of fine meal. Add milk a little at a time to make a very stiff dough. Work until dough is smooth and blisters well. If using a dough hook, beat mixture for 15 minutes or until it is smooth, blistered, and no longer sticks to bowl. If working by hand, knead dough by picking up the mass and slapping it down against the board until it is shiny and blistered. This could take 30 minutes or more. Or put into the bowl of a food processor and process 3 minutes with a steel blade, then knead as usual. Roll out dough to ½-inch thickness on board. Cut with small biscuit cutter and prick from top through to bottom with tines of a fork. Preheat the oven to 300°.

Place the biscuits on a greased baking sheet and bake for 45 minutes. Biscuits should be lightly colored but not browned.

Note: *Traditionally the dough for beaten biscuits was literally beaten with a hammer—often on a tree stump in the backyard—until it blistered. The process sometimes took an hour or more if there was a large quantity of dough.*

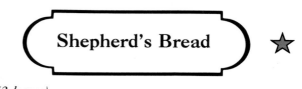

Shepherd's Bread

(2 loaves)

1 cup milk
¼ cup sugar
1 tablespoon salt
4 tablespoons butter
2 envelopes dry yeast
1½ cups water
8 cups flour, approximately

Scald the milk in a saucepan. Cool slightly. Stir in the sugar, salt and butter. Cool. In a bowl add the yeast to the warm water. Stir until dissolved. Add the cooled milk and stir. Stir in half the flour. Beat until smooth. Stir in additional flour to make a soft dough. Turn the dough out onto a well floured board and knead at least 10 minutes or until smooth and elastic. Place in a greased bowl. Let rise until double in bulk. Punch dough. Let rest 15 minutes. Divide the dough in half. Shape each half into a ball and set on a greased baking sheet. Let rise until doubled in bulk. Preheat the oven to 400°.

Bake for 20 minutes or until loaves sound hollow when tapped on the bottom.

Stollen

(2 loaves)

½ cup milk
½ cup sugar
  Pinch of salt
½ pound (2 sticks) butter
 2 envelopes dry yeast
½ cup warm water
 5 cups flour, approximately
 2 eggs
¼ teaspoon mace
 1 cup raisins
 1 cup candied fruits (citron, pineapple, etc.),
  chopped
 1 cup chopped almonds
 2 tablespoons sugar
 1 teaspoon cinnamon
  Powdered sugar

In a saucepan heat the milk to boiling. Remove from the heat and stir in the sugar, salt, and half of the butter. Cool. Dissolve the yeast in the warm water and add to the milk mixture. Add 2 cups of the flour and the eggs and mace. Turn the dough into the bowl of an electric mixer or food processor and beat with a dough hook for 5 minutes, or process for 60 seconds. Stir in the fruits and almonds. Stir in enough additional flour to make a soft dough. Turn out onto a floured board and knead until smooth and

shiny, at least 5 minutes. Place the dough in a greased bowl. Cover and let rise until double in bulk. Punch down. Knead again to remove air bubbles. Divide the dough into 2 pieces. Roll each into a 15″ × 9″ oval. Melt the remaining butter. Generously brush the dough with the melted butter. Mix together the cinnamon and sugar and sprinkle over the loaves. Fold each piece in half lengthwise. Lay the dough on a baking sheet and curve into a slight crescent shape. Cover and let rise until double in bulk. Preheat the oven to 350°.

Bake for 30 minutes. Sprinkle with powdered sugar while hot.

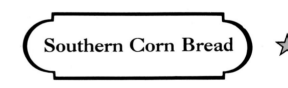

Southern Corn Bread

(10 servings)

 3 whole eggs
 2 cups buttermilk or 1¾ cups sweet milk
  mixed with ¼ cup vinegar
⅓ cup butter, melted
1½ teaspoon salt
 3 teaspoon baking powder
 2 cups yellow cornmeal
 1 tablespoon white flour

Preheat the oven to 450°.

In a small bowl beat the eggs well. Add the buttermilk and melted butter and stir well to combine. In a separate bowl sift together all the dry ingredients. Combine the milk and egg mixture with the dry ingredients, stirring just until moist. Pour the mixture into a well greased, 13″×9″×2″ pan. Bake for about 20 minutes. Cut into 2-inch squares to serve. Split the squares and butter them while they are still hot.

Note: *This corn bread is also excellent cold.*

Parker House Rolls

(24 rolls)

2 cups milk
4 tablespoons (½ stick) butter
3 tablespoons sugar
2 teaspoons salt
2 packets dry yeast
4 tablespoons warm water
6 cups flour
4 tablespoons (½ stick) butter, melted

In a saucepan heat the milk and add the butter, sugar, and salt. Stir until melted. Remove from the heat. Dissolve the yeast in the warm water. Stir into the milk. Stir in the flour. Knead until smooth and elastic. Cover and let rise until doubled in bulk. Punch down the dough and roll into a rec-

tangle ¼-inch thick. Cut the dough into rounds with a large biscuit cutter. Brush the tops with melted butter. Make a crease across the center of each roll with the back of a knife. Fold rolls over. Place rolls on baking sheet about one inch apart. Cover and let rise until doubled in bulk. Preheat the oven to 400°.

Bake for 30 minutes.

Corn Sticks

(12 servings)

¾ cup all-purpose flour
 2 teaspoons baking powder
 2 tablespoons sugar
¾ tablespoon salt
¾ cup yellow cornmeal
 1 egg
 2 tablespoons butter, melted
¾ cup milk

Preheat the oven to 425°. Grease generously 12 iron corn stick molds.

Into a large bowl sift the flour, baking powder, sugar, and salt. Add the cornmeal. In a separate bowl beat the egg and then add the melted butter and the milk. Pour into the dry ingredients. Stir just to mix. Pour into molds. Bake for 25 minutes or until golden brown.

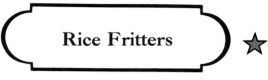

Swedish Cherry Coffee Cake

(6–8 servings)

⅔ cup butter
⅓ cup sugar
4 eggs, beaten
  Salt
1 teaspoon ground cardamom
4 cups flour
¾ cup half and half
1 package dry yeast, softened in ¼ cup
  water

Filling:
½ cup butter
½ cup sugar
½ cup ground almonds
½ cup cherry preserves (homemade, if
  possible)

In a bowl cream together the butter and sugar until light and fluffy. Beat in the eggs. In a separate bowl stir together the salt, cardamom, and flour. Add the flour to the sugar mixture, alternating with the half and half and yeast. Spread the dough into two 9-inch square pans. Mix together filling ingredients and spread on top of the dough. Cover pans lightly and let rise until double in bulk. Preheat the oven to 375°.

Bake for 20 minutes. Serve warm or at room temperature with plenty of fresh butter.

Rice Fritters

(6–8 servings)

1½ cups cooked rice
⅓ cup cracker crumbs
½ cup shredded cheese
1 teaspoon minced onion
2 tablespoons flour
1 tablespoon chopped fresh parsley
  Salt and freshly ground pepper
3 eggs, separated
  Bread crumbs
  Fat for deep frying

In a large bowl combine the rice, cracker crumbs, cheese, onion, flour, and parsley. Season with salt and pepper. Stir in the egg yolks. In a separate bowl beat the egg whites until stiff. Fold into the rice mixture. Form the mixture into cakes. Dredge in the bread crumbs, knocking off any excess. Fry the cakes in hot deep fat until golden brown. Drain.

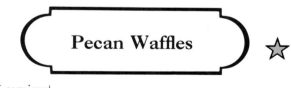

Pecan Waffles

(6 servings)

1 cup sifted cake flour
1 cup unbleached flour
2 teaspoons baking powder

½ teaspoon baking soda
  Salt
2 tablespoons brown sugar
3 eggs separated—yolks beaten, whites
  beaten until stiff peaks form
1½ cups buttermilk
4 tablespoons (½ stick) butter, melted
¾ cup chopped pecans

In a large bowl mix together all the dry in-gredients. Add the egg yolks, buttermilk, and melted butter. Stir in the pecans. Fold in the beaten egg whites. Pour into a hot waffle iron and bake until golden.

Sally Lunn Bread

(Makes 1 loaf)

1 package dry yeast
¼ cup warm water
¾ cup warm milk
3 tablespoons butter
2 tablespoons sugar
2 whole eggs, beaten
3½–4 cups flour
1 teaspoon salt

In a bowl dissolve the yeast in the warm water. Stir in the warm milk. In a separate bowl cream together the butter and sugar until light and fluffy. Beat in the eggs. Combine the flour and salt. Add alternately with the yeast mixture to the egg mixture. Knead lightly on a floured board. Cover and let rise until doubled in bulk. Punch down. Grease a tube pan well and fill with dough. Let rise at least 1 hour. Preheat the oven to 300°.
  Bake for 1 hour.

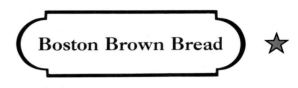

Boston Brown Bread

(Makes 1 loaf)

½ cup yellow cornmeal
½ cup whole wheat flour
½ cup rye flour
½ teaspoon baking soda
  Pinch of salt
½ cup molasses
1¼ cups buttermilk
½ cup raisins (optional)
1 empty 1-pound coffee can, well greased
  and lined on the bottom with parchment
  or waxed paper

Mix the dry ingredients together in a large bowl. Stir in the molasses and buttermilk and mix well. Add the raisins if desired. Pour the mixture into the prepared coffee can. Cover with foil and tie foil on with string. Set the can on a rack in a deep kettle that has a tight-fitting lid. Pour in boiling water until it is halfway up the side of the can. Cover the kettle and steam for at least 1½ hours. Uncover the can and dry the top of the bread by placing the can in a hot (400°) oven for 5 to 6 minutes. Remove the bread from the can immediately. Cool. Slice with a serrated blade, wire, or thread.

Salads

California Fruit Salad

(4–6 servings)

    1 pineapple
    2 kiwifruits
    ½ canteloupe
    1 pint fresh strawberries, washed but not
        stemmed
        Sugar
        Sour cream

Peel the pineapple and slice into wedges. Peel and slice the kiwi and canteloupe. Arrange the fruit on a serving plate. Decorate with fresh strawberries. Serve with bowls of sugar and sour cream.

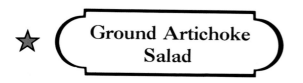

Ground Artichoke Salad

(4 servings)

    1 pound Jerusalem or ground artichokes
    3 tablespoons lemon juice
    5 tablespoons olive oil
        Salt and freshly ground black pepper
    1 tablespoon minced onion or 1 bunch
        scallions, sliced
    2 tablespoons chopped parsley
    2 slices bacon, fried crisp and crumbled

Scrub the artichokes and peel them with a vegetable peeler. Cut into ½-inch pieces and cover with boiling, salted water. Add 2 tablespoons lemon juice. Simmer 5 to 10 minutes until the chokes are crisply tender. Drain and cool. In a bowl beat together the oil and remaining lemon juice. Season with salt and pepper. Beat in the onion. Pour over the artichokes and marinate for 30 minutes. Just before serving stir in the parsley and bacon.

Note: *Ground artichoke is a colloquial name for Jerusalem artichoke.*

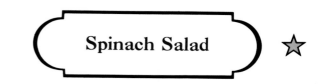

Spinach Salad

(4–6 servings)

    1 pound fresh spinach
    ¼ pound bacon, cut in 1-inch pieces
    ¼ pound mushrooms, sliced
    2 bunches scallions, sliced
    ½ cup vinaigrette

Wash the spinach thoroughly. Stem the leaves and tear into serving-size pieces. Arrange in a salad bowl. In a skillet fry the bacon until crisp. Drain on absorbent paper. Toss the spinach with the bacon, mushrooms, and shallots. Pour on the vinaigrette, toss and serve.

Waldorf Salad

(4 servings)

3 cups diced apples
½ cup chopped walnuts
1 cup chopped celery
¾ cup homemade mayonnaise
½ teaspoon celery seed
   Whole nuts

In a large bowl mix together the apples, walnuts, and celery. Stir in the mayonnaise and celery seed. Garnish with whole nuts.

Ziti Salad with Green Pepper

(6 servings)

¾ pound ziti, cooked just until tender and drained
¼ cup vinaigrette
1 bunch scallions, chopped
1 clove garlic, minced
1 cup Monterey Jack cheese, cubed
½ cup oil-cured black olives
1 large green pepper, seeded and chopped
2 tablespoons chopped parsley
   Salt and freshly ground pepper
   Lettuce

In a large bowl toss the ziti with all other ingredients except the lettuce until well mixed. Season with salt and pepper. Refrigerate for 1 hour. Serve on a bed of lettuce.

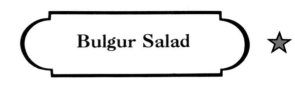

Bulgur Salad

(6 servings)

½ pound bulgur wheat
2 bunches scallions, thinly sliced
½–¾ cup finely chopped fresh parsley
2 large tomatoes, peeled, seeded, and chopped
3 tablespoons chopped walnuts
¼ cup olive oil
4 tablespoons lemon juice
   Salt and freshly ground pepper

Soak the bulgur in water to cover for one hour. Drain and press out the moisture with hands. Spread on a clean towel to dry. When the wheat is dry, put in a salad bowl and add the scallions, parsley, tomatoes, and walnuts. Add the oil and lemon juice, tossing well. Season well with salt and pepper. Refrigerate 2 hours.

Note: *Bulgur wheat is a type of cracked, parboiled wheat that is a staple Middle Eastern food. It can be substituted for rice in many instances, although it needs little cooking. Simple rehydration with hot or cold water is all that is necessary.*

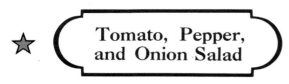

Tomato, Pepper, and Onion Salad

(4 servings)

Lettuce
2 large tomatoes, sliced
2 large green peppers, seeded and sliced
   in rings
2 medium onions, thinly sliced
½ cup spicy vinaigrette
1 tablespoon chopped fresh basil

Line serving plates with lettuce. Arrange the tomatoes, green peppers, and onions in overlapping circles. Sauce with vinaigrette and top with basil.

Caesar Salad

(6 servings)

1 head romaine lettuce, washed and torn
   into pieces
⅓ cup olive oil
2 cloves garlic, finely minced
3 tablespoons lemon juice
   Salt and freshly ground black pepper
1 egg, coddled (simmered 2 minutes)
3–4 anchovy fillets
¼ cup grated parmesan cheese
1 cup garlic croutons

Arrange lettuce in a large wooden bowl. Pour the olive oil over the lettuce and toss. Add the lemon juice, salt, and pepper and toss lightly. Break the egg onto the salad, add the anchovies, and toss gently. Sprinkle with cheese and croutons. Toss just before serving.

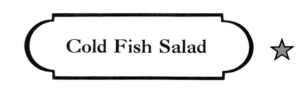

Cold Fish Salad

(4 servings)

1 pound cold poached fish (rockfish, bass,
   snapper, etc.)
1 head Boston lettuce
1 red onion, halved and thinly sliced
1 large green pepper, seeded and chopped
1 cup stuffed olives
2 hard-boiled eggs, chopped
4 anchovy fillets, chopped
⅓ cup olive oil
1 tablespoon mustard
3 tablespoons vinegar
1 clove garlic, minced
   Salt and freshly ground pepper
   Chopped anchovy

Flake the fish with a fork. Wash the lettuce, dry, remove any stems, and tear into pieces. In a large bowl toss together the fish, lettuce, onion, green pepper, olives, and eggs. In another bowl beat together the oil, mustard, vinegar, garlic, and salt and pepper to taste. Pour the dressing over the salad and toss well. Garnish with chopped anchovy.

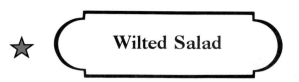

Wilted Salad

(4 servings)

2 heads leaf lettuce, spinach, dandelion
greens, or a mixture of them
2 slices bacon, cut into ¼-inch strips
¼ cup vinegar
1 teaspoon sugar
1 tablespoon chopped parsley

Wash the greens and toss in a salad bowl.
In a skillet fry the bacon until crisp. Remove
from the skillet with a slotted spoon and
drain. Add the vinegar and sugar to the bacon drippings and bring to a boil. Pour over
the greens. Toss lightly, and top with bacon
and parsley. Serve immediately.

Orange Chicken Salad

(2 servings)

1 cup chopped cooked chicken
2 bunches scallions, sliced
¼ cup mayonnaise
¼ cup sour cream
  Salt and freshly ground white pepper
¼ cup chopped celery
1 tablespoon chopped fresh parsley
1 tablespoon chopped fresh basil
  Lettuce
2 oranges, peeled and sectioned

In a large bowl mix together all the ingredients except the lettuce and oranges. Chill.
Arrange the salad on a bed of lettuce. Surround with fresh orange sections.

Boiled Dressing Cole Slaw

(8–12 servings)

½ cup milk
½ cup vinegar
½ cup water
1 teaspoon dry mustard
¼ cup sugar
½ teaspoon salt
2 whole eggs, well beaten
  Salt and freshly ground pepper
2 tablespoons butter
2 tablespoons flour
1 medium head cabbage, grated

In a saucepan mix together the vinegar,
water, mustard, sugar, salt, and milk. Heat
just until fully dissolved. Remove from the
heat and add the beaten egg slowly, stirring
all the time. Season with salt and pepper. In
a small bowl mix the butter and flour with a
little of the hot liquid to make a paste. Add
the paste to the liquid. Cook slowly, stirring
constantly, just until thick. Cool. In a large
bowl toss the dressing well with the grated
cabbage. Chill the cole slaw before serving.

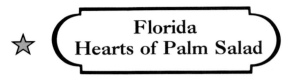

Florida Hearts of Palm Salad

(6 servings)

¼ cup shredded carrots
1 tablespoon slivered green pepper
1 tablespoon minced onion
1 small can hearts of palm, cut in fine julienne
1 tablespoon chopped fresh oregano
  Salt and freshly ground pepper
3 tablespoons lime juice
3 tablespoons mayonnaise
  Red pepper sauce
  Lettuce

Toss the vegetables and seasonings together with the lime juice. Season the mayonnaise with red pepper sauce to taste. Stir into the vegetables. Serve on lettuce leaves.

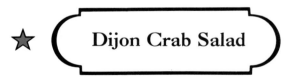

Dijon Crab Salad

(4 servings)

12 ounces crabmeat, well-picked over
1 stalk celery, chopped
½ cucumber, peeled, seeded, and finely sliced
1 tablespoon shredded carrot
½ apple, seeded and diced—but not peeled
  Lettuce leaves

Dressing:
3 tablespoons Dijon mustard
3 tablespoons white wine vinegar
  Salt and freshly ground pepper to taste
1 tablespoon chopped parsley
¾ cup salad oil

In a large bowl gently toss together the salad ingredients. To make the dressing beat together the mustard and vinegar in a small bowl. Season with salt, pepper, and parsley. Beat in the oil a little at a time until the oil is incorporated and the dressing is thick. Toss the salad with ⅓ cup dressing and mound on lettuce leaves. Serve remaining dressing separately.

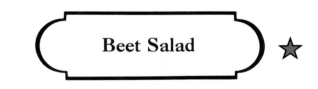

Beet Salad

(6 servings)

3 large boiled beets, diced
1 small onion, very thinly sliced
2 hard-cooked eggs, diced
1 cup thin green beans, steamed and cooled
  Salt and freshly ground black pepper
  Lettuce

Vinaigrette:
1 tablespoon hot mustard
2 tablespoons vinegar
  Salt and freshly ground black pepper
1 egg yolk
⅓ cup salad oil

In a bowl combine the beets, onion, eggs, and green beans. Season with salt and pepper. To make the vinaigrette, in a small bowl beat together the mustard, vinegar, salt, pepper, and egg yolk. Beat in the salad oil. Toss the vegetables with the dressing and chill. Serve the salad on a bed of lettuce.

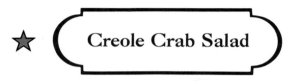

Creole Crab Salad

(4–6 servings)

12 ounces crabmeat
½ cup thinly sliced celery
1 tablespoon capers
1 bunch scallions, thinly sliced
½ green pepper, minced
½ cup homemade mayonnaise
   Red pepper sauce to taste
   Lettuce or fresh spinach
2 ripe tomatoes, cut in wedges
2 hard cooked eggs, cut in quarters
   Fresh parsley, minced
   Lemon wedges

In a bowl toss the crabmeat, celery, capers, scallions, and green pepper together with the mayonnaise until well coated. Season with red pepper sauce to taste. Arrange the salad on a bed of lettuce or fresh spinach. Garnish with the tomato and egg wedges. Sprinkle with parsley. Serve with lemon wedges.

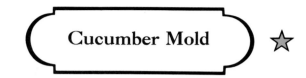

Cucumber Mold

(8 servings)

¼ cup distilled white vinegar
1 tablespoon tarragon vinegar
¾ cup water
3 tablespoons sugar
1 teaspoon salt
   Red pepper to taste
½ teaspoon Worcestershire sauce
½ cup chopped onion
2 cloves garlic, crushed
3 tablespoons unflavored gelatin
½ cup chopped celery
3 medium-sized cucumbers, shredded
½ cup mayonnaise
½ cup heavy cream, whipped
3–4 drops green food coloring (optional)

In a saucepan mix together the vinegars and water. Add the sugar, salt, red pepper, Worcestershire, onion, garlic, and gelatin. Heat the mixture over low heat. Remove and let cool for 10 to 15 minutes. To the cooled vinegar-water mixture add the celery and cucumbers. Refrigerate until partially set. Fold in the mayonnaise and whipped cream. If desired, add just enough food coloring to give the mixture a delicate green tint. Rinse a one-quart ring mold with cold water. Shake out the excess water and fill the mold with the cucumber mixture. Refrigerate for 3 to 4 hours.

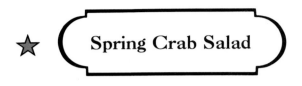

Spring Crab Salad

(4 servings)

2 pineapples, cut in half lengthwise, center
    scooped out
1 pound Maryland backfin crabmeat,
    cartilage removed
1 cup pineapple, chopped
½ cup chickpeas (optional)
½ cup fresh parsley, chopped
¼ cup walnuts, chopped
2 medium apples, sliced ¼-inch thick
2 tablespoons lemon juice
    Lettuce or romaine

Celery Seed Dressing:

½ cup cider vinegar
¾ cup salad oil
3½ tablespoons confectioners' sugar
½ teaspoon salt
½ teaspoon paprika
¼ cup onion, chopped
¼ cup pineapple
½ tablespoon celery seed

In a medium bowl combine crabmeat,
pineapple, chickpeas, parsley, and walnuts
and toss gently. Place sliced apples in a bowl
and cover with the lemon juice. Line pineapples with lettuce or romaine. Mound one
fourth of the crab mixture on each lettuce
bed. Arrange apple slices around crab mix-

ture. Top with a small piece of apple. Refrigerate until ready to serve.

To make the dressing, combine all ingredients in a blender and liquify. Refrigerate
and serve chilled.

Sautéed Mushroom Salad

(4 servings)

2 tablespoons olive oil
1 clove garlic, minced
1 tablespoon chopped parsley
½ pound wild mushrooms (shiitake, chanter-
    elles, cepes, etc.)
    Mixed salad greens such as: cress, radic-
    chio, endive, red-leaf lettuce, arrugula,
    mache, dandelion greens
¼ cup vinaigrette
    Salt and freshly ground pepper
    Chopped parsley

In a small skillet heat the oil and saute
the garlic for one minute. Stir in the parsley
and mushrooms. Toss until heated through.
Keep warm. Toss the salad greens with the
vinaigrette. Arrange the greens on service
plates. Top each with a large spoonful of
mushrooms. Season with salt and pepper.
Garnish with chopped parsley and serve
while the mushrooms are still warm.

Spring Crab Salad ▶

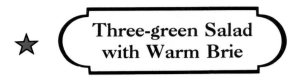

Three-green Salad with Warm Brie

(8 servings)

½ cup olive oil
¼ cup freshly-squeezed lemon juice
   Dijon mustard
   Salt and freshly ground black pepper
   Any three varieties of salad greens,
   washed, dried, and torn
 8 small wedges Brie cheese
   Chopped chives or parsley

In a covered jar combine the oil, lemon juice, and mustard, and season to taste with salt and pepper. Shake well, and set aside at room temperature for at least 1 hour.

To serve, preheat the oven to 350°. Toss the greens with the dressing and arrange on individual salad plates. Heat Brie in oven for 3 minutes. Top each serving with a wedge of warm Brie and garnish with chopped chives or parsley.

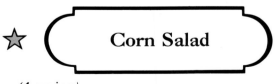

Corn Salad

(4 servings)

 2 cups fresh corn, cut from the cob
 1 small onion, finely minced
½ green pepper, seeded and finely minced
   Salt and freshly ground pepper

Dressing:
 2 tablespoons mustard
 2 tablespoons vinegar
 1 tablespoon white wine
   Salt and freshly ground pepper to taste
 1 teaspoon thyme
 1 tablespoon chopped parsley
½ cup salad oil
   Lettuce

In a large bowl toss together the corn, onion, and green pepper. Season with salt and pepper. To make the dressing beat together the mustard and vinegar. Beat in the wine, salt, pepper, and parsley. Beat in the salad oil a little at a time until the sauce is thick. Toss the corn with the dressing and mound on a bed of lettuce.

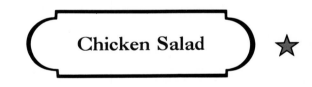

Chicken Salad

(6 servings)

 3 cups boiled chicken meat, diced or cut into
   large pieces
 1 cup thinly sliced celery
 2 bunches scallions, thinly sliced
½ green pepper, thinly sliced
 1 cup homemade mayonnaise
 1 tablespoon hot mustard
 2 tablespoons chopped fresh basil
   Red pepper sauce to taste
   Salt and freshly ground black pepper
   Lettuce
   Whole basil leaves

In a large bowl mix together all ingredients except the lettuce and whole basil leaves. Season with salt and pepper. Serve on a bed of lettuce, garnished with whole basil leaves.

Hot German Potato Salad

(8 servings)

8 large potatoes, diced with skins on
½ pound bacon
3 tablespoons bacon drippings
1 small onion, finely chopped
½ cup celery, finely chopped
2 dill pickles, finely chopped
⅓ cup water
¾ cup vinegar
2 teaspoons sugar
½ teaspoon salt
½ teaspoon paprika
½ teaspoon dry mustard
   Chopped parsley
   Chopped chives

In a covered saucepan simmer the potatoes until tender. Drain and set aside. In a skillet fry the bacon until crisp. Remove the bacon, drain, and crumble, reserving 3 tablespoons drippings. Saute the onion and celery in the drippings until translucent. Add the chopped pickles, water, and vinegar and bring to a boil. Add the seasonings, potatoes, and bacon, stirring gently until well mixed. Serve at once, garnished with chopped parsley and chives.

Taco Salad

(4–6 servings)

1 pound ground beef
1 small onion, minced
3 tablespoons tomato sauce
1 tablespoon chopped green chilies
1 teaspoon chili powder
¼ cup red wine
1 package tortilla chips
½ head iceberg lettuce, shredded
2 tomatoes, cut in wedges
1 bunch scallions, sliced
1 avocado, peeled and sliced
½ cup black olives
1 cup cheddar cheese, shredded
   Vinaigrette dressing

In a heavy skillet saute the beef. Add the onion and cook until tender. Stir in the tomato sauce, green chilies, chili powder, and red wine. Simmer 10 minutes. Arrange the corn chips on serving plates. Top with the meat mixture. Garnish with lettuce, tomatoes, scallions, avocado, and olives. Top with cheddar cheese. Moisten with vinaigrette.

West Indies Salad

(6 servings)

1 medium onion, thinly sliced
1 pound fresh lump crabmeat
    Salt and freshly ground white pepper
½ cup peanut oil
⅓ cup cider vinegar
½ cup ice water

Spread half of the onion slices over the bottom of a large bowl. Cover with separated crab lumps and then remaining onion. Add salt and pepper to taste. Beat the oil, vinegar, and water together in a small bowl. Pour the dressing over the crabmeat, cover, and marinate for 2 to 12 hours. Toss lightly before serving.

Lentil Salad

(4 servings)

1 cup brown lentils
    Salt and freshly ground pepper
¼ cup olive oil
3 tablespoons vinegar
2 cloves garlic, minced
1 onion, halved and thinly sliced
¼ pound bacon, fried until crisp and
    crumbled
1 tomato, peeled, seeded, and chopped

Soak the lentils for 2 hours in cold water to cover. Drain. Simmer the lentils, covered, in a large kettle in water to cover for 30 minutes, or until lentils are tender. Season with salt and pepper, and cool to room temperature. Beat together the olive oil, vinegar, garlic, and salt and pepper to taste. Add the onion slices. Drain the lentils and put in a bowl. Toss with the bacon and dressing. Garnish with chopped tomato and let stand for 2 hours or more.

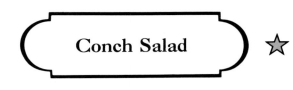

Conch Salad

(6 servings)

1 pound conch, diced
½ pound tomatoes, peeled, seeded, and diced
1 green pepper, seeded and diced
1 stalk celery, diced
1 large onion, diced
1 small cucumber, peeled, seeded, and diced
⅓ cup fresh lime juice
    Cayenne pepper
    Salt to taste

Combine all the ingredients in a glass bowl. Stir well. Marinate for 2 hours. Serve on a bed of lettuce.

Note: *Conch is available fresh in many fine seafood shops.*

Grilled Quail with Nasturtium Flowers

(8 servings)

Dressing:
2 tablespoons red wine vinegar
1 tablespoon Pommery mustard
1 teaspoon finely chopped garlic
2 tablespoons capers
2 tablespoons extra virgin olive oil
1 teaspoon salt
   Freshly ground pepper

8 quail, oven ready
1 tablespoon olive oil
   Salt and freshly ground pepper
1 bunch arugula, rinsed and dried, stems removed
1 bunch radicchio, cored and cut into 2-inch slices
1 bunch radicchio leaves, pulled from stems, rinsed and dried
24 nasturtium flowers

Preheat the broiler to 550°.

To make the dressing, in a mixing bowl whisk together the vinegar, mustard, garlic, and capers. Continue whisking and gradually add olive oil, a pinch of salt, and two or three grindings of pepper.

Place the quail in a shallow roasting pan, brush them with the olive oil, and leave them breast side down. Sprinkle with salt and pepper. Heat the pan on the top of the stove until the fat starts to sizzle. Place the quail in the broiler—or on a preheated barbecue grill—and cook for about 7 minutes.

Remove the quail from the heat. With a knife, remove the meat from each side of the breasts. Remove the legs, separating the thighs from the drumsticks. Remove the bones from the thighs.

In a large mixing bowl combine the arugula, sliced radicchio, dressing, salt, and pepper, and toss well. Place 3 or 4 radicchio leaves on each plate, with the round sides on the edges of the plates. Distribute the dressed salad greens among the plates, and serve the quail over them. Decorate the salads with the nasturtium flowers.

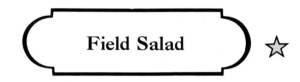

Field Salad

Young beet greens
Young dandelion greens
Purslane
Lambs lettuce (Mache)
Any young, edible wild green

Dressing:
3 tablespoons cider vinegar
2 tablespoons mustard
   Salt and freshly ground black pepper
½ cup olive oil or peanut oil

In a salad bowl toss the greens together.

To make the dressing, whisk together the vinegar, mustard and seasonings in a small bowl. Whisk in the oil. Toss the dressing with the greens.

Molded Cranberry Salad

(8 servings)

1 package (16 oz.) fresh cranberries
2 cups water
1½ cups sugar
2 packages lemon gelatin
⅔ cup chopped celery
½ cup chopped walnuts
½ cup sour cream
½ cup whipped cream

In a saucepan simmer the cranberries in the water and sugar until the berries begin to pop. Remove pan from the heat. Stir the gelatin into the cranberries until dissolved. Chill slightly. Stir in the celery and nuts. Pour into a lightly oiled mold. Refrigerate until set, at least 4 hours. Unmold. Fold sour cream gently into whipped cream. Serve with salad.

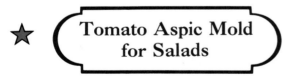

Tomato Aspic Mold for Salads

(6 servings)

2 envelopes unflavored gelatin
3½ cups tomato juice or vegetable juice cocktail
⅓ cup minced green pepper
1 tablespoon grated onion
⅓ cup finely chopped celery

In a small bowl sprinkle the gelatin over 1 cup of the juice. When soft, pour into a saucepan and heat gently until gelatin is dissolved. Cool, stir in remaining juice, and chill slightly. Stir the green pepper, onion, and celery into the aspic mixture. Pour into a lightly oiled mold and chill until firm. Unmold on lettuce and fill.

Note: *Foods for which this mold is a welcome accompaniment include chicken salad, cold boiled shrimp, and lobster salad.*

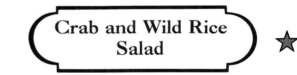

Crab and Wild Rice Salad

(8 servings)

2 cups cooked wild rice
12 ounces lump crab meat
1 tablespoon lemon juice
½ green pepper, finely chopped
½ red pepper, finely chopped
1 medium avocado, peeled and diced
1 bunch scallions, thinly sliced
1 tablespoon chopped parsley
1 tablespoon Dijon-style mustard
3 tablespoons red wine vinegar
   Salt and freshly ground pepper
1 egg yolk
½ cup salad oil, or ¼ cup salad oil and ¼ cup olive oil
   Leaf lettuce

Chill the rice. In a mixing bowl toss the crab with the lemon juice. Add the rice, peppers, avocado, scallions, and parsley, and toss gently. In a small bowl beat the mustard and vinegar until well mixed. Add the salt and pepper. Beat in the egg yolk and then beat in the oil. Pour the dressing over the salad and toss lightly. Serve on a bed of leaf lettuce.

Cobb Salad

(4–6 servings)

½ head iceberg lettuce, shredded
½ cup watercress, chopped
½ head romaine, cut up
 1 cup arrugula, cut up
¼ cup minced chives
 1 poached chicken breast, shredded
¼ pound bacon, fried crisp and crumbled
 1 avocado, peeled and sliced
 1 large tomato, cut in wedges, or 1 cup
   cherry tomatoes, halved
 2 hard-boiled eggs, cut in wedges
 4 tablespoons Roquefort cheese, crumbled
½ cup vinaigrette

In a salad bowl toss the greens with the chives. Arrange the chicken, bacon, avocado, tomato, and eggs on the lettuce. Sprinkle with Roquefort cheese. Just before serving toss with vinaigrette.

Creole Mixed Green Salad

(6 servings)

Mixed greens: leaf lettuce, romaine, and
   watercress
¼ pound bacon, cubed, fried until crisp, and
   drained
 1 cup broccoli flowerets
½ cup cucumber slices
 1 large tomato, cut in wedges
 1 carrot, sliced

Dressing:
 1 egg yolk
 2 tablespoons white wine or cider vinegar
 1 tablespoon Dijon mustard
   Salt and freshly ground white pepper
   Red pepper sauce to taste
½ cup peanut oil

Wash and dry salad greens. Toss together in a salad bowl and then arrange on serving plates. Garnish with bacon and raw vegetables.

To make the dressing, beat together the egg yolk, vinegar, mustard, and seasonings. Beat in the peanut oil a little at a time.

Drizzle the dressing over the greens before serving.

Meat Main Dishes

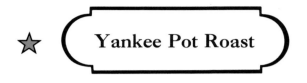

Yankee Pot Roast

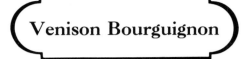

Venison Bourguignon

(6–8 servings)

1 3-pound pot roast of beef, chuck, etc., in
  one piece
1 teaspoon salt
¼ teaspoon pepper
  Flour
2 tablespoons bacon fat or butter
1 cup water or ½ cup water and ½ cup
  hearty red wine
8 small potatoes, peeled
8 small carrots, peeled
8 small onions, peeled
1 small turnip, peeled and cut in 4 pieces

Sprinkle the roast with salt and pepper.
Dredge in flour, knocking off the excess.
Heat the fat or butter in a heavy kettle.
Brown the meat on all sides in the hot fat.
Pour in the water or water and wine. Simmer, covered, at least 2½ hours or until
meat is very tender. Forty minutes before
serving add the potatoes, carrots, onions,
and turnip. Check from time to time, adding
a little more water if necessary. When the
meat is cooked remove from the kettle and
slice. Surround with the vegetables. Boil the
remaining liquid for 1 minute and serve
alongside.

(6 servings)

1 3–4 pound venison roast
2 cups red wine
¼ cup lime juice
¼ cup lemon juice
10 whole cloves
2 cloves garlic, crushed
1 onion, sliced thin
1 carrot, sliced thin
  Salt to taste
  Whole grain pepper
1 teaspoon dried thyme
3 tablespoons butter
2 tablespoons Cognac or brandy
3 slices bacon, cubed
½ pound fresh mushrooms, quartered
½ pound boiling onions, peeled

Marinate the venison overnight in the
wine, lime juice, lemon juice, cloves, garlic,
onion, carrot, salt, pepper, and thyme. Turn
several times while marinating.
Drain the meat, reserving the marinade,
and pat dry. Cut the venison into 2-inch
cubes. In a heavy kettle or skillet melt the
butter and brown the meat a little at a time
until all is well colored. Pour on the Cognac,
ignite, and stir until the flames die down.
Strain the marinade and add to the meat.
Simmer, covered, for 1 hour. Fry the bacon

until crisp. Drain on absorbent paper. Add the bacon, mushrooms, and onions to the venison and simmer, covered, for 30 minutes more. Serve with freshly cooked noodles.

Kalua Pig

(8–10 servings)

6–8 pounds fresh ham or pork shoulder
2½ tablespoons coarse salt (Kosher)
   Ti leaves and/or banana leaves, or enough corn husks to cover roast with thick layer of leaves
   Salt
½ cup boiling water
   Foil

Preheat the oven to 500°.

Make shallow incisions in the pork roast. Sprinkle coarse salt over the roast. If using ti leaves, remove the fibrous backbone. Wrap the roast in leaves or corn husks and tie securely with string. Wrap the entire roast in foil. Place on a rack in a shallow roasting pan and roast for 30 minutes. Lower the temperature to 400° and roast for 4½ hours.

Remove the foil and string. Discard the ti leaves or corn husks. Cut or tear the pork into bite-sized pieces that can be eaten by hand. Pour the boiling water over them. Season to taste with salt. Serve in individual bowls. The rind may be removed from the pork roast, placed on a rack and roasted separately during the last thirty minutes or placed in a 450° oven for 15 minutes. Cut crisp rind and divide it among bowls of kalua pig.

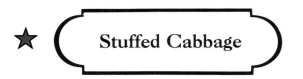

Stuffed Cabbage

(6 servings)

1 medium cabbage
⅔ pound ground beef
¼ pound sliced bacon, cut in 1-inch pieces and fried crisp
1 onion, chopped
1 green pepper, seeded and chopped
1 clove garlic, minced
½ cup grated cheddar cheese
1 egg, beaten
½ cup fresh bread crumbs
½ cup milk
   Salt and freshly ground pepper
1 teaspoon ground thyme

Clean the cabbage. Remove the stem and hollow out the inside of the cabbage. In a bowl mix together the other ingredients. Pack the meat mixture into the cabbage. Wrap in cheesecloth. Steam the cabbage until tender, at least 1 hour. Serve, cut in wedges, with any spicy tomato sauce.

Spareribs with Sauerkraut

(4 servings)

2 pounds spareribs
  Salt and freshly ground pepper to taste
3 cups Sauerkraut
⅓ cup brown sugar

Preheat the oven to 325°.
Sprinkle the spareribs with salt and pepper. Arrange the sauerkraut in the bottom of a baking dish. Lay the ribs out on the sauerkraut. Bake for 2 hours. Sprinkle the ribs with the brown sugar and bake 30 minutes longer.

Nevada Beans

(10–12 servings)

6 slices bacon, cut into ½-inch pieces
1 large onion, chopped
1 16-ounce can baked beans
1 15-ounce can red kidney beans, undrained
1 15-ounce can butter beans, drained
½ cup catsup
¼ cup prepared mustard
¼ cup Worcestershire sauce
2 tablespoons brown sugar
1 tablespoon dark molasses

Preheat the oven to 350°.
In a skillet cook the bacon and onion until the onion is tender, about 10 minutes. In a large bowl combine the bacon and onion with the beans, catsup, mustard, Worcestershire sauce, brown sugar, and molasses. Pour into a greased 2-quart casserole. Bake, uncovered, for 1 hour.

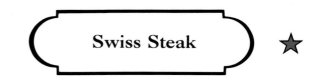

Swiss Steak

(4–6 servings)

2 pounds round steak in one piece
  Flour
  Salt and freshly ground pepper
2 tablespoons butter
1 tablespoon oil
3 large onions, thinly sliced
1 clove garlic, minced
5 large tomatoes, peeled, seeded, and chopped
3 cups beef stock or bouillon

Dredge the steak in flour that has been seasoned with salt and pepper. In a deep skillet melt the butter with the oil and brown the meat well on both sides. Add the onions, garlic, tomatoes, and stock. Cover and simmer 2 hours, until meat is very tender. Uncover and raise the heat to thicken the sauce a little. Check the seasonings. Serve the steak with the sauce in a separate dish.

Note: *Noodles, rice, or boiled potatoes are excellent accompaniments for this dish.*

Baked Beans

(6 servings)

1½ pounds pea beans or white navy beans,
    well picked over
1 tablespoon peanut oil
1 onion, peeled
    Salt and freshly ground pepper
3 tablespoons brown sugar
1 teaspoon dried mustard
½ cup molasses
½ pound salt pork in one piece, scored
    nearly through to rind
    Boiling water or 1 part cider and 1 part
    water

Soak the beans overnight in water to
cover.

Drain the soaked beans. Place in a saucepan. Add water to cover and 1 tablespoon oil
(to prevent foaming). Simmer for 15 to 20
minutes and drain, but reserve cooking liquid. Place the onion in the bottom of a bean
pot or covered casserole. Pour in the parboiled beans. In a bowl mix together the salt
and pepper, sugar, mustard, molasses, and
half of the reserved cooking liquid. Pour
over the beans. Bury the salt pork just below
the surface of the beans and add boiling water just to cover the beans. Cover the casserole and bake at 275° for 6 hours, or until
beans are very tender. Check every hour and
add boiling water if necessary to keep beans

covered. Uncover the casserole during the
last half hour of baking. Do not add more
liquid.

Green Chili Stew

(6 servings)

    Lard or cooking oil
  2 pounds lean chuck, cut into ½-inch cubes
½ medium onion, chopped
  4 medium potatoes, peeled and diced
    (optional)
  4 medium zucchini, peeled and diced
    (optional)
12 large fresh green chilies, roasted, peeled,
    and cut in pieces
  1 clove garlic, finely chopped
  1 teaspoon salt
6–7 cups water

In a large, deep, heavy pan heat the lard
and brown the meat. Add the onion. If desired, add the potatoes and brown them with
the meat. When the meat and onion and
potatoes have been browned, drain off any
excess fat. Add the zucchini, if desired,
chilies, garlic, salt, and water. Bring to a boil
and simmer for at least ½ hour. Ladle into
bowls and serve with homemade bread. The
stew should be eaten with a spoon, like a
hearty soup.

Note: *A 7-ounce container of frozen chopped
green chilies or 2 4-ounce cans of chopped green
chilies can be substituted for the fresh green chilies.*

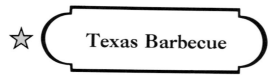

Texas Barbecue

Texas-style barbecues are like everything else in Texas—big. Three or four kinds of meat are cooked, including huge pieces of beef, sides of spareribs, chicken halves, and sometimes even wildly spiced sausages. There are also salads, beans, homemade breads and biscuits, and lots of cold drinks. Sometimes these barbecues are held in remote areas and simply getting there is enough effort to work up an appetite equal to the task of attacking the mounds of food.

Just as there are companies in Rhode Island and Massachusetts that specialize in making clambakes, in Texas there are organizations that do everything for a barbecue except provide the guests to eat the food. In fact, there may even be companies that will do that!

Even without any professional help, it is possible to have a reasonable facsimile of an authentic Texas barbecue anywhere in the U.S., provided you can find someone with a field, or large backyard, who does not object to having a pit dug in it.

Dig a pit about 3½ feet wide, 2½ feet deep, and as long as is needed to cook all the meat

Beef Brisket
(or for larger parties,
a haunch or quarter of beef)
Chicken Halves
Ribs
(beef or racks of pork spareribs
depending on the local custom)
Barbecue Sauce
Chorizo Sausages
Cole Slaw
Barbecued Beans
Sourdough Bread
Assorted Pickles

at hand. Fill the pit with good hardwood, or untreated charcoal (not briquets). The fire should burn for about 4 hours, as it is the heat from the coals that cooks the meat, not the flames from the fire. It is also best to have a separate small fire nearby to provide a fresh supply of hot coals when the time comes to grill the ribs, chicken, and sausages.

While the fire is burning, wash, dry, and rub the brisket with warm salt water. Wrap the meat in clean cheesecloth that has been dampened with salt water, and then wrap it in burlap. Wet the burlap.

When there is a good bed of red-hot coals 6 to 8 inches deep, sprinkle the coals with a very light layer of sand to prevent flare-ups and start laying the meat into the pit. If at all possible have a grid or heavy wire screen supported by stones about halfway down into the pit. Place the basted packages of meat on the grid and then cover the pit with damp canvas, sealing the edges of the canvas with dirt or sand to keep in the heat and steam. If a grid is not available, be sure to dampen the burlap-wrapped packages thoroughly before placing them directly on the coals.

Large pieces of meat, such as a quarter or haunch, will require 6 to 8 hours of cooking time. Large pieces of brisket will require at least 6 hours, as the fibrous cut requires long cooking to make it tender.

About 2 hours before the beef should be ready, open the canvas and partially unwrap the meat. Begin basting it with the barbecue sauce and continue about every 15 minutes until well done. A small, clean rag mop is the perfect basting tool.

At the same time as the fire is opened, put a new grid or grill over one end of the pit. Arrange on it the chicken, sausage, and spareribs. If necessary, shovel coals under the grid from the small reserve fire. Baste everything well with barbecue sauce every 15 minutes.

While the chicken and ribs are cooking, set out salads, bread, beans, and relishes. Substantial plates and real knives and forks are a must with this style of cookout. No paper plates and plastic cutlery for such a gargantuan feast. Have lots of cold drinks handy to quench the fires of thirst.

When everything is done, including the chicken and ribs, serve the meats very hot. Another bowl of sauce might be placed on the table for those who like their meat powerfully spicy.

Notes: *Allow ½ pound of ribs and ¼ chicken for each diner, as well as about ½ to ¾ pound of beef and several sausages. For small barbecues, ask your butcher for the largest possible cuts of beef brisket. Leave some of the fat on the beef to provide moisture and to help tenderize these somewhat tough cuts of meat. A shoulder, haunch (steamboat roast), or quarter can be roasted in the same way. These cuts are more tender, but require long cooking times in the pit.*

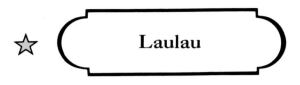

Laulau

(6 servings)

36 luau (taro) or fresh spinach leaves
3 pounds fresh pork shoulder or leg
1½ pounds salted butterfish or similar salt
  fish, soaked in water for several hours if
  very salty
2 tablespoons rock salt
12 ti leaves (corn husks can be substituted)
6 cooking bananas or plantains
6 sweet potatoes

Wash the luau or spinach leaves thoroughly, through several rinsings. Strip the stem and fibrous part of the veins from the back of the luau leaves, if using, by pulling gently with the tip of a knife from the stem to the edge of the leaves. Discard the stems and veins. Place the pork in a bowl, add the salt, and work together thoroughly. Divide the ingredients into six equal portions, one portion per laulau. Arrange 5 or more luau leaves, the largest on the bottom, in the palm of the hand. If using spinach, arrange a small handful of spinach in a flat layer. Add the pork, fat side up, then a layer of butterfish. Fold the luau leaves or ends of spinach over the pork and fish to form a bundle (puolo). Prepare each ti leaf by cutting the stiff rib partially through and stripping it off. Place each laulau on the end of a ti leaf and wrap tightly. Wrap with another leaf in the opposite direction, forming a flat package. Tie securely with string or the fibrous part of the ti leaves. Steam the laulaus for 4 to 6 hours. Add the sweet potatoes and bananas for the last hour. Remove the string from the laulaus and serve.

Note: *This dish can also be served as an appetizer. This recipe will provide 12 appetizer servings.*

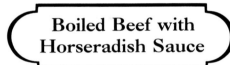

Boiled Beef with Horseradish Sauce

(8 servings)

4 pounds beef brisket or round
1 small whole onion
1 carrot, cut in chunks
1 stalk celery, with leaves, cut in chunks
1 leek, washed and cut up
1 cup red wine
  Water
  Salt and freshly ground pepper
  Fresh parsley

Sauce:
½ teaspoon mustard
½ cup horseradish
1 teaspoon chopped parsley
½ cup cooking liquid
  Salt and freshly ground pepper
½ cup sour cream

Place the meat and vegetables in a heavy kettle. Add the wine and enough water to cover. Bring to a boil. Skim. Add salt and pepper to taste and several sprigs of parsley. Reduce heat and simmer 2½ hours until meat is very tender. Take out and reserve ½ cup cooking stock.

To make the sauce mix together the mustard, horseradish, parsley, and stock. Season. Simmer 2 minutes. Stir in the sour cream. Remove from heat and serve with the beef.

★ Red Flannel Hash

(4 servings)

2 tablespoons butter
1 cooked onion, chopped
1 boiled potato, chopped
1 cup boiled beets, chopped
2 cups cooked corned beef, chopped
½ cup cream
  Salt and freshly ground pepper

Preheat the oven to 375°.

In a heavy oven-proof skillet melt the butter and stir in all the ingredients. Place the skillet in the oven and bake until well browned. Serve with Horseradish Cream Sauce.

Note: *This dish is made from the leftovers of a New England Boiled Dinner. (See page 159.)*

Buffalo Stew ★

(8–10 servings)

½ cup all-purpose flour
¼ teaspoon black pepper
3½ pounds buffalo meat or stewing beef
  cut into 1-inch cubes
⅓ cup oil
3 cups beef stock
3 tablespoons tomato paste
2 tablespoons Worcestershire sauce
¼ teaspoon thyme
2 cups sliced celery
2 medium-size potatoes, cubed
1½ cups sliced carrots
1½ cups sliced onions
1 cup peas (frozen if fresh are unavailable)

Combine the flour and pepper in a plastic bag. Add the meat cubes, a few pieces at a time, and toss to coat evenly. In a large Dutch oven brown the meat in the oil. Add the beef stock, tomato paste, Worcestershire sauce, and thyme. Cover and simmer 40 minutes. Add the celery, potatoes, carrots, and onions. Simmer, covered, 35 minutes longer or until tender. Add the peas and cook, covered, 5 minutes more.

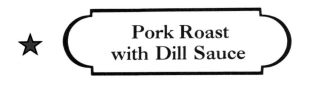

Pork Roast with Dill Sauce

(8 servings)

1 fresh pork shoulder with the skin left on
Salt
Ground ginger
⅓ cup fresh dill leaves
Freshly ground black pepper
1 cup dry white wine

Sauce:
2 tablespoons butter
1 tablespoon flour
½ cup degreased drippings from roasting pan
½ cup heavy cream
¼ cup minced dill leaves
1 teaspoon ground ginger
Salt and freshly ground black pepper

Preheat the oven to 350°.

Slash the pork skin in a fine diamond pattern. Rub the surface with salt and ground ginger. Make deep cuts in the pork with a sharp knife. Stuff the slits with the dill leaves. Salt and pepper the surfaces of the roast. Place in a roasting pan, pour in the wine, and roast 25 minutes per pound. DO NOT BASTE.

To prepare the sauce, melt the butter in a saucepan, stir in the flour, and cook until golden brown. Pour in the degreased cooking liquid and cream. When thickened, stir

in the dill, ginger, and salt and pepper to taste. Serve in a separate dish.

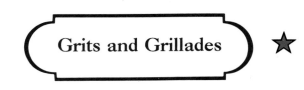

Grits and Grillades

(4–6 servings)

2 pounds veal or beef round, thinly sliced
6 tablespoons bacon drippings or salad oil
4 tablespoons all-purpose flour
1 medium onion, chopped
1 cup peeled and cubed tomatoes
1½ cups water
1 green pepper, chopped
1 clove garlic, chopped
1 bay leaf
1 tablespoon chopped parsley
2 teaspoons salt
1 teaspoon red pepper sauce
½ teaspoon thyme
3 cups hot cooked grits

In a deep skillet brown the meat in hot oil. Remove the meat. Add the flour and brown, stirring constantly. Add the onion and tomatoes. Simmer for a few minutes. Add the meat, water, pepper, garlic, bay leaf, parsley, salt, red pepper sauce, and thyme. Cover and simmer for 1½ hours or until the meat is very tender, adding water if necessary to make the sauce the consistency of thick gravy. Serve grillades with a portion of hot grits on the side.

★ Sauerbraten

(8–10 servings)

4 pounds rump roast in one piece
2 cups vinegar
2 cups dry white wine
3 onions, sliced
3 carrots, sliced
6 whole cloves
1 teaspoon black peppercorns
4 tablespoons butter
1 teaspoon ground ginger or 5 ginger snaps

Place the meat in a large glass or pottery bowl. Add the vinegar, white wine, onions, and carrots. Stir in the cloves and peppercorns. Marinate the meat in the liquid for 2 days, turning every 12 hours.

Remove the meat from the marinade. In a heavy kettle melt the butter and brown the meat on all sides. Pour in 1 cup of marinade. Cover the kettle and simmer at least 2 hours until meat is very tender. Add more marinade from time to time if necessary. Remove the meat from the kettle and keep warm. Stir the ginger into the sauce in the kettle—or, if a thicker sauce is necessary, break up the ginger snaps and stir into the sauce. Simmer until the cookies melt into the sauce. Slice the meat and serve with the sauce.

Country Ham in Red Eye Gravy ★

(3 servings)

1 large slice smoked, sugar-cured ham
½ cup strong black coffee

In a hot skillet fry the ham slice until browned on both sides. Remove ham, set aside, and keep warm. Pour the coffee into the skillet. Stir well, scraping up any drippings in the bottom of skillet. Pour the gravy over the ham.

Serve with grits, Fried Apples, and lots of steaming black coffee.

Cushion Roast Lamb ★

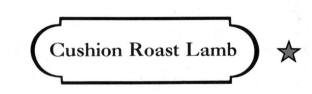

(6–8 servings)

2 cloves garlic, finely chopped
1 cup chopped cooked spinach
⅓ cup heavy cream
    Salt and freshly ground pepper to taste
2 square-cut lamb shoulders, boned and sewn together, skin sides out, with a pocket in one side left open for stuffing (finished roast looks like a square, flat cushion)

Preheat the oven to 300°.

In a bowl mix together the garlic, spinach, cream and salt and pepper. Stuff the roast and sew or skewer the pocket closed. Salt and pepper the surface of the meat and place it on a rack in a roasting pan. Roast for 25 to 30 minutes per pound.

Note: *Have the butcher bone the roasts and sew them together.*

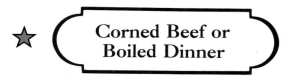

Corned Beef or Boiled Dinner

(6–8 servings)

1 3–4 pound piece of corned beef
6–8 medium beets
1 head cabbage, quartered
6–8 medium potatoes
6–8 medium carrots
1 white turnip, quartered
6–8 small onions

Place the meat in a large kettle and add water to cover. Cover the kettle and simmer gently for 3 hours. While the meat is cooking, simmer the beets in water in a separate saucepan until tender.

When the meat is cooked add the cabbage, potatoes, turnip, carrots, and onions. Simmer 30 minutes more, or until the vegetables are tender. Drain the meat and slice. Arrange on a serving platter. Arrange the vegetables, including the beets, around the meat. Garnish with parsley and serve with Horseradish Cream Sauce and mustard.

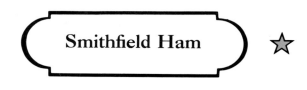

Smithfield Ham

(25 servings)

1 whole sugar-cured ham, uncooked
Water
1 cup brown sugar
2 tablespoons prepared hot mustard
Whole cloves

Scrub the ham well. Soak overnight, changing water once.

Drain the ham. Cover with fresh water and simmer gently 15 to 20 minutes per pound. Allow the ham to cool in the water. Drain, remove the skin and all but a thin layer of fat. Cool completely.

Preheat the oven to 325°.

Slash the fat in a diamond pattern. In a small bowl mix together the brown sugar and mustard and spread over the ham. Press a whole clove into each diamond. Bake the ham for 45 minutes.

Cool to lukewarm and slice *very* thin.

Note: *See the Resource Guide for information on ordering Smithfield ham.*

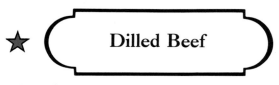

Dilled Beef

(6 servings)

3 tablespoons oil
3 pounds beef chuck, cut into 2-inch cubes
3 cups beef stock
1 tablespoon chopped dill
10 peppercorns, crushed
1 cup red wine
  Salt
2 tablespoons flour
2 tablespoons butter
  Fresh dill sprigs

In a deep kettle heat the oil and brown the beef a little at a time. When all the beef is browned return to the kettle. Add the stock, dill, peppercorns, red wine, and salt to taste. Simmer until very tender. Mix the flour and butter into a paste. Stir into the sauce a little at a time. Cook until thick. Garnish with fresh dill.

Barbecued Ribs Northwestern

(6 servings)

3 pounds fresh spare ribs
  Salt and pepper
1 cup Northwestern Barbecue Sauce

If the spare ribs are to be grilled at a picnic site, parboil them at home by simmering gently in water for 30 minutes on top of the stove. Drain the ribs and dry them well. At the site, salt and pepper the parboiled ribs and brush generously with Northwestern Barbecue Sauce. Place over hot coals and grill about 30 minutes, turning after 15 minutes. Baste frequently with barbecue sauce.

Note: *Parboiling serves two purposes in this case. It cuts down on the grilling time while insuring that the pork is thoroughly cooked, and it helps produce a juicier finished product.*

Barbecued Pork

(8–14 servings)

1 fresh ham, or fresh pork shoulder, with skin on (cooking time will be less for a shoulder)
  Salt water, warmed
  Peanut oil
1 tablespoon crushed red pepper
1 cup cider vinegar
½ cup brown sugar
2 cups peanut oil

Barbecue Sauce:
1 teaspoon crushed red pepper
½ cup cider vinegar
⅓ cup brown sugar
1 teaspoon red pepper sauce

Brush the ham or shoulder with the warm salt water. Place on a grill over hot coals, skin side up. Place a drip pan underneath it. Brush again with salt water. Roast about 3 hours, covered. If necessary, add more coals. Brush with salted water until the skin begins to crisp. Brush with oil and turn the roast skin side down. In a saucepan heat the pepper, vinegar, brown sugar and peanut oil. Baste the roast from time to time when it begins to look dry. Roast 2 to 3 hours longer. When the skin is very crisp and the roast is fully cooked and tender, remove it from the grill. Remove the meat from the bones and chop it up by hand—not a grinder. Chop the skin separately.

In a large bowl blend the red peppers, vinegar, brown sugar and hot sauce. Add the chopped meat and mix thoroughly with the hot sauce. Serve on hamburger buns or plain. Serve with cole slaw and more hot sauce.

Note: *This dish is traditionally prepared in a pit outdoors, but a very good substitute can be prepared in a covered charcoal grill.*

(*4 servings*)

  2 eggs, beaten
¼ cup milk
1½ pounds round steak, sliced and pounded

1 cup flour, seasoned with salt and freshly
  ground pepper
2 tablespoons butter
¼ cup oil
  Cream Gravy

In a bowl beat the eggs and milk together. Dip the steaks into the egg mixture and then into the flour. In a heavy skillet melt the butter and oil. Fry the steaks until brown on the underside, then turn and fry until the second side is browned. Cover and cook 15 to 20 minutes over medium heat until meat is tender. Remove cover and continue cooking over medium-high heat until meat is crisp on the outside. Drain steaks well and serve with Cream Gravy.

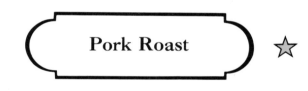

(*6–8 servings*)

1 6–7 pound loin of pork
  Prepared mustard
  Salt and freshly ground pepper
  Flour

  Preheat the oven to 450°.
  Paint the roast with the mustard. Season with salt and pepper. Sift a thin layer of flour over the meat. Roast for 30 minutes. Reduce the heat to 300° and cook for 30 minutes per pound.

North Carolina Barbecue

Southern barbecue traditionally means a barbecued pig, pit cooked and awash with a hot basting sauce. A whole pig will serve 75 people; a suckling pig will serve about 12. Properly served, the meat of the cooked pig is broken up along with the crisp bits of skin (although some cooks keep the skin separate in order to retain its crispness) and again mixed with quantities of the basting sauce.

Served with sliced tomatoes, fried potatoes, cole slaw, and lots of buttered corn bread, barbecued pork is a heavenly dish. Children like it piled into hamburger buns, too. In the Deep South, soft drinks accompany a barbecue, but ice-cold beer is also excellent.

Barbecued pig
Sliced Tomatoes
French-fried potatoes
Cole slaw
Pickles
Corn bread
Beer
Soft drinks

Order the pig (preferably grain fed and about 75 pounds in weight) in advance from your butcher, or through a local restaurant. Have the pig opened flat by splitting it from neck to tail and cracking the pelvis and ribs. Have the butcher clean it and remove the head and the feet up to the elbow joint.

Dig a pit 16 inches deep and as wide and long as the pig, allowing room on one side to add coals from time to time. Fill the pit with good hardwood, or unprocessed charcoal. Do not use gasoline or charcoal lighter to light the fire. Light the fire and burn until there is a good layer of coals—at least one inch.

Keep a separate fire burning in a shallow pit to provide fresh coals for replenishing the cooking pit.

Place heavy wire screening or iron poles every 6 to 8 inches along the top of the pit, at a level which will keep the pig about a foot above the bed of coals.

Rub the pig inside and out very well with warm salt water before placing it skin side up on the grid over the coals. A 60-pound pig (after preparation) will take about 8 to 10 hours to cook. (A small barbecue can be made with a suckling pig of about 20 pounds, which will require about 4 hours cooking time and will have a more delicate flavor than a more fully grown pig.) Leave the pig skin side up for about 4 hours, or until the skin begins to drip fat. Brush occasionally with warm salt water. At that time, oil the skin liberally with plain unsalted oil. Carefully turn the pig skin side down. (Many expert barbecuers believe that this method holds in the juices and the flavors of the sauce. There are others that don't turn the pig until about an hour before it is completely cooked. Do whichever appeals to you most.) From time to time, whenever the meat begins to look a little dry, brush the surface with a mixture of crushed red pepper, cider vinegar, brown sugar, and about ½ gallon of unsalted vegetable oil. A new little rag mop makes an excellent basting tool.

When the skin is crisp and the pig is fully cooked, remove it from the heat. On a large table, chop the meat by hand into small pieces. In a large clean washtub, mix the cut pork thoroughly with a barbecue sauce made of crushed red peppers, cider vinegar, brown sugar, hot pepper sauce, but no oil—there is sufficient fat in the meat itself. Work the sauce in well with wooden spoons, or even better, with your hands. Serve each person some crisp skin along with the barbecued meat.

Note: *North Carolina purists prefer a basting sauce of vinegar and crushed red pepper only.*

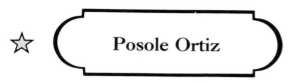

Posole Ortiz

(4 servings)

2 cups frozen white *posole* (hominy)
1 quart water
1 pound pork shoulder or pork chops, cubed
⅛ teaspoon oregano
1 teaspoon whole black peppercorns
⅓ cup chopped onion
4 dried red chile peppers, crumbled
Salt

In a large, heavy pot mix together all the ingredients. Bring to a boil and simmer, covered, for about 2½ hours or until the hominy is soft but not mushy. Season with salt to taste.

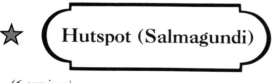

Hutspot (Salmagundi)

(6 servings)

6 medium onions, diced
6 carrots, diced
8 potatoes, peeled and diced
½ cup heavy cream
2 tablespoons butter
Salt and freshly ground pepper
½ pound thick-sliced bacon

In a kettle of salted water boil the onions and carrots until very tender. Drain. Boil the potatoes in salted water until tender. Drain. Add the potatoes to the carrots and onions. Mash thoroughly. Stir in the cream and butter. Season with salt and pepper. Fry the bacon until crisp. Drain. Serve Hutspot with bacon.

Variation: *This dish can also be made by simmering 1½ pounds beef brisket in salted water. When really tender add the onions and carrots. Then proceed as above, removing beef before mashing vegetables. Slice beef and serve on a bed of mashed vegetables.*

Rechauffé

(6 servings)

2 tablespoons bacon fat
3 onions, sliced
1½ cups well-seasoned beef stock
2 cups cooked beef or pork, cubed
Salt and freshly ground pepper
3 medium potatoes, diced
2 carrots, sliced
½ cup prunes, plumped

In a large pot melt the fat and saute the onions just until transparent. Add the stock, meat, salt, pepper, potatoes, and carrots. Simmer 30 minutes until the potatoes and carrots are tender. Serve on a platter surrounded by the prunes.

Note: Rechauffé *literally means "reheated," and this recipe uses cooked meat.*

Country Stuffed Cabbage Leaves

(8 servings)

1 large head cabbage
½ cup rice
2 tablespoons vegetable oil
1 small onion, grated
1 pound ground beef
½ pound ground pork or veal
2 eggs
1 teaspoon salt
¼ teaspoon pepper
2 8-ounce cans tomato paste
1 cup tomato puree
1 cup water
1 large onion, thinly sliced
¼ cup vinegar (optional)
3 strips bacon, cooked and
   crumbled (optional)

Remove core from cabbage. Place cabbage right side up in 2 inches of boiling water. Steam 5 minutes. Remove cabbage and carefully peel off outer leaves; set aside to cool. Return cabbage to boiling water for 5 more minutes and peel off leaves again, repeating this procedure until you have removed all of the leaves. Reserve 10 to 12 large, undamaged cabbage leaves to use as cover leaves.

Cook rice in boiling water for 10 minutes. Drain and rinse immediately with cold water. Drain again and set aside.

In a heavy skillet heat the oil and cook the onion until it is wilted but not browned. In a bowl combine beef and pork or veal with eggs, rice, salt, and pepper. Add meat mixture to skillet and stir until ingredients are thoroughly combined and the meat is browned. Remove from skillet and refrigerate until cool enough to handle.

Place a meatball-sized amount of meat mixture in one of the smaller cabbage leaves. Fold the edges of the leaf over the filling and tuck in the ends; set aside, seam side down. Repeat until the meat mixture has all been used. Preheat the oven to 325°.

Line the bottom of a heavy baking dish or a Dutch oven with the remaining small cabbage leaves. Arrange stuffed cabbage leaves on top, seam side down. In a bowl stir together the tomato paste, tomato puree, and water and pour the mixture over the stuffed cabbage. Top with onion slices and add vinegar, if desired. Bake, covered, for 1 hour. (Stuffed cabbage can be refrigerated overnight and finished before serving.)

Dip reserved large cabbage leaves in simmering water until barely wilted. Place 2 or 3 stuffed cabbage leaves in the center of each large leaf and fold sides and ends over to make a package. Place in serving dish, seam side down; repeat with remaining large leaves. Ladle sauce over stuffed cabbage. Top with crumbled bacon, if desired.

Seafood Main Dishes

◄ *Jambalaya*

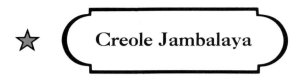

Creole Jambalaya

(8–10 servings)

4 tablespoons (½ stick) butter
1 pound Andouille sausage or Creole
    smoked sausage
½ pound country ham or boiled ham, in
    pieces
4 tablespoons flour
3 medium white onions, finely chopped
6 scallions with their green tops, chopped
1 small green pepper, chopped
4 cloves garlic, minced
4 large tomatoes, peeled and chopped
1 bay leaf
½ teaspoon thyme leaves
⅛ teaspoon ground cumin
⅛ teaspoon ground cloves
⅛ teaspoon ground allspice
¼ teaspoon cayenne or more to taste
    Freshly ground black pepper to taste
3 cups beef stock
2 pounds raw shrimp, peeled
½ pound cooked chicken, in pieces
2 cups raw rice
    Salt

In a thick-bottomed pot or Dutch oven melt the butter, cook the sausage and ham until lightly browned, and then stir in the flour. Add the onions, scallions, green pepper, and garlic, and cook until the vegetables are soft and transparent. Stir in the tomatoes and their juice. Add the bay leaf, thyme, cumin, cloves, allspice, cayenne, black pepper, and the beef stock and mix well. Add the raw shrimp and the chicken. Stir in the raw rice. The liquid in the pot should just cover the contents; add more stock if necessary. Season with salt. Simmer, covered, until the rice is done. A jambalaya should not be soupy. Correct seasoning and serve at once.

Note: *Creole or Andouille is different than French tripe sausage. See the Resource Guide for information on ordering.*

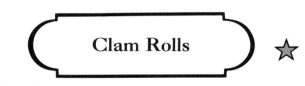

Clam Rolls

(4 servings)

24 clams, in the shell
    Flour or cornmeal for dredging
    Salt and freshly ground white pepper
    Fat for deep frying
4 hot dog buns, sliced vertically
    Butter
½ cup tartar sauce

Steam the clams in a large pot over boiling water just until they open. Remove from shells and roll in flour seasoned with salt and pepper. Let dry for 5 minutes. Fry in hot deep fat until golden. Drain and keep warm. Split the rolls, brush the cut sides with butter and run under the broiler until golden. Place six clams on each roll and top with tartar sauce. Serve hot.

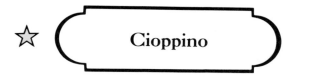

Cioppino

(8 servings)

½ cup olive oil
1 green pepper, seeded and chopped
1 onion, chopped
2 or more cloves garlic, minced
3 or 4 tomatoes, peeled, seeded, and chopped
½ cup tomato sauce
2 cups red wine
¼ cup chopped parsley
   Salt and freshly ground pepper
1 pound shrimp in shells
1 quart clams in shells
1 lobster in the shell cut in serving pieces
1 sea bass, striped bass, red snapper, or
   other firm-fleshed fish
¼ cup chopped parsley

In a deep kettle heat the oil and add the green pepper, onion, and garlic. Saute until the vegetables are transparent. Stir in the tomatoes, tomato sauce, red wine, parsley, and salt and pepper to taste. Simmer 20 minutes. Add the shrimp, clams, and lobster pieces. Simmer 10 minutes. Clean the fish and cut into pieces. Add to the stew. Cook 10 minutes. Stir in the parsley and serve very hot in large bowls, accompanied by good crisp bread.

Note: Cioppino *is a fishermen's stew with an Italian accent.*

Black Bass with Morels

(4 servings)

1 smallmouth bass, cleaned and scaled
⅓ cup lime juice
¼ pound (1 stick) butter
1 bunch scallions, white parts only, sliced
¼ pound dried morels, plumped in hot water
   and thoroughly washed
1 teaspoon chopped fresh basil
¼ cup heavy cream
   Salt and freshly ground pepper
½ cup bread crumbs
½ cup dry white wine

Preheat the oven to 350°.
Sprinkle bass inside and out with lime juice. In a small skillet melt half the butter and saute the scallions until transparent. Drain the morels, add to the scallions, add the basil and cook 3 minutes, adding butter if needed. Stir the cream into the sauce, and reduce until thickened. Season with salt and pepper. Roll the fish in breadcrumbs. Melt 2 tablespoons butter in a skillet and saute the fish until golden, about 2 minutes per side. Pour in the white wine. Add the scallions, morels, and basil. Cover and bake for 15 minutes. Serve the fish with the sauce.

Note: Morels *are wild mushrooms prized for their delicate, exquisite flavor.*

★ Baked Trout

(6 servings)

6 large trout fillets, skin on
  Salt and freshly ground pepper
2 tablespoons lemon juice
½ cup heavy cream
½ cup grated cheddar cheese

Preheat the oven to 450°.

Butter the inside of a glass or ceramic baking dish. Arrange the trout in one layer, skin side down. Sprinkle with salt and pepper and drizzle with lemon juice. Pour the cream around the fillets and sprinkle with cheese. Bake for 20 minutes. Serve very hot.

☆ Special Abalone Steaks

(4 servings)

1 cup bread crumbs
¼ cup ground almonds
  Flour for dredging
  Salt and freshly ground pepper
4 abalone steaks, pounded thin
2 eggs, beaten with ¼ cup water
¼ pound (1 stick) butter
¼ cup dry white wine
  Lemon wedges
  Chopped fresh parsley

In a bowl stir together the bread crumbs and ground almonds. Season the flour with salt and pepper. Dredge the pounded steaks in flour. Dip in the egg and roll in breadcrumb mixture. Knock off the excess. In large heavy skillet melt the butter and saute the abalone quickly, about 2 minutes on each side. Set aside and keep warm. Deglaze the pan with white wine. Boil quickly, stirring up all bits in the pan. Season with salt and pepper. Pour over the abalone. Garnish with lemon wedges and chopped parsley.

Note: *Abalone is a shellfish primarily found off the West Coast. It is frequently available fresh in fine fish markets. Short cooking is necessary, as long exposure to heat makes it tough. Abalone is frequently pounded, like veal, to make it more tender.*

Catfish Bake ☆

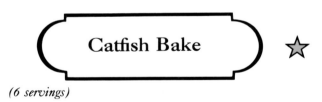

(6 servings)

1 pound catfish fillets
1 cup bread crumbs
3 tablespoons butter
1 cup artichoke hearts, quartered
8 eggs
4 tablespoons water
  Salt and freshly ground pepper
1 large red pepper, seeded, and cut into cubes
1 cup fresh corn, cut from the cob

½ cup heavy cream
½ cup grated cheese

Preheat the oven to 375°.

Roll the catfish fillets in the bread crumbs. In a skillet melt the butter and fry the fillets until golden. Drain. Fry the artichoke hearts until just golden. In a bowl beat the eggs with the water and salt and pepper until light and fluffy. Stir in the artichoke hearts, red pepper, corn, and cream. Stir in the cheese. Generously butter a rectangular baking dish. Pour the egg mixture into the baking dish. Arrange the fried fillets in the mixture. Bake until set, about 15 or 20 minutes.

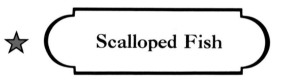

Scalloped Fish

(6 servings)

1 cup soft bread crumbs
1 cup dry bread crumbs
¾ cup butter
2 pounds fish fillets, cut into serving-size pieces
　Salt and freshly ground pepper
　Mace
1 tablespoon lemon juice
2 tablespoons chopped parsley
⅔ cup half and half

Preheat the oven to 375°.

In a bowl stir together the bread crumbs and butter. Spread half of the mixture in a shallow baking dish. Arrange the fish fillets over the crumbs. Season with salt, pepper, mace, and lemon juice. Pour the half and half over all. Stir the parsley into the remaining crumbs. Top the fish mixture with the parslied crumbs. Bake for 30 minutes.

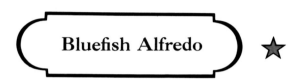

Bluefish Alfredo

(6 servings)

2 pounds bluefish, cut into 1-inch strips
1 cup white wine
　Salt and freshly ground pepper
1 teaspoon oregano
½ cup finely chopped parsley
½ cup almonds, chopped
12 cherry tomatoes
3 cups medium noodles, cooked
¼ cup chopped parsley
¼ cup grated Romano cheese
1 tablespoon olive oil

Preheat the oven to 400°.

Soak the fish in white wine for 10 minutes. Mix together salt, pepper, oregano, parsley, and almonds and spread on a plate. Roll the fillet strips in the mixture and then roll each up around a cherry tomato. Arrange the rolls in a lightly greased baking dish. Bake for 10 minutes. Toss the cooked noodles with the ¼ cup parsley, cheese, and olive oil. Arrange in a serving dish. Top with the fish and serve at once.

★ Outdoor Fish Fry

I remember my Louisiana grandmother reminiscing about fish fries along the bayous before the turn of the century. They were festive occasions, when seldom-seen neighbors and friends came together for a day filled with eating, games, and catching up on all the news. When people rode horseback or in open carriages for several hours to get to the fry, it was important to serve plenty of ice cold drinks and mountains of fried fish and hushpuppies.

People rarely arrive at a fry on horseback these days, but the fresh air still provides guests with ravenous appetites; a lot to eat is a must.

Fried Fish
Hushpuppies
Cole Slaw
Pickles
Potato Chips
Tartar Sauce
Beer
Soft Drinks or Iced Tea

For an outdoor fry, use a heavy pan made of black steel or stainless steel, or one of the commercial steel roasting pans that measure about 4″ × 18″ × 24–30″. *Do not* use galvanized metal.

For about 30 people you will need to do the following:

Bring two gallons of oil (vegetable oil, or preferably peanut oil, which does not smoke and has a high flash temperature) to a temperature of 400°–450°. It is best to use a frying

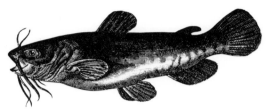

thermometer to be sure of the temperature. Guard against having the oil too hot and risking a dangerous overflow when you add the fish. Gas, oil, electricity or a wood fire can be used to provide the heat.

Use about 1 pound of fillets or fish per person. Thick fillets are better than thin ones, as they do not tend to curl so much. Sea trout, flounder, sea mullet, catfish, and croakers all make good fillets. Brim, crappy, and any perch can be scaled, cleaned, and cooked whole. A good firm fish is best (not an oily variety such as bluefish); many southern experts prefer catfish.

In a large paper bag mix about 10 pounds of finely ground cornmeal with salt and pepper. Spread the seasoned cornmeal into a large flat pan and dredge the fish or fish fillets well.

Deep-fry the fish in the hot oil for 3 to 5 minutes. (If the fish is cold to start, it will take longer for the oil to come back to a temperature of 400°.) There is no need to turn the fish if it is cooked in deep fat. Bring the oil back to a temperature of 400° after each batch of fish

has been cooked. At 400° oil will not penetrate the fish or make it greasy. When the cornmeal is nicely browned, the fish will be cooked. Do not overcook. Place the fried fish in a pan lined with absorbent paper and salt it lightly to taste.

After all the fish has been cooked, drop the hushpuppy batter (see page 263) by tablespoonfuls into the still-hot fat and cook for about 8 minutes, or until the hushpuppies are crisp and golden brown.

Often the fish is served with pepper vinegar (apple cider vinegar in which whole hot red peppers have been soaked), and some people prefer their hushpuppies with butter. It's always good to have plenty of both.

To serve the fry, have long oilcloth-covered tables set with paper plates, forks, knives, pickles, chips, bowls of tartar sauce and shakers of pepper vinegar. Start the serving line by having the guests pick up plates and utensils, and then lead them by the fryer where they will use tongs to serve the fish and hushpuppies. Then they can help themselves to the accompaniments.

Fried Herring

(4–6 servings)

4 tablespoons dry bread crumbs
  Salt
2 pounds small herring, cleaned and boned
3 tablespoons butter

Season the bread crumbs with salt. Roll the fish in bread crumbs until well coated. Melt the butter in a heavy skillet and fry the fish until well browned on each side. Serve with Onion Sauce.

Bluefish Rollups

(6 servings)

2 pounds bluefish fillets, cut in strips 1 inch
  wide
4 tablespoons butter
4 tablespoons flour
  Salt and freshly ground pepper
¼ cup sherry
2 cups milk
5 tablespoons chopped parsley
  Cooked rice

Preheat the oven to 425°.

Roll up each fish fillet strip in the form of a turban. Arrange the roll-ups in a lightly greased baking dish. Melt the butter in a saucepan. Stir in the flour and cook gently for 3 minutes. Do not brown. Stir in salt and pepper to taste. Stir in the sherry, milk, and chopped parsley. Simmer until the sauce begins to thicken. Spoon the sauce over the fillets. Bake for about 12 minutes. Serve the roll-ups on bed of rice.

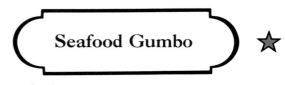

Seafood Gumbo

(6–8 servings)

 ¼ pound bacon or salt pork, diced
 3 tablespoons oil
 3 tablespoons flour
 2 large onions, minced
 2 cups fresh okra, sliced
 3 cloves garlic, minced
 3 large tomatoes, peeled and chopped
2–3 quarts liquid (water, chicken stock,
     clam juice, or a combination)
 2 pounds shrimp, cleaned
 6 hard-shell crabs, quartered
 1 cup diced ham (optional)
½–1 pound fresh lump crab meat
     Salt and freshly ground pepper
     Red pepper sauce to taste
     Worcestershire sauce to taste
 1 teaspoon filé powder
 2 tablespoons parsley
     Cooked rice

In a large cast-iron skillet saute the bacon or salt pork until transparent. Remove the pieces and set aside. In another pan heat 1 tablespoon of the bacon fat with the oil and stir in the flour to make a roux. Add the onion, okra, and garlic to the remaining bacon fat and saute until golden. Add the tomatoes and cook until the liquid has been absorbed. Add the roux and stir in the liquid. Simmer over a low flame for 30 minutes. Add the shrimp and hard-shell crabs and simmer for 30 minutes more. Stir in the reserved bacon or salt pork pieces, ham, crab meat, salt and pepper to taste, red pepper and Worcestershire sauce. Simmer until thoroughly heated. If too thick, adjust with extra liquid. Stir in the filé powder and sprinkle with parsley. Serve in a deep bowl over a scoop of rice.

Note: *Filé powder, which is ground up sassafras leaves, is used as a thickener. It must be added just before serving, as excessive heat makes the powder form strings. See the Resource Guide for ordering information.*

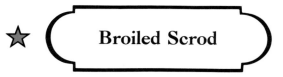

Broiled Scrod

(2 servings)

1 small scrod (young cod), cleaned and dressed
2–3 tablespoons butter, melted
Salt and freshly ground pepper
1 tablespoon chopped parsley
Lemon wedges

Split the whole fish down the back. Lift out the back bone. Brush inside and out with the melted butter and season with salt and pepper. Lay flesh side down on a hot grill or lock inside a fish griller. Grill or broil 5 to 7 minutes. Brush again with butter and turn over. Grill until skin is crisp and flesh just flakes easily. Sprinkle with parsley and serve immediately with lemon wedges.

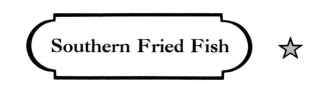

Southern Fried Fish

(12 servings)

3 cups finely ground cornmeal
Salt and freshly ground pepper
3 pounds fish fillets—sea trout, flounder, catfish, or croaker
Oil for deep frying, heated to 400°

In a large flat pan mix the cornmeal with salt and pepper. Dredge the fish in the cornmeal. Drop the fillets a few at a time into the hot fat. When the cornmeal is browned, the fish is cooked. Be careful not to overcook. Drain on absorbent paper and salt lightly. Bring the oil back up to 400° before frying each new batch. If Hushpuppies are also on your menu, fry them in the same batter as soon as the fish is finished. Serve with pepper vinegar—vinegar in which hot red peppers have been soaked.

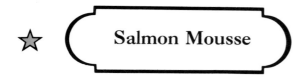

Salmon Mousse

(6 entreé servings or 10 appetizer servings)

2 envelopes unflavored gelatin
½ cup dry white wine
2 thick slices onion
3 tablespoons lemon juice
2 cups cold poached salmon
¼ cup tomato paste
2 cups whipping cream
1 tablespoon chopped parsley
1 teaspoon dill
½ teaspoon chervil
8 drops red pepper sauce

In a saucepan dissolve the gelatin in the wine and heat until completely dissolved. Pour into a blender or food processor. Add the onion and lemon juice and blend. Add the salmon and tomato paste and blend again. Keeping the motor on, pour in 1 cup whipping cream. Add the seasonings. Add the remaining cup whipping cream and blend. Pour into an oiled 6-cup mold. Chill until firm.

Note: *This is delicious served with Caviar Dip.*

Redfish Court Bouillon

(6–8 servings)

Fish Stock:
(2 quarts)
1 pound fish bones and heads
1½ quarts water
2 cups dry wine, red or white
   Bouqet garni of thyme, parsley
1 celery stalk with leaves
1 medium onion stuck with 2 cloves
1 carrot, cut into pieces
1½ teaspoons salt

Court Bouillon:
6 tablespoons salad oil or bacon fat
6 tablespoons all-purpose flour
½ cup finely chopped onion
½ cup finely chopped celery
½ cup finely chopped scallions
2 teaspoons finely chopped garlic
3 cups peeled and coarsely chopped tomatoes
1 cup tomato puree
1 cup finely chopped green peppers
1 cup fish stock
½ cup dry red wine
½ teaspoon thyme, crumbled
¼ teaspoon marjoram, crumbled
¼ teaspoon ground allspice
2½ pounds redfish (red drum) or red snapper fillets, skinned and cut into strips
¼ cup white wine

2 tablespoons fresh lemon juice
2 teaspoons red pepper sauce
  Cooked rice

To make the fish stock, simmer the fish and water in a covered pot for 20 minutes. Strain. Add the remaining ingredients to the strained liquid and simmer, covered, for 20 minutes more. Strain again.

To prepare Redfish Court Bouillon, in a heavy 4- or 5-quart pot heat the oil and add the flour. Cook over low heat, stirring constantly, until dark brown, being careful not to let it burn (this could take 15 minutes). Add the onion, celery, scallions, and garlic. Simmer about 5 minutes, stirring occasionally, until the vegetables are soft. Add the tomatoes, tomato puree, green peppers, fish stock, red wine, thyme, marjoram, and allspice. Cook uncovered over medium heat for 15 minutes, stirring occasionally. Dip the fish in the white wine and add to the mixture in the pot, coating each piece well. Stir in the lemon juice and red pepper sauce. Reduce heat to low. Simmer, tightly covered, for 20 minutes, or until fish flakes easily when touched gently with a fork. Serve at once from a heated serving bowl, accompanied by hot cooked rice.

Planked Shad

(8-10 servings)

¼ cup Worcestershire sauce
2 tablespoons butter
1 tablespoon lemon juice
   Salt and freshly ground pepper
   Red pepper sauce to taste
1 large shad, cleaned and split down the backbone
1 hardwood plank, wide enough to nail the fish on it, skin side down

In a saucepan boil together the Worcestershire sauce, butter, lemon juice, and salt, pepper, and red pepper sauce to taste. Nail the shad to the plank and suspend over a wood or charcoal fire. Baste the fish every 45 minutes. Cook over the fire for 3½ to 4 hours.

Note: *This is an outdoor event—usually an occasion for local politicians to come calling. For one fish, the plank can be suspended about 18-20 inches above a medium-hot charcoal fire. Normally the fire would be made of hardwood and the rack would be about 30 inches above the fire. The long cooking time is required to soften the hundreds of small bones for which shad is famous.*

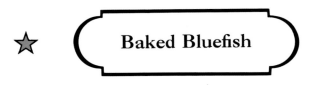

Baked Bluefish

(8 servings)

3 pounds bluefish fillets
Salt and freshly ground pepper
2 tablespoons minced onion
1–2 tablespoons mayonnaise
Paprika

Preheat the oven to 350°.
Wash the fish and dry them thoroughly. Place the fish in a single layer on a large sheet of aluminum foil, skin side down, and place foil on a shallow baking pan. Season the fish with salt and pepper to taste and sprinkle with the minced onion. Smooth a thin layer of mayonnaise over the entire fish and sprinkle with paprika.

Loosely seal the aluminum foil over the fish. Bake, covered, for 40 minutes. Uncover fish and bake until lightly browned, about 10 minutes.

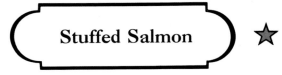

Stuffed Salmon

(4 servings)

1 whole small salmon or large salmon trout
  (3–4 pounds)
Salt and freshly ground pepper
3 tablespoons butter
½ cup chopped celery
½ cup chopped onions
2 cups dry bread crumbs
1 tablespoon dried dill
¼ cup dry white wine
2 tablespoons oil

Clean the salmon. Sprinkle the cavity with salt and pepper. In a skillet melt the butter, add the celery and onions, and saute until transparent. Stir in the bread crumbs, salt and pepper to taste, dill, and white wine. Remove from heat. Preheat the oven to 350°.

Stuff the salmon with the mixture and secure with skewers. Arrange the stuffed fish in an oiled baking dish and brush with the oil. Bake 10 to 12 minutes per pound, but no longer than 40 minutes.

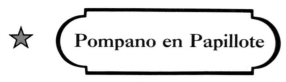

Pompano en Papillote

(6 servings)

6 pompano fillets
1½ cups Fish Stock (see page 176) or clam
   juice
4 tablespoons butter
2 tablespoons chopped scallions
1 cup small shrimp, cooked until barely
   opaque
1 cup crabmeat
1 clove garlic, minced (optional)
6 large heart-shaped pieces of parchment
   paper
2 tablespoons flour
   Salt and freshly ground pepper
¼ cup sherry

Preheat the oven to 400°.

Poach the pompano fillets in fish stock for 5 minutes. Remove the fillets, drain and set aside. Strain the stock and reserve 1 cup.

In a skillet melt 2 tablespoons of the butter and saute the scallions, shrimp, crabmeat, and garlic for 2 to 3 minutes. Oil the parchment hearts. Arrange one pompano fillet on one half of each parchment heart. Melt the other 2 tablespoons butter in a small saucepan. Stir in the flour, salt, and pepper. Cook over low heat 2 or 3 minutes. Stir in the reserved fish stock and the sherry Simmer until thick. Stir in the shrimp and crabmeat. Spoon the seafood mixture over

the fillets. Fold the top half of each paper heart over the filling and seal the edges by folding them in and pressing down hard. Transfer the packets to a baking sheet and bake for 15 minutes or until paper puffs up. Serve very hot, slitting each packet with a knife to release the steam.

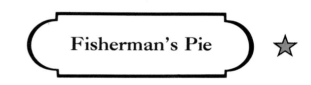

Fisherman's Pie

(4–6 servings)

2 tablespoons butter
2 tablespoons flour
   Salt and freshly ground pepper
1 cup milk
2 cups cooked fish, shrimp, crabmeat or any
   combination of these
½ cup peas
1 small onion, diced
1 tablespoon minced green pepper

Topping:
½ cup cracker meal
2 tablespoons parmesan cheese
4 tablespoons butter, melted

In a heavy saucepan melt the butter, add the flour, and cook 5 minutes without browning. Season with salt and pepper. Stir in the milk and cook, stirring, until thick. Stir in the seafood, peas, onion, and green pepper. Preheat the oven to 375°.

Butter a baking dish. Turn the fish mixture into the dish. To make the topping, in a bowl toss the cracker meal with the cheese and butter. Spread on top of the seafood. Bake for 20 minutes.

Variation: *Add ¼ cup sherry to cream sauce if desired.*

Eggplant and Oysters

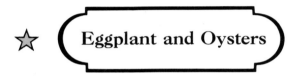

(2–3 servings)

1 medium eggplant
1 pint oysters
½ stick butter
¼ cup minced onion
1 clove garlic, minced
½ cup Italian seasoned bread crumbs
  Salt and freshly ground pepper
  Thyme

Halve the eggplant lengthwise and scoop out the flesh, leaving about ½ inch inside the skin. Chop the eggplant flesh. Cut the oysters into bite-size pieces. Melt the butter in a skillet and saute the onion and garlic until transparent. Add the oysters. Cook 1 minute. Stir in the bread crumbs and seasonings. Preheat the oven to 350°.

Pile the eggplant mixture into the eggplant halves and arrange in a buttered baking dish. Bake for 35 minutes.

Eggplant Stuffed with Crabmeat

(6 servings)

2 large eggplants
1 pound small shrimp, boiled and shelled
12 ounces crabmeat, well picked over
3 tablespoons butter
1 green pepper, seeded and chopped
1 onion, chopped
2 tomatoes, peeled, seeded, and chopped
1 cup rice, cooked
3 cloves garlic, minced
  Salt and freshly ground pepper
3 tablespoons chopped parsley
½ cup grated cheddar cheese
10 large okra, sliced and steamed 5 minutes

Preheat the oven to 325°.

Cut the eggplants in half, scoop out the inside and chop, reserving the eggplant shells. Chop the shrimp and toss with the crabmeat. In a heavy skillet melt the butter and saute the green pepper and onion until onion is transparent. Add the chopped eggplant and dry out over low heat. Add the tomatoes and rice. Simmer 5 minutes. Stir in the garlic and season with salt, pepper, and parsley. Stir in the crabmeat and shrimp. Pile the mixture into the eggplant shells. Top with grated cheese. Arrange sliced okra around the edges of the eggplant. Bake until the cheese is melted and bubbly, about 15 to 20 minutes. Serve very hot.

New England Clambake

Rhode Island and Massachusetts are the clambake capitals of America. Professionals abound in these states who will arrange and prepare bakes at the drop of a hat for any occasion and for any number of people.

On a hot summer day, with good friends all around, a clambake is truly a meal for kings. But you cannot be dainty; the bake is meant to be eaten out of hand. Luckily, most of the best bakes are held at the seashore—or at least somewhere close to water—and there is always somewhere to wash your sticky fingers.

Commercial fishermen in the Northeast have perfected the individual clambake, which is now available by mail. While the ingredients are fresh and good, there is definitely something missing from the stove-top version of this feast.

Eating soft clams—the highpoint of the bake—is an art easily learned. Remove the clam from the shell and pick it up by the long neck. Swish the body in clam broth or warm water to remove any sand, then dip in melted butter and eat. Many people discard the neck, but it is just the tough outer skin that should be rejected. This can be easily peeled off with your fingers.

Clambakes for more than fifteen people require a good deal of planning, and some expertise; but with a little effort the smaller bakes can be easy, delicious, and fun.
For an early afternoon bake, preparations should begin practically at dawn. The bake must be heated for at least 2 hours before serving time, which does not include the time to

Soft-shell clams
Chicken
Firm-fleshed fish (haddock, cod, bluefish, etc.)
Lobster (optional)
Sweet Italian sausages
or Spanish chorizos
Corn on the cob
Small sweet onions
Sweet potatoes
White potatoes
Melted butter
Beer
Watermelon, well chilled

dig the pit, line it with stones, build and light the fire, or the time to prepare the food.

Prepare a large square pit on the beach, well above the high tide line. Line it with large dry stones. It is important that the stones be totally dry—otherwise the heat will cause any moisture in them to expand and the rocks may explode. Pile firewood evenly over the dry stones. Light the fire and continue burning, adding wood if necessary, until the stones give off a great deal of steam when sprinkled with water. This could take 2 or 3 hours.

While the stones are heating, prepare the food. Wash and soak the clams in fresh water into which a little cornmeal has been stirred. Allow them to stand in the water for at least 2 hours. Discard any clams that do not shut tightly when touched. Count on a peck for every 2 diners.

Husk the corn. Allow two ears per person.

Allow 1 small lobster per person if they are included in the bake. (Lobsters must be alive before being put into the pit.)

Cut the chickens into serving pieces and put each piece into a waxed-paper sandwich bag. Allow 2 pieces for each diner.

Put 2 sausages each into waxed-paper sandwich bags, allowing 1 bag per person.

Wash, but do not peel the potatoes.

Cut the fish into serving-sized pieces and place each piece in a waxed-paper sandwich bag. Allow 1 bag per person.

When all the food is ready to be cooked, arrange each type of food in a separate wooden frame, each with a bottom of galvanized screen. Or carefully arrange foods on grilling racks.

Once the stones are very hot, rake away the coals and quickly heap several bushels of wet rockweed on top of the stones. You will need a layer of seaweed about 1½ feet thick. Place the flats of food on top of the seaweed—in the following order: potatoes on the bottom, then onions, chicken, and sausage. Next add the corn, lobster, fish and finally—on top—the clams. The moisture from the opening clams and the bursting water pods of the seaweed traditionally give off the moisture that produces the steam for cooking. Cover everything with wet canvas to hold in the steam. Be sure to anchor the canvas with sand or more large stones.

The bake can be opened after about 1½ hours. The clams are served first with melted butter, while the other flats of food are covered again and left to cook until the clams have been eaten.

Once the clams have been consumed, serve the rest of the food. The lobsters should be accompanied by more melted butter. If anyone has room, watermelon makes the perfect dessert.

Note: *For small bakes of 6 to 12 people, a clean oil drum, open at both ends and sunk into the sand about half way, makes an excellent "pit." Line the drum with stones and then build a fire as you would in a pit. When the stones are hot, remove the coals with a shovel and continue as for a large bake. Cover everything with wet canvas and allow to steam.*

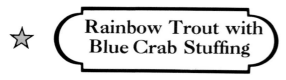

Rainbow Trout with Blue Crab Stuffing

(8 servings)

¼ pound (1 stick) butter or margarine
½ cup chopped onion
⅓ cup chopped celery
⅓ cup chopped green pepper
2 cloves garlic, crushed
½ cup chopped pimiento
1 pound blue crab claw meat, picked over
2 eggs, slightly beaten
½ teaspoon seafood seasoning
1 teaspoon salt
½ teaspoon pepper
1 teaspoon Worcestershire sauce (optional)
1 teaspoon horseradish (optional)
2 cups fresh bread crumbs
1 large, fresh rainbow trout
  Butter
  Paprika

In a heavy skillet melt the butter and saute the onion, celery, green pepper, garlic, and pimiento until onion is transparent. Remove from heat. Add crabmeat, eggs, seafood seasoning, salt, pepper, Worcestershire sauce, and horseradish. Stir in bread crumbs gradually until mixture holds together well. Adjust seasonings to taste.

Preheat the broiler. Wipe the cavity of the trout with damp absorbent paper. Dot with butter. Stuff loosely with crabmeat mixture; do not pack tightly. Place the fish on its side in a shallow baking pan. Dot the skin with additional butter. Add just enough water to cover the bottom of the pan. Broil 3 to 5 inches from heat for 10 minutes. Sprinkle with paprika and additional bread crumbs, if you wish. Broil 10 minutes longer or until meat flakes easily but is still moist.

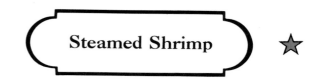

Steamed Shrimp

(6 servings)

1 cup dry white wine
½ cup water
1 small onion, thinly sliced
1 stalk celery, thinly sliced
1 large carrot, thinly sliced
2 tablespoons chopped parsley
2 sprigs fresh thyme
1 tablespoon "crab boil" seasonings
1½ pounds small shrimp, washed and drained
  Hot seafood sauce

In a large pot bring all of the ingredients except shrimp and seafood sauce to a boil and let boil for 10 minutes. Add the shrimp and cover. Simmer 5 to 10 minutes. Remove from the heat and let cool in the liquid. Drain well. Pile the shrimp in a bowl and serve with hot seafood sauce.

Note: *See Resource Guide for information on ordering "crab boil" seasonings. Old Bay is the brand most often used.*

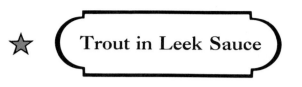

Trout in Leek Sauce

(6 servings)

¾ pound (3 sticks) butter
18 2-ounce trout fillets
1½ cups leeks, white part only, julienned
1½ cups white onions, julienned
 1 medium tomato, peeled, seeded, and cut
   into thin strips
¼ teaspoon oregano
¼ teaspoon salt
½ teaspoon garlic powder
½ teaspoon black pepper
⅔ teaspoon cayenne pepper
¼ teaspoon powdered thyme
⅛ teaspoon paprika
½ teaspoon onion powder
1½ cups white wine
1½ cups greatly reduced fish stock (from 4–5
   cups originally)
 18 fresh whole mushrooms, stems removed
1½ cups heavy cream

Place all the ingredients except the cream in a large pan. Simmer, covered, for 5 to 6 minutes or until the fish is done, being careful not to overcook the fish. Remove the fish from the pan to six warm plates, placing three fillets on each plate. Place one mushroom on each fillet. Cook and stir the leek sauce, uncovered, over relatively high heat until the liquid is reduced. Add the cream, and simmer the sauce until it is reduced again and a thick-cream-sauce consistency is achieved. Top each serving of fish and mushrooms with ½ cup of sauce and serve.

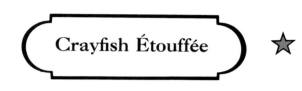

Crayfish Étouffée

(6 servings)

4–5 pounds fresh crayfish
 4 tablespoons butter
 2 large onions, chopped
 2 cloves garlic, minced
¼ cup chopped scallions
 1 tablespoon chopped parsley
 2 tablespoons tomato paste
   Cayenne pepper to taste
 1 tablespoon flour
⅔ cup warm water
   Salt and freshly ground pepper
   Cooked rice

Boil the crayfish for 5 minutes. Drain, cool slightly, and peel.

In a deep heavy skillet melt the butter and add the onions, garlic, scallions, and parsley. Saute just until golden. Stir in the tomato paste and cayenne. In a small bowl mix together well the flour and water and then beat into the sauce. Cook 5 minutes. Add the crayfish, cover and simmer 20 to 30 minutes. Season with salt and pepper. Serve very hot with rice.

Notes: Etouffée *means "smothered" in French. See the Resource Guide for information on ordering crayfish.*

Mesquite-Grilled Scallops

(4 servings)

2 shallots, minced
½ cup dry white wine
  Salt and freshly ground pepper
2 sticks (½ pound) unsalted butter, cut into small cubes
2 tablespoons orange juice
1 tablespoon grated orange rind
1 tablespoon oil
1 teaspoon soy sauce
8 large scallops, split horizontally into 2 pieces
  Fresh chervil

In a saucepan boil the shallots, wine, salt, and pepper until reduced by half. Reduce the heat and beat in the butter a little at a time, whisking constantly. Do not let the butter melt. Keep the saucepan cool by removing from the heat occasionally. When all the butter has been added, the mixture should be thick and creamy. Strain the sauce. Beat in the orange juice and orange rind. Keep the sauce warm but not hot enough to melt the butter. Mix together the oil and soy sauce. Brush the scallops with the mixture. Grill quickly over hot Mesquite charcoal, turning once. Do not overcook. Place 4 pieces of scallop on each serving plate. Sauce with the orange butter sauce and garnish with fresh chervil.

Note: *It is important that the butter emulsify and not melt. You do not want to see golden liquid, but a pale yellow frothy mixture. The bottom of the pan should never become too hot to touch. This sauce is traditionally served warm, not hot.*

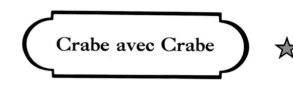

Crabe avec Crabe

(4 servings)

  Vegetable oil or fat for deep frying
8 medium-size soft-shell crabs
  Milk
  Corn flour, or unbleached flour
4 tablespoons butter
1 pound lump crabmeat, backfin if possible
3 tablespoons lemon juice
  Red pepper sauce to taste

Heat the oil in a deep fat fryer to 365°.
Dip the crabs in the milk and then dredge in the corn flour, patting gently to knock off the excess flour. Place the crabs in the frying basket, and fry briefly until light golden brown. Remove the crabs and keep hot. In a skillet melt the butter and add the lump crabmeat and lemon juice. Cook just long enough to heat the crabmeat through, stirring very gently in order not to break up the lumps of meat. Stir in the red pepper sauce. Arrange the fried crabs on a serving plate, cover with the crabmeat lumps, and drizzle with the butter-lemon sauce from the pan.

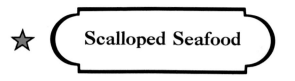

Scalloped Seafood

(6–8 servings)

¼ cup butter
½ pound mushrooms, sliced
¼ cup flour
2 cups milk
½ teaspoon salt
⅛ teaspoon paprika
¾ pound haddock, flounder, cod, or other fish
    fillets, cut into bite-size pieces
1 pound cooked scallops
1 pound cooked and cleaned shrimp
½ cup plain bread crumbs
3 tablespoons butter, melted

Preheat the oven to 350°.

In a heavy saucepan melt the butter, add the mushrooms, and saute until golden. Remove the mushrooms and stir in the flour. Gradually add the milk and cook over medium heat, stirring constantly, until thickened and smooth. Add the seasonings and cook gently for 2 minutes. Add the fish pieces to the sauce along with the other seafoods and the sauteed mushrooms. Turn the mixture into an ovenproof casserole. Mix together the bread crumbs and butter. Spread the bread crumbs on top of the fish, and bake for 20 to 25 minutes, or until mixture bubbles on top.

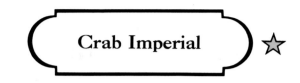

Crab Imperial

(4 servings)

12 ounces crabmeat, well picked over
 3 tablespoons butter
 1 tablespoon finely chopped onion
 1 tablespoon finely chopped green pepper
 1 tablespoon flour
    Salt and freshly ground pepper
½ cup half and half
½ cup soft white bread crumbs
 1 teaspoon Worcestershire sauce
⅓ cup mayonnaise
    Juice of half a lemon
    Red pepper sauce

In a small skillet melt 2 tablespoons of the butter, add the crabmeat, and toss to coat with the butter. In a large skillet melt the remaining tablespoon butter and saute the onion and green pepper until golden. Stir in the flour and salt and pepper. Stir in the half and half and simmer, stirring, until thick. Stir in the bread crumbs, Worcestershire sauce, mayonnaise, and lemon juice. Stir in the crabmeat. Season with red pepper sauce to taste. Preheat the oven to 450°.

Lightly grease clean crab shells, molds, or a small casserole. Spread the crab mixture in the shells. Bake for 15 minutes until very hot.

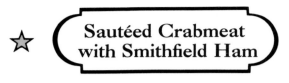

Sautéed Crabmeat with Smithfield Ham

(6 servings)

  5 tablespoons butter
  2 thin slices Smithfield ham, chopped
  ½ cup chopped green pepper
  ¼ cup chopped onion
  2 pounds crabmeat
    Cooked rice

In a heavy skillet melt the butter and saute the ham, green pepper, and onion until tender. Add the crabmeat. Cook over low heat until lightly browned, about 5 minutes. Serve with hot fluffy rice.

Note: *See the Resource Guide for information on ordering Smithfield ham.*

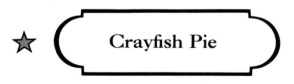

Crayfish Pie

(6 servings)

    Pie crust for a 1-crust pie
  4 pounds crayfish
  5 tablepoons butter
  1 small onion, chopped
  ½ green pepper, minced
  3 tablespoons chopped parsley

  3 tablespoons minced celery
  1 bunch scallions, finely sliced
  3 tomatoes, peeled, seeded, and chopped
  2 tablespoons butter
  2 tablespoons flour
  1 cup half and half
  ⅓ cup well-seasoned chicken stock
  2 hard boiled eggs, chopped
  ½ cup bread crumbs
    Salt
    Cayenne pepper

Preheat the oven to 350°. Roll out dough and fit into a 9-inch pie plate.

In a large pot boil the crayfish for 5 minutes. Peel, and chop off the tails. In a heavy skillet melt the butter and saute the onion, pepper, parsley, celery, and scallions until transparent. Add the tomatoes, cover, and simmer 5 minutes. In a saucepan melt the 2 tablespoons butter, stir in the flour and cook until golden brown; do not let it burn. Pour in the half and half and cook, stirring, until thick. Add to crayfish mixture. Stir in the chicken stock, eggs, bread crumbs, and seasonings. Cook 5 minutes. Fill the pie shell and bake for 30 minutes until pastry is browned.

Notes: *The same filling can be used to make small turnover pastries. See the Resource Guide for information on ordering crayfish.*

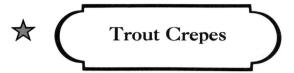

Trout Crepes

(5 servings)

Crepes:
2/3 cup flour
2 small eggs, beaten
1/2 cup milk
1 tablespoon oil
Pinch of salt
Pinch of freshly ground pepper
1 1/2 teaspoons oil for frying

Filling:
12 ounces trout fillets
1/2 cup chopped parsley
1 cup fresh mushrooms, sliced
1/4 cup black olives, sliced
1/2 tablespoon butter
2 tablespoons white wine
3 tablespoons mayonnaise
1/8 teaspoon pepper
1/2 teaspoon salt
1/4 teaspoon beau monde seasoning or
    celery salt

Sauce:
2 tablespoons butter
1 cup sliced fresh mushrooms
1/2 cube chicken bouillon
2 tablespoons flour
2 cups half and half

Paprika
Slices of stuffed green olive (optional)
Sprigs of fresh dill (optional)

Preheat the oven to 350°.

Combine the crepe batter ingredients in a small bowl, mix well, and set aside.

In a shallow casserole dish combine fillets, parsley, mushrooms, olives, butter and wine. Cover and bake for 10 to 15 minutes. In a bowl, combine the mayonnaise with the spices. Drain the fish and vegetables and add them to the mayonnaise mixture, stirring gently. Place in a warm oven until ready to use.

Brush a 6-inch diameter skillet lightly with oil. Pour 1 1/2 tablespoons of crepe batter into the skillet, swirl around until skillet is covered, and fry until golden, turning once. Repeat until you have 10 crepes. Separate crepes with absorbent paper and place in a warm oven.

To make the sauce, saute the mushrooms in the butter until tender. Stir in the flour. Add the chicken bouillon, stirring to avoid lumps. Slowly add the cream, and heat sauce until boiling.

Spoon about 2 tablespoons of the filling on each crepe, roll up, and pour sauce over each. Sprinkle with paprika and garnish each serving with slices of green olive and a sprig of fresh dill if desired.

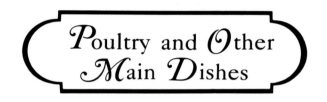

Poultry and Other Main Dishes

◄ *Fried Chicken*

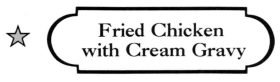

Fried Chicken with Cream Gravy

(4–6 servings)

> 2 frying chickens (2½-3 pounds each), cleaned
> Salt and freshly ground black pepper
> 3 cups flour
> 1½ teaspoons salt
> 3 teaspoons ground black pepper
> Vegetable oil for frying
> Butter

Cream Gravy:
> 3 tablespoons cooking oil in which chicken was fried
> 3 tablespoons seasoned flour left from dredging chicken
> All browned bits left in oil from frying chicken
> 1½ cups cold milk

Cut the chicken into serving-size pieces. Pat dry with paper towels. Season the flour with salt and pepper. Dredge the chicken pieces in the seasoned flour. In a heavy iron skillet or in an electric skillet heat equal parts of oil and butter to a total depth of 1 inch to 375°. Add the chicken pieces, but do not crowd the skillet. Cook on one side until brown. Turn the chicken. Cover and cook an additional 15 to 20 minutes. Uncover and fry until crisp, turning once more. Remove from skillet and drain on absorbent paper.

To make the gravy, remove all but 3 tablespoons oil from the skillet. Stir in the seasoned flour, scraping up browned bits. Cook, stirring, 2 minutes to make a roux. Add the cold milk and stir over medium heat until thickened. Taste and correct seasonings. Serve with the chicken and potatoes, rice, or biscuits.

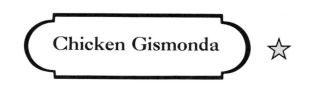

Chicken Gismonda

(4 servings)

> 2 whole chicken breasts, boned and split
> Salt and freshly ground pepper
> Freshly rolled bread crumbs
> 5 tablespoons butter
> 1½ pounds spinach, thoroughly washed and stemmed
> ½ pound mushrooms, thinly sliced
> 3 tablespoons cream
> 3 tablespoons finely chopped parsley

Season the chicken breasts with salt and pepper. Dredge in bread crumbs, knocking off excess. In a skillet melt half the butter and saute the chicken breasts until golden brown and cooked through, about 15 minutes. Set aside and keep warm.

Steam the spinach just until tender. Drain thoroughly and keep hot.

Add the remaining butter to a skillet and saute the mushrooms until just tender. Stir in the cream and simmer for 2 minutes.

Arrange the spinach on serving plates. Top with chicken breasts and spoon mushrooms over all. Garnish with chopped parsley.

Lemon Chicken

(6 servings)

2 pounds boneless chicken breasts
½ cup flour
2 teaspoons salt
½ teaspoon freshly ground pepper
   Dash cayenne pepper (optional)
8 tablespoons butter
4 tablespoons oil
1 tablespoon fresh or ¼ teaspoon dried tarragon (optional)
5 tablespoons freshly squeezed lemon juice
5 tablespoons chopped fresh parsley
1 lemon, thinly sliced
   Fresh parsley

Flatten the chicken by pounding it gently between layers of waxed paper. In a plastic bag combine the flour, salt, pepper, and cayenne pepper. Add the chicken and shake to coat evenly. In a skillet melt 4 tablespoons butter and the oil. Brown the chicken on both sides until just tender. Do not overcook. Remove, set aside, and keep warm.

Melt the remaining 4 tablespoons butter and add the tarragon (if desired), lemon juice, and parsley. Heat to simmering. Return the chicken to the skillet and cover with sauce. Serve immediately, garnished with lemon slices and parsley.

Chicken Stew with Dumplings

(4 servings)

1 3½-pound frying chicken, cut up
   Salt and freshly ground pepper
¼ cup white wine
   Water

Dumplings:
2 cups flour
1 teaspoon salt
2 teaspoons baking powder
3 tablespoons butter
¾ cup milk

Place the chicken in a kettle with a close-fitting lid. Season with salt and pepper. Add the wine and enough water to cover. Simmer 30 minutes.

To make the dumplings, stir together the flour, salt, and baking powder. Cut in the butter until the mixture resembles coarse meal. Add the milk to make a thin dough. Drop by spoonfuls onto the chicken. Cover tightly and cook for 30 minutes without opening. Serve from kettle.

Chicken Hash

(4–6 servings)

3 tablespoons butter or chicken fat
2 tablespoons flour
2 cups chicken stock
4 cups diced cooked chicken
⅛ teaspoon dried thyme
  Salt and freshly ground pepper
  Freshly chopped parsley
  Buttered egg noodles

Preheat the oven to 350°.

In saucepan melt the butter and stir in the flour. Cook 3 minutes, but do not brown. Add the chicken stock, stirring constantly. Simmer gently for 5 minutes. Add the chicken, thyme, salt, and pepper. Generously butter an oven-proof casserole. Fill with the chicken mixture. Bake for 20 minutes. Garnish with freshly chopped parsley. Serve over hot, freshly buttered egg noodles.

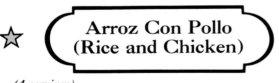

Arroz Con Pollo (Rice and Chicken)

(4 servings)

2 slices salt pork, ¼ inch thick, cut into
  1-inch pieces
1 frying chicken, cut up
2 tablespoons olive oil
3 cloves garlic, minced
1 green pepper, seeded and minced
2 onions chopped
1 tomato, peeled, seeded, and chopped
  Saffron to taste
3 cups water
1½ cups raw rice

In a large skillet fry salt pork until crisp. Remove with a slotted spoon and reserve. Brown the chicken pieces in the pork fat.

In a heavy kettle heat the olive oil and saute the garlic, pepper, onions, and tomato until onion is transparent. Add the saffron, water, browned chicken and rice. Stir gently. Cover and cook over low heat, stirring occasionally, for about 1 hour, or until chicken is tender and rice is cooked.

Szechuan Chicken

(4–6 servings)

¼ cup dry sherry
¼ cup soy sauce
¼ cup water
2 tablespoons sugar
1 ounce fresh ginger, thinly sliced
1 teaspoon dried hot chilies, crushed
2 tablespoons peanut oil
½ pound shallots, peeled and halved
  lengthwise
¼ pound small mushrooms, halved or
  quartered
1 pound boneless chicken breast, cut in thin
  strips

In a saucepan bring the sherry, soy sauce, water, sugar, ginger, and chilies to a boil. Boil until reduced by half. Remove from heat.

In a wok or heavy pan, heat the oil. Saute shallots and mushrooms for 2 to 3 minutes. Add chicken and reduced liquid. Simmer just until chicken is cooked through. Serve with rice or noodles.

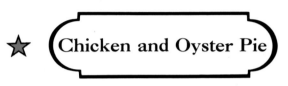

Chicken and Oyster Pie

(6 servings)

3 cups diced cooked chicken (poached
  is best)
2 dozen small oysters
2 tablespoons butter
1 teaspoon sage
  Salt and freshly ground pepper
2 tablespoons butter
2 tablespoons flour
2 cups milk
  Pastry for 1-crust pie

Butter an oven-proof casserole. Combine the oysters and chicken and arrange in the casserole. Dot with butter, season with sage, salt, and pepper.

In a heavy saucepan melt the other 2 tablespoons of butter, stir in the flour, and cook 5 minutes without browning. Season with salt and pepper to taste. Stir in the milk and cook over low heat until thick.

Pour the sauce over the chicken and oysters. Preheat the oven to 400°.

Roll the pastry very thin. Cover the dish with the pastry and crimp around the edges. Bake for 30 minutes. Serve hot.

Note: *If desired, ¼ pound sliced mushrooms can be added to the chicken and oyster combination.*

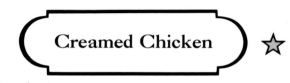

Creamed Chicken

(4 servings)

2 tablespoons butter
1 large onion, finely chopped
2 tablespoons flour
2 cups scalded milk
  Salt and freshly ground white pepper
3 cups cooked chicken, diced
1 cup sliced mushrooms, sauteed in 1
  tablespoon butter
¼ cup chopped chives
1 tablespoon chopped parsley
  Cooked rice

In a heavy saucepan melt the butter, add the onion, and saute until transparent. Stir in the flour. Cook gently—do not brown—for 5 minutes. Stir in the milk at once. Add salt and pepper to taste. Stir in the chicken, mushrooms, and chives. Garnish with a little chopped parsley. Serve beside mounds of fluffy rice.

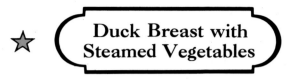

Duck Breast with Steamed Vegetables

(4 servings)

Marinade
¼ cup honey
1 tablespoon soy sauce
½ cup pineapple juice

Boned breasts of 2 Long Island ducklings,
2½–3½ pounds each
2 medium zucchini, peeled and cut into
1-inch pieces
1 pound baby carrots, peeled
1 bunch broccoli, trimmed, florets only
½ pound asparagus spears, trimmed
1 tablespoon butter, melted

In a large bowl or pan combine the marinade ingredients. Place the breasts in the marinade. Refrigerate for 24 hours.

Preheat the broiler to 550°.

Score the fatty sides of the breasts of the ducklings and place in the broiler (or over a preheated charcoal fire) for 7 to 10 minutes on each side.

Steam vegetables separately until each is just tender. Toss in hot melted butter just before serving.

Remove the skin from each duck breast and slice the breasts on an angle with a sharp knife. Arrange the slices of duck breast on each of 4 dinner plates. Arrange the vegetables around the duck.

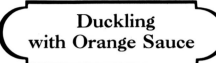

Duckling with Orange Sauce

(4 servings)

1 5-pound duckling
Salt and freshly ground pepper
3 oranges
1 cup orange marmalade
½ cup well-seasoned duck or veal stock
¼ cup Grand Marnier
½ cup dry white wine

Preheat the oven to 350°.

Rub the cavity of the duck with salt and pepper. Prick the skin all over with a sharp fork. Set the duckling on a rack and roast for about 1½ hours.

While the duckling is roasting, peel one orange. Cut the peel into thin strips. Blanch for five minutes in boiling water. Drain. Slice the orange into thin slices. Melt the marmalade in a saucepan. Add the orange peel, stock, and Grand Marnier. Season with salt and pepper. Simmer to reduce. Peel the remaining oranges and break into sections. Add any juice to the sauce. Transfer the roasted duck to a serving platter. Deglaze the pan with the white wine. Simmer long enough to scrape up all the browned pieces. Add to the sauce. Boil hard for 5 minutes. Arrange the orange sections around the duck. Lay the orange slices on the duck breast. Spoon some of the sauce over the duck. Serve the duck very hot and pass the remaining sauce separately.

Grilled Duck Breast with Steamed Vegetables ▶

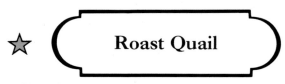

Roast Quail

(4 servings)

4 tablespoons butter
8 small quail
½ cup white wine
Salt and freshly ground pepper
8 rounds of toast, buttered
Fresh parsley

Preheat the oven to 400°.

In a large skillet melt the butter and brown the birds on all sides. Arrange in a baking dish. Pour the wine and remaining butter from the skillet around the birds. Sprinkle with salt and pepper. Roast, covered with foil, for 45 minutes, basting frequently. Serve each bird on a buttered toast round and pass remaining pan juices. Garnish with parsley.

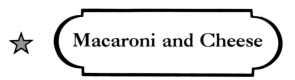

Macaroni and Cheese

(4 servings)

1½ cups milk, scalded
1 cup fresh soft bread crumbs
1½ cups grated cheddar cheese
1 cup cooked macaroni
3 eggs, separated
Salt
2 tablespoons melted butter

Preheat the oven to 375°.

Pour the hot milk over the bread crumbs and cheese. Stir until the cheese melts. Add the macaroni, egg yolks, salt, and butter. In another bowl beat the egg whites until stiff peaks form. Fold the egg whites into the macaroni mixture. Pour into a well-greased casserole. Bake for 30 minutes. Serve very hot.

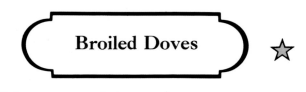

Broiled Doves

2 doves per serving
Salt and freshly ground pepper
Butter or margarine
1 cup water
½ cup dry white wine

Split doves down the back and wash thoroughly. Salt and pepper both sides generously. Grease bottom of broiler pan with butter or margarine and place doves in pan, breast side down. Put ½ teaspoon of butter on each dove. Start cooking doves in a cold broiler on high temperature. Brown on both sides. Add 1 cup of water and ½ cup dry white wine to the pan. Reduce the oven temperature and bake at 400° for another hour, basting frequently with drippings and adding water or wine as needed.

Note: *The pan gravy is delicious with rice or grits.*

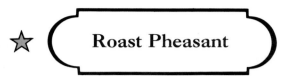

(6–8 servings)

2 pheasant, cleaned and trussed
  Salt and freshly ground pepper
3 slices bacon, cut in half
1 cup dry white wine
½ cup chicken stock

Preheat the oven to 400°.
  Rub the pheasants with salt and pepper. Cover each breast with 3 half-slices of bacon. Set the birds on a rack in a covered roaster. Pour the wine and stock around the birds. Cover and roast for 40 minutes. Uncover, remove the bacon and roast 15 minutes more, basting frequently.

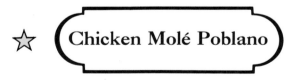

(4–6 servings)

1 large chicken
1 onion, quartered
  Salt
½ cup olive oil
1 onion, chopped
3 green poblano chilies
4 whole tomatoes, peeled, seeded, and chopped
3 cloves garlic
¼ cup bread crumbs
¼ cup ground peanuts
¼ cup ground almonds
½ teaspoon cinnamon
6 peppercorns, cracked
2 squares unsweetened chocolate, grated
2 cups well-seasoned chicken stock (from poaching chicken)
1 tablespoon sesame seeds, toasted

Place the chicken in a pot. Add the quartered onion and water to cover. Simmer until tender, about 1 hour. Remove the chicken from the stock, reserving 2 cups of the liquid. Preheat the oven to 400°.
  Brush the chicken with oil and place in a roasting pan. Roast until golden (or chicken can be cut up, dried and browned in 3 tablespoons oil). When golden, return the chicken to the empty pot. Pour the reserved stock around the chicken. In the bowl of a food processor process the chopped onion, chilies, tomatoes, garlic, crumbs, and nuts until just blended and still a little grainy. Beat in the spices and chocolate. Heat 4 tablespoons olive oil in a small pan. Add the chilie and chocolate mixture. Cook, stirring, for 5 minutes. Spread the chocolate mixture over the chicken. Cover and simmer for 2 hours, basting every 15 minutes. To serve, spoon sauce over chicken and sprinkle with sesame seeds.

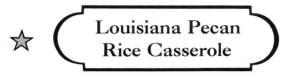

Louisiana Pecan Rice Casserole

(8 servings)

  1 cup long-grain rice, preferably Louisiana
    Pecan Rice
  3 whole chicken breasts, skinned, boned,
    and cut into bite-size pieces
  4 tablespoons butter
    Salt and freshly ground white pepper
    to taste
1½ pounds shrimp, shelled and deveined
    Juice of 1 lemon
  4 cups Light Wine Sauce
  ½ cup day-old bread crumbs
  1 cup cooked green beans or peas

Light Wine Sauce:
  1 clove garlic, minced
  3 tablespoons butter
1½ tablespoons flour
1½ cups well-seasoned chicken broth
  ½ cup dry white wine

Cook rice according to package directions.

In a skillet, lightly saute the chicken in the butter. Season with salt and white pepper.

To make the sauce, saute the garlic in the butter until wilted but not browned. Stir in the flour. Add the broth slowly, stirring constantly. Simmer 5 minutes. Add the wine; simmer 5 minutes longer.

Preheat the oven to 325°.

Drop shrimp into boiling salted water with the lemon juice. Cook until pink, about 2 minutes. Drain and rinse with cold water.

In a buttered casserole combine rice, chicken and shrimp with Light Wine Sauce. (The dish can be refrigerated overnight at this point and finished just before serving.) Top with bread crumbs. Bake 15 to 20 minutes. Add hot green beans or peas and spoon sauce over the top to glaze the vegetables.

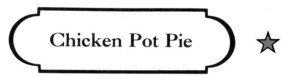

Chicken Pot Pie

(6 servings)

1 large chicken, cut into at least 8 serving
  pieces
5 large potatoes, well washed and thinly
  sliced
3 large onions, thinly sliced
  Salt and freshly ground pepper
½ pound pot pie noodles, or 2 sheets of fresh
  pasta dough cut into 2-inch squares
2 or more cups chicken stock, or water

Generously butter a heavy casserole that can be used on top of the stove. Place a thin layer of potato slices in the bottom of the casserole. Add a layer of chicken, another layer of potatoes, and a layer of onions. Season with salt and pepper and add a single layer of noodles or pasta squares. Continue layering the ingredients until the casserole is filled, finishing with a layer of potatoes. Add the stock to fill the casserole half way. Cover tightly and cook over low heat until tender, about 2 to 2½ hours.

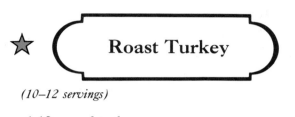

Roast Turkey

(10–12 servings)

1 12-pound turkey
  Salt
1 pound bacon, diced
3 onions, chopped
⅓ cup celery, chopped
¼ cup chopped parsley
5 tablespoons butter
¼ cup white wine
6 cups day old bread, torn into chunks
3 teaspoons poultry seasoning
Gravy;
  Neck and giblets from turkey
½ cup white wine
3 tablespoons flour
  Salt and freshly ground pepper

Remove the giblets and neck from the turkey and set aside. Salt the turkey inside and out. In a skillet fry the bacon until fat is rendered. Add the onions, celery, and parsley. Cook until the vegetables are transparent. Stir in the butter and wine. Simmer 5 minutes. Pour over the bread and toss until well mixed. Toss with poultry seasoning.

Preheat the oven to 375°.

Stuff the cavity and neck of the turkey. Spread 2 tablespoons softened butter over the breast and legs of the turkey. Place in a roasting pan and tent with aluminum foil. Roast for 3 to 3½ hours, basting every 30 minutes. Remove foil for last 30 minutes to brown skin. When the turkey is roasted, remove it to a serving platter and set aside to keep warm.

To make the gravy, while the turkey is roasting, simmer the neck and giblets in water to cover with ½ cup white wine for at least 2 hours. Cool in the stock. Pull the meat off the bones and chop the giblets. Set aside.

Once the turkey has been roasted and set aside, add 3 tablespoons flour to the pan drippings. Stir well to pick up all the browned bits. Cook over low heat until browned. Stir in the giblet stock. Season with salt and pepper. Stir in shredded meat and giblets. Heat well. Serve with the turkey.

Bacon and Cheese Scrambled Eggs

(3–4 servings)

6 slices bacon, fried, drained, and crumbled
½ cup grated cheddar cheese
8 eggs, broken and lightly beaten
3 tablespoons butter

In a skillet melt the butter, add the eggs, and stir gently. Add the cheese and stir until nearly melted. Stir in all but 2 tablespoons bacon. Garnish with remaining bacon.

Stewed Pheasant with Dumplings

(6–8 servings)

2 pheasants, cut into serving-size pieces
2 large tomatoes, peeled, seeded, and
   chopped
½ small head of cabbage, cut up
3 large carrots, cut up
3 large onions, chopped
2 cups white wine
   Salt and freshly ground pepper
2 teaspoons thyme
2 large potatoes, peeled and cubed
1 cup cubed pumpkin or other yellow squash

Dumplings:
2 cups flour
1 tablespoon baking powder
   Salt
1 egg, beaten
¾ cup or more milk

   Place the pieces of pheasant in a heavy
kettle. Add the tomatoes, cabbage, carrots
and onions. Add the white wine and enough
water to cover the pheasant and vegetables.
Season with salt, pepper, and thyme. Simmer until the vegetables are nearly tender.
Add the potatoes and pumpkin. Simmer until tender.
   To make the dumplings, stir together the
flour, baking powder, and salt. Add the egg
and milk. Drop by spoonfuls into the boiling
stew. Cover and steam for 15 minutes.

Chicken Luau

(8–10 servings)

2 frying chickens, cut up
4 tablespoons butter
1½ tablespoons salt
1½ cups water
   Salt and freshly ground pepper to taste
2 pounds taro leaves or fresh spinach
2 cups coconut milk

   In a large skillet brown the chicken in the
butter. Add the salt and water. Simmer 30
minutes or until the chicken is tender. Remove the chicken and reserve. Season the
broth with salt and pepper and set aside.
   Wash the taro or spinach leaves and break
them into large pieces. In a covered saucepan cook the leaves without additional water
over low heat until wilted. Add 1 cup of hot,
but not boiling, coconut milk to the taro or
spinach and simmer for 2 minutes. Arrange
the chicken pieces in the center of a large,
deep dish. Arrange the spinach in coconut
milk around the chicken pieces. Heat the
remaining cup of coconut milk with the
chicken broth and pour over the chicken
and spinach.

Note: *Taro or Ti leaves are the large blade-
shaped leaves of the taro plant. They are available fresh in Hawaii. The taste is very similar to
spinach, and large spinach leaves make a good
substitute.*

Chicken Liver and Mushroom Pie

(6 servings)

¼ pound thick-sliced bacon
  Pastry for 1-crust pie
4 tablespoons butter
1 large onion, chopped
1 pound chicken livers, cut in half
  Flour
1 pound mushrooms, cut in quarters
  Salt and freshly ground pepper
½ cup well-seasoned chicken stock
½ cup dry red wine
1 tablespoon chopped parsley

Preheat the oven to 375°.

In a skillet cook the bacon until crisp. Drain. Roll out the pastry and line a 9-inch pie pan. Line the pastry with parchment paper and fill with rice or beans. Bake for 15 minutes. Remove the paper and rice and let the shell cool.

In a heavy skillet melt the butter and saute the onion until transparent. Dredge the chicken livers in flour and fry quickly in the pan with the onions. Remove the chicken livers and set aside. Saute the mushrooms until golden brown. Remove from the skillet. Stir in 1 tablespoon flour and season with salt and pepper. Cook until well browned. Slowly add the stock and wine. Simmer until thickened. Add the bacon, mushrooms and chicken livers. Pour

into the baked shell. Garnish with parsley. Heat at 375° for 8 minutes. Serve hot.

Crab-stuffed Chicken Breast

(6 servings)

6 chicken breast halves, skinned and boned
3 tablespoons mayonnaise
  Salt and freshly ground white pepper
¼ teaspoon seafood seasoning
12 ounces crabmeat
6 small slices Gruyere cheese
3 slices boiled ham, cut in half
  Flour
1 egg beaten with 1 cup water
½ cup bread crumbs
1 tablespoon chopped parsley
2 tablespoons oil

Pound the chicken breasts between 2 sheets of wax paper until they are very thin. In a bowl mix together the mayonnaise, seasonings and crabmeat. Mound the crabmeat on the end of each chicken breast. Top with cheese and ham slices. Roll up the breasts around the filling, pricking to seal. Roll the breasts in flour, dip in the egg wash and then roll in crumbs that have been mixed with parsley. Preheat the oven to 400°.

Heat the oil in a skillet and brown the breasts all over. Arrange on a lightly greased baking sheet and bake for 10 to 15 minutes. Serve very hot.

Vegetables

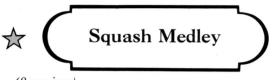

Squash Medley

(8 servings)

2 tablespoons butter
1½ pounds zucchini, thinly sliced
1½ pounds yellow squash, thinly sliced
1 small onion, finely chopped
   Salt and freshly ground pepper to taste

In a skillet melt the butter and saute the zucchini, squash, and onion until crisply tender. Season with salt and pepper.

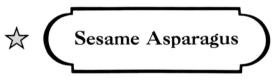

Sesame Asparagus

(4 servings)

1½ pounds fresh asparagus, washed and cut
   into 1½-inch lengths
3 tablespoons olive oil
3 tablespoons toasted sesame seeds
   Salt and freshly ground pepper

In a steamer or saucepan with steamer insert steam the asparagus until just tender. In a skillet or wok heat the oil. Toss the asparagus in the hot oil until heated through. Sprinkle with sesame seeds and season with salt and pepper. Toss well and serve very hot.

Red Cabbage with Apples and Port

(6 servings)

3 tablespoons red wine vinegar
⅓ cup water
2 tablespoons butter
1 small head red cabbage, finely shredded
¼ cup brown sugar
2 Granny Smith apples, peeled and sliced
½ cup port
   Salt and freshly ground pepper

In a kettle heat the vinegar and water and add the butter and cabbage. Sprinkle the brown sugar over the cabbage. Cover and simmer 1 hour. Add the apples, port, and salt and pepper to taste. Simmer 30 minutes more.

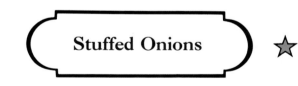

Stuffed Onions

(6 servings)

½ cup dry bread crumbs
3 tablespoons butter, melted
6 medium onions, hollowed out
½ green pepper, finely diced
¾ cup soft bread crumbs
¼ pound spicy sausage, crumbled and sauteed
2 egg yolks, beaten

¼ **cup heavy cream**
  Salt and freshly ground pepper

Preheat the oven to 350°.

Toss the dry bread crumbs with the melted butter and set aside. Chop the onion removed from the shells. Toss with green pepper, soft crumbs, sausage, egg yolk, and heavy cream. Season with salt and pepper. Stuff into onion shells. Sprinkle with buttered crumbs. Lightly oil a rectangular baking dish. Arrange the onions in the dish and bake for 45 minutes.

Note: *Onions can be hollowed out with a melon baller.*

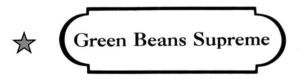

Green Beans Supreme

(4–6 servings)

  1 **pound green beans, trimmed and sliced
    diagonally**
  2 **tablespoons butter**
  3 **tablespoons minced onion**
  3 **tablespoons minced red pepper**
  ⅓ **cup minced celery**
  ⅓ **cup fresh parsley, chopped**
  2 **cloves garlic, minced**
    Salt and freshly ground pepper
  1 **teaspoon thyme**

Steam green beans until crisply tender. In a large skillet, melt the butter and saute the onion, red pepper, and celery until the vegetables are transparent but not browned. Stir in the parsley and garlic. Add the green beans, salt, pepper, and thyme. Toss gently until heated through. Serve very hot.

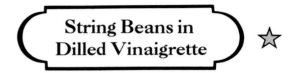

String Beans in Dilled Vinaigrette

(8 servings)

  2 **pounds fresh string beans**
    Salt to taste
  1 **large onion, thinly sliced**
  3 **sweet red peppers, thinly sliced**

Vinaigrette:
⅓ **cup salad oil**
¼ **cup wine vinegar**
½ **teaspoon salt**
¼ **teaspoon pepper**
  3 **tablespoons chopped fresh dill**

In a large saucepan cook the string beans in boiling salted water for 7 minutes. Drain the beans and cool in cold water. Toss the onion and red pepper slices with the green beans.

To make the vinaigrette, in a jar with a tight fitting lid thoroughly combine oil, vinegar, salt, pepper, and dill.

Pour dressing over vegetables and serve.

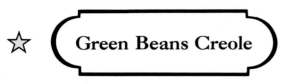

Green Beans Creole

(4–6 servings)

1 pound green beans, trimmed
2 tablespoons butter
½ green pepper, cored, seeded, and chopped
½ yellow or red pepper, cored, seeded, and
  chopped
  Salt and freshly ground pepper

Cook green beans in boiling salted water
to cover until just tender, about 10 minutes,
or steam gently until just tender. Drain and
keep warm.

In a small skillet melt the butter and saute
the chopped peppers gently until tender
crisp. Combine peppers with green beans.
Season with salt and pepper. Serve warm.

Baked Asparagus

(4 servings)

¾ cup bread crumbs
1 pound asparagus, washed and trimmed
1 cup grated cheddar cheese
1 tablespoon butter
1 tablespoon flour
  Salt and freshly ground pepper
⅔ cup milk
1 teaspoon Worcestershire sauce
3 tablespoons toasted almonds

Preheat the oven to 350°.

Butter a rectangular casserole. Layer the
crumbs, asparagus, and ¾ of the cheese in
the casserole. Set the remaining cheese
aside. Melt the butter in a saucepan. Stir in
the flour and cook for 3 minutes. Do not
brown. Add salt and pepper to taste. Stir in
the milk all at once and simmer until thickened. Stir in the Worcestershire sauce. Pour
the sauce over the asparagus. Top with the
remaining cheese and the almonds. Bake for
35 minutes.

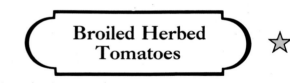

Broiled Herbed Tomatoes

(8 servings)

8 large tomatoes, cored and halved but not
  peeled
¼ cup (½ stick) butter
  Salt and freshly ground black pepper to
  taste
½ cup bread crumbs
½ cup chopped parsley
½ cup chopped chives

Preheat the broiler. Arrange the tomato
halves on a cookie sheet or in a baking pan,
cut side up. Place about ½ teaspoon butter
on each tomato half. Sprinkle with salt and
pepper, bread crumbs, parsley, and chives.
Broil 5 to 7 minutes, until lightly browned
and bubbling.

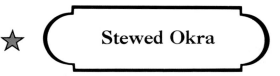

(4–6 servings)

1 pound okra
1 cup chicken stock
1 cup Stewed Tomatoes
   Salt and freshly ground black pepper
¼ pound salt pork, diced
1 tablespoon butter, softened
1 tablespoon flour
2 tablespoons chopped fresh parsley
   Parsley sprigs

Place the okra in a heavy saucepan. Add the chicken stock, tomatoes, and salt and pepper to taste. Bring to a boil. In a skillet saute the salt pork until crisp. Drain. Stir into the okra. Simmer for about 30 minutes. In a small bowl cream the butter and flour. Stir into the okra. Stir until thickened. Serve very hot garnished with parsley sprigs.

(6 servings)

   Pastry for a 1 crust pie
3 large ripe tomatoes, peeled and thickly
   sliced
   Salt and freshly ground pepper
½ teaspoon dried basil

1 cup grated cheddar cheese
3 eggs
2 tablespoons flour
1 cup heavy cream

Preheat the oven to 400°.

Roll out the pastry and line a 9-inch pie pan. Bake for 5 minutes. Cool. Arrange the tomato slices in the bottom of the pie shell. Season with salt, pepper, and basil. Top with grated cheese. In a mixing bowl beat the eggs with the flour. Stir in the cream. Pour over the cheese and tomatoes. Bake for 15 minutes, reduce heat to 325° and bake for 35 to 40 minutes more or until filling is set. Serve hot or lukewarm.

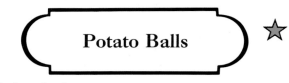

(4–6 servings)

3 cups mashed potatoes
1 egg, beaten
⅓ cup onion, minced
   Salt and freshly ground pepper
   Flour for dredging
   Fat for deep frying

In a bowl mix the potatoes with the egg and onion. Season with salt and pepper. Shape into 1-inch balls and dredge in flour. Fry in hot deep fat just until golden brown.

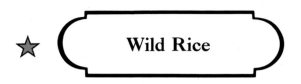

Wild Rice

(4–6 servings)

1 cup wild rice
  Boiling water
  Salt

In a saucepan cover the wild rice with boiling water. Let stand 10 minutes. Drain. Cover the rice a second time with boiling water. Let stand 10 minutes. Drain. Place the rice in a heavy saucepan. Cover with boiling salted water and simmer just until the water is absorbed. Remove the saucepan from the heat. Cover with absorbent paper and a lid. Let stand 10 minutes before serving.

Delmonico Potatoes

(4–6 servings)

2 tablespoons butter
2 tablespoons flour
1 cup milk
  Salt and freshly ground black pepper
3 large potatoes, boiled, peeled, and cubed
½ small onion, thinly sliced
½ cup grated cheese
2 tablespoons butter
½ cup bread crumbs

Preheat the oven to 375°.

In a saucepan melt the butter and stir in the flour. Simmer for 3 minutes. Pour in the milk all at once and stir. Cook over low heat until thick and season with salt and pepper. Stir in the potatoes and onion. Butter a baking dish. Layer half the potatoes in the dish. Top with a layer of half of the cheese. Follow with another layer of potatoes and one of cheese. In a skillet melt the butter and stir in the crumbs. Arrange over the potatoes and cheese. Bake for 30 minutes until cheese is melted and crumbs are golden brown.

Cole Slaw

(8–10 servings)

1 large head cabbage, finely chopped
2 small green peppers, finely chopped
1 sweet onion, finely chopped
1 red pepper or pimiento, finely chopped
  Celery seed
  Salt and freshly ground pepper
¾ cup peanut oil
¾ cup vinegar
1½ cups sugar

Layer the vegetables in a bowl. In a saucepan bring to a boil the oil, vinegar, and sugar. Cool. Pour over the vegetables in the bowl and toss. Refrigerate 2 hours.

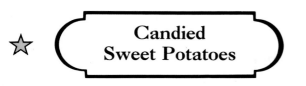

Candied Sweet Potatoes

(6 servings)

3 pounds yams or sweet potatoes
1 cup brown or white sugar
1 cup water or apple cider
  Cinnamon
3 tablespoons butter
  Granulated sugar

Boil the sweet potatoes in their skins. Cool slightly and cut into rounds. Arrange the potatoes in a flat, buttered baking dish. In a saucepan combine the sugar, water or cider, cinnamon, and butter. Bring to a boil. Pour the syrup over the potatoes. Cover with foil and bake at 300° for 1½ hours. Remove the foil, sprinkle with granulated sugar, and broil for 1 minute. Serve very hot.

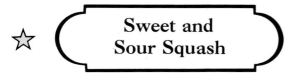

Sweet and Sour Squash

(6 servings)

¼ pound salt pork, diced
2 onions, sliced
1 green pepper, seeded and cut in chunks
1 clove garlic, minced
2 pounds hubbard squash or pumpkin, or any yellow-fleshed squash

½ cup brown sugar
  Salt
½ cup cider vinegar
½ teaspoon cornstarch (optional)

In a skillet saute the salt pork until golden. Remove and set aside. Saute the onions, pepper, and garlic until the onions are transparent. Add the squash, brown sugar, salt to taste, and vinegar. Simmer, covered, until the squash is tender. If desired, thicken with a ½ teaspoon cornstarch dissolved in 2 tablespoons of water. Heat, uncovered, until thick.

Sauerkraut

(6 servings)

3 cups sauerkraut
2 tablespoons bacon grease
1 onion, thinly sliced
1 cup dry white wine
1 teaspoon caraway seed

In a sieve rinse the sauerkraut in cold water and set aside. In a heavy skillet melt the bacon grease. Saute the onion until transparent, but not browned. Add the sauerkraut and cook for 5 minutes. Add the wine and the caraway seed and simmer, covered, for 30 minutes. Uncover and boil off most of the liquid. Serve very hot.

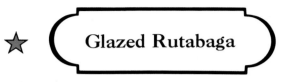

Glazed Rutabaga

(6 servings)

1 large rutabaga, peeled and cut into julienne
2 tablespoons butter
1 tablespoon sugar
  Salt and freshly ground white pepper to
  taste

Steam the rutabaga until crisply tender. In a skillet melt the butter and sugar and add the rutabaga, salt, and pepper. Cook, tossing constantly, until strips are well coated with the glaze. Serve very hot.

Note: *Rutabaga is sometimes called yellow turnip.*

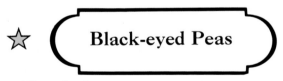

Black-eyed Peas

(12 servings)

4 pounds shelled fresh black-eyed peas
1 pound thick-sliced breakfast bacon, cut
  into ¾-inch pieces
4 onions, finely chopped (about 2 cups)
4 large cloves garlic, finely chopped
  Water to cover peas by 1 inch
1 tablespoon plus 1 teaspoon salt
½ teaspoon red pepper sauce

Rinse the peas and pick over to clean.

In a large pot saute the bacon pieces until crisp. Set aside. Saute the onions and garlic in 3 tablespoons bacon fat until transparent. Add the peas and stir. Cover with water. Simmer 1 hour, covered, stirring and checking occasionally to see if additional water is needed. Add salt and red pepper sauce. Simmer an additional 30 minutes, uncovered, stirring occasionally and checking moisture. Taste to correct seasoning. Add the cooked bacon.

Note: *Cooking time for black-eyed peas varies with freshness and maturity. Late in the season they will take longer to cook and will absorb more water.*

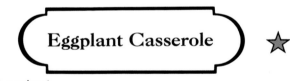

Eggplant Casserole

(6 servings)

¼ cup olive oil
2 cloves garlic, minced
1 onion, chopped
½ green pepper, minced
5 tomatoes, peeled, seeded, and chopped
½ pound fresh mushrooms, sliced
1 medium eggplant, peeled and cubed
  Salt
2 tablespoons chopped parsley
2 eggs, beaten
½ cup grated parmesan cheese
½ cup bread crumbs
2 tablespoons butter

Preheat the oven to 375°.

Heat the oil in a heavy skillet. Saute the garlic and onion with the pepper until transparent. Add the tomatoes, mushrooms, and eggplant. Simmer until the eggplant is tender. Season with salt and the chopped parsley. Spoon the mixture into a buttered casserole. In a bowl beat together the eggs and cheese. Stir into the vegetables. Top with the crumbs, dot with butter, and bake for 25 minutes.

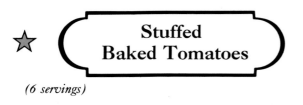

Stuffed Baked Tomatoes

(6 servings)

6 ripe but firm tomatoes
1 clove garlic, minced
  Salt and freshly ground pepper to taste
4 tablespoons butter, softened
⅓ cup bread crumbs
1 tablespoon chopped parsley

Preheat the oven to 375°.

Cut the tops off the tomatoes. Scoop out the pulp and chop. In a bowl mix the chopped tomatoes with the garlic, salt, pepper, and half the butter. Stuff the mixture back into the tomatoes. In a small skillet melt the remaining butter and toss with the bread crumbs and parsley. Top the tomatoes with the crumb mixture. Arrange in a greased baking dish. Bake for 20 minutes.

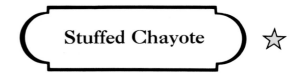

Stuffed Chayote

(4 servings)

2 medium chayote
½ pound hot, spicy sausage
1 medium onion, chopped
½ cup bread crumbs
1 teaspoon dried thyme
  Salt and freshly ground pepper
  Chopped fresh thyme

In a saucepan boil the unpeeled chayotes in water to cover, until nearly tender. Drain and cool. Cut in half lengthwise and scoop out and reserve the flesh, leaving a wall about ¼-inch thick all around. Preheat the oven to 350°.

In a skillet saute the sausage until browned, breaking it up with a fork. Saute the onion in the rendered fat. Stir in the crumbs, thyme, and seasoning. Chop up the flesh of the chayotes and stir into the filling. Stuff the chayotes with the filling. Bake for 25 minutes. Garnish with chopped thyme.

Note: *Chayote is a summer squash, but it is usually available year round. It is known also as mirliton, vegetable pear and by several Caribbean names. Zucchini, yellow or patty pan squash can be substituted.*

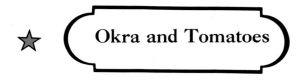

Okra and Tomatoes

(4–6 servings)

  4 slices thick-cut bacon
½ green pepper, diced
  1 small onion, finely diced
  2 cups okra, thinly sliced
  5 large tomatoes, peeled, seeded, and chopped
    Red pepper sauce
    Salt and freshly ground black pepper

In a skillet fry the bacon until crisp. Drain on absorbent paper and crumble. Pour off all but 3 tablespoons bacon grease. Add the green pepper and onion. Saute until the onions are transparent, but not browned. Add the okra and saute 3 minutes, stirring constantly. Stir in the tomatoes. Cover and simmer 15 minutes. Season to taste with red pepper sauce, salt and pepper. Stir in the bacon bits and serve very hot.

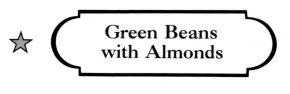

Green Beans with Almonds

(4 servings)

  1 pound very thin green beans
  2 tablespoons butter

¼ cup slivered almonds or sliced almonds
¼ cup sliced scallions
    Salt and freshly ground pepper

In a large pot steam beans until tender, but still very green. In a large skillet melt the butter, add the almonds and saute until golden brown. Add the scallions and cook gently until tender. Add the beans and salt and pepper to taste. Toss until hot and well combined.

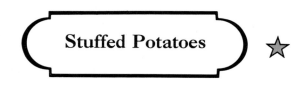

Stuffed Potatoes

(4–6 servings)

4–6 large baking potatoes, wiped with olive oil
    and baked until tender
  3 tablespoons olive oil
½ cup sliced mushrooms
¼ cup bean sprouts
¼ cup sliced scallions
½ teaspoon dried basil
¼ teaspoon dried thyme
    Salt and freshly ground pepper

Preheat the oven to 450°.
Cut open the top of each potato and scoop out half the inside. Reserve for another dish. In a skillet heat the oil and saute the other vegetables lightly for 5 minutes. Season with the basil, thyme, salt, and pepper. Stuff the potatoes and bake for 10 minutes.

Stuffed Potatoes and Green Beans with Almonds ►

Cut Green Beans with Spaetzle Dumplings

(4 servings)

2 tablespoons diced bacon
1 pound green beans, washed and cut
   into 1-inch lengths
2 large onions, thinly sliced
4 tomatoes, chopped
   Salt and freshly ground pepper to taste
½ cup water
   Chopped fresh parsley

Spaetzle Dumplings:

1 cup flour
1 teaspoon baking powder
   Salt and freshly ground white pepper
½ beaten egg
½ cup milk
1 tablespoon butter
2 tablespoons melted butter

In a skillet fry the bacon until crisp. Add the remaining ingredients, except parsley, and simmer 20 minutes until most of the water has evaporated.

To make the dumplings, in a bowl mix together the flour, baking powder, and salt and pepper to taste. Stir in the beaten egg, milk, and butter. Push the batter through a colander into boiling, salted water. Boil 3 minutes. Drain and toss with 2 tablespoons melted butter.

Add the dumplings to the green beans and toss. Garnish with chopped parsley.

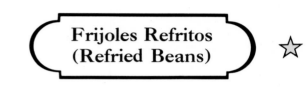

Frijoles Refritos (Refried Beans)

(6 servings)

8 ounces small, dried red pinto beans
5–6 cups water
1 large onion, finely chopped
2 cloves garlic, finely minced
1 tablespoon bacon drippings
1½ teaspoons salt
8 tablespoons lard or bacon drippings

In a large saucepan combine the beans, water, ½ cup onion, garlic, and 1 tablespoon bacon drippings. Bring to a boil, cover, and simmer 1½ to 2 hours or until very tender. Add the salt and cook 15 minutes more. In a large, heavy skillet heat the lard or bacon drippings. Add the remaining onion and cook until soft. Add enough beans to cover the bottom of the skillet. Turn heat to high. Mash beans, adding liquid from beans as needed. Continue this process until all beans are mashed and mixture becomes paste. Cook 15 to 20 minutes more, or until beans are semi-dry and edges are crispy. Serve immediately.

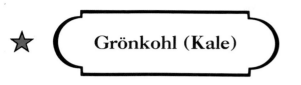

Grönkohl (Kale)

(6 servings)

1½ pounds fresh kale, washed and stemmed
¼ cup finely diced lean bacon
    Salt and freshly ground black pepper
3 tablespoons butter, melted

In a large saucepan or skillet simmer the kale with the bacon in salted water to cover for about 25 minutes. Drain well. Season with freshly ground pepper and toss with hot melted butter.

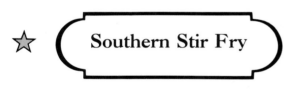

Southern Stir Fry

(6 servings)

3 tablespoons peanut oil
1 cup peeled and very thinly sliced sweet onions
1 cup washed, unpeeled, and very thinly sliced zucchini
½ cup seeded and very thinly sliced green pepper
½ cup seeded and very thinly sliced red pepper
⅓ cup seeded and very thinly sliced yellow pepper

½ teaspoon thyme
½ teaspoon rosemary
    Salt and freshly ground pepper to taste
1 tablespoon chopped fresh parsley

Heat the oil in a heavy wok or skillet. Add the onions and saute until transparent. Add the zucchini and toss for 3 minutes over the heat. Add the peppers, thyme, rosemary, and salt and pepper. Toss for another 3 or 4 minutes over the heat. Serve very hot with a sprinkling of fresh parsley.

Corn Pudding

(6–8 servings)

2 egg yolks, beaten
1½ cups grated corn or kernel corn
1 tablespoon finely chopped onion
½ cup milk or half and half
    Salt and freshly ground white pepper to taste
2 egg whites, beaten until stiff peaks form

Preheat the oven to 350°.
In a mixing bowl beat the egg yolks, corn, onion, milk or half and half, salt, and pepper until well mixed. Fold in the egg whites. Pour into a well-greased, 1-quart baking dish and set the dish in a pan of boiling water. Bake for 40 to 45 minutes or until set.

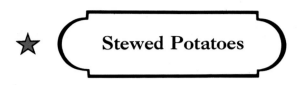

Stewed Potatoes

(4 servings)

1 tablespoon butter
1 small onion, thinly sliced
½ teaspoon salt
   Freshly ground black pepper
½ cup Stewed Tomatoes
2 cups uncooked potatoes, diced
1 tablespoon minced parsley
¼ cup cream

In a saucepan melt the butter and saute the onions until transparent. Add the salt, and pepper to taste. Stir in the tomatoes and potatoes. Add enough water to cover and cook until tender. Stir in the parsley and cream and heat thoroughly. Serve hot.

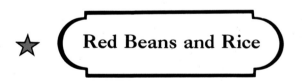

Red Beans and Rice

(4 servings)

1 pound dried red kidney beans
1 large onion, finely chopped
3 cloves garlic, minced
2 tablespoons chopped parsley
   Salt and freshly ground pepper
   Cooked rice or 1 cup uncooked rice

Soak the beans overnight. Drain.

Add fresh water to cover at least 2 inches above the beans. Add the onion, garlic, and parsley. Simmer, covered, 2 hours, until creamy but not mushy. Season with salt and pepper. Serve over fluffy, cooked rice.

Note: *Some Southerners add uncooked rice about 30 minutes before the beans are done. Then the dish is served stirred together.*

Wild Mushroom Saute

(4–5 servings)

1 pound wild mushrooms
5 tablespoons butter
4 cloves garlic, minced
2 tablespoons chopped parsley
   Salt and freshly ground pepper
¼ cup dry white wine

Clean the mushrooms and cut in halves or quarters if they are very large. Melt the butter in a heavy skillet. Saute the mushrooms for 3 minutes. Add the garlic and parsley. Cook, stirring, for 3 to 4 minutes. Season with salt and pepper. Stir in the wine. Cook for 3 minutes and serve on buttered toast, over Polenta, or as an accompaniment to grilled meat.

Note: *Be sure to buy the wild mushrooms from a reputable picker.*

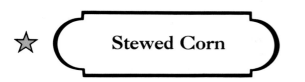

Stewed Corn

(6 servings)

2 tablespoons butter
3 cups fresh corn cut from the cob
⅓ cup heavy cream
　Freshly ground white pepper
　Salt

In a heavy saucepan melt the butter and add the corn, cream and a generous amount of pepper. Salt to taste. Simmer, covered, very gently (in a double boiler if you like) 15 to 20 minutes.

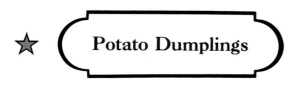

Potato Dumplings

(6 servings)

6 medium potatoes, boiled and finely chopped
　Salt and freshly ground pepper
2 tablespoons butter
1 teaspoon nutmeg
4 eggs, well beaten
3 tablespoons flour
1½ cups fresh bread crumbs
　Flour for dredging

In a bowl mix together all the ingredients. Form into small balls. Dredge in flour. Drop into boiling, salted water. Cover and simmer for 15 minutes or until light.

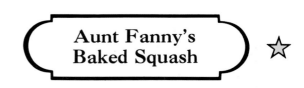

Aunt Fanny's Baked Squash

(6 servings)

3 pounds yellow summer squash, washed and diced
½ cup chopped onions
½ cup bread crumbs
2 eggs
　Dash of red pepper sauce
1 tablespoon sugar
1 teaspoon salt
½ teaspoon black pepper
¼ pound (1 stick) butter
¼ cup bread crumbs for topping

Preheat the oven to 375°.
In a steamer or saucepan with steamer insert steam the squash for 5 minutes. Drain thoroughly. In a bowl combine the squash and all the other ingredients except ½ the butter and the ¼ cup bread crumbs. In a small saucepan melt the remaining butter. Turn the squash mixture into a baking dish, spread melted butter over the top, and sprinkle with the bread crumbs. Bake for 1 hour.

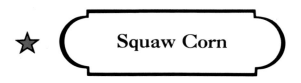

Squaw Corn

(4–6 servings)

4 slices bacon, cut in 1-inch pieces
½ cup chopped onion
¼ cup chopped green pepper
2 cups corn, cut from the cob
1 egg
¼ cup heavy cream
    Salt and freshly ground white pepper

In a skillet fry the bacon until crisp. Add the onion and pepper and cook gently until the onion is transparent. Add the corn, egg, cream, and salt and pepper to taste. Simmer gently for 10 minutes. Serve hot.

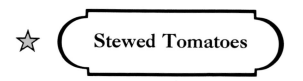

Stewed Tomatoes

(6 servings)

4 tablespoons butter
½ green pepper, finely chopped
2 bunches scallions, white parts only, finely sliced
1 clove garlic, minced
5 large tomatoes, peeled, seeded, and chopped
¼ cup sugar

⅓ cup dry white wine
    Salt and freshly ground black pepper
½ teaspoon thyme
½ cup soft bread crumbs

In a heavy saucepan melt the butter and saute the pepper, scallions and garlic until just tender but not browned. Add the tomatoes, sugar, wine, salt, pepper, and thyme. Simmer 15 minutes. Stir in the bread crumbs and cook 5 minutes longer.

Note: *Some people eat hominy grits and stewed tomatoes stirred together. Don't knock it until you try it!!!*

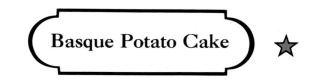

Basque Potato Cake

(6 servings)

3 tablespoons butter
4 large potatoes, boiled just until tender, drained until dry, and thinly sliced
2 small onions, peeled and very thinly sliced
2 eggs
2 tablespoons cream
    Salt and freshly ground pepper
6 slices bacon, cooked until crisp and then crumbled

In a heavy skillet melt 2 tablespoons butter. Add the potatoes and onions, mix together, and then pack down. When brown on the bottom, place a plate on top of the skillet. Invert the skillet, turning the potato cake out onto the plate. Slide potato cake back into the skillet. Cook until browned on underside. In a bowl beat the eggs and cream together with salt and pepper to taste. Pour over the potatoes. Cover and cook for 15 minutes. Invert potato cake onto serving plate and top with crumbled bacon.

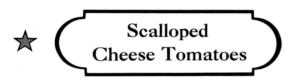

Scalloped Cheese Tomatoes

(4 servings)

3 tablespoons butter
6 large tomatoes, peeled, seeded, and chopped
1 clove garlic, minced
¼ teaspoon oregano
2 teaspoons sugar
½ cup toasted bread crumbs
1 cup thinly sliced onions
¾ cup grated cheddar cheese
¼ cup dry white wine

Preheat the oven to 350°.

In a skillet melt the butter and saute the tomatoes for 5 to 7 minutes. Add the garlic, oregano, and sugar. Layer the bread crumbs, tomatoes, onions, and cheese in a shallow baking dish. Pour wine over all. Bake for 45 minutes.

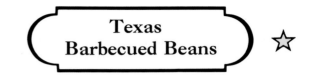

Texas Barbecued Beans

(8 servings)

4 cups plain pork and beans
⅓ cup catsup
⅓ cup brown sugar
2 tablespoons prepared mustard
½ teaspoon hot chili powder
½ cup HOT Texas barbecue sauce
2 onions, chopped and fried in bacon fat until limp
8 slices of salt pork or bacon

Preheat the oven to 350°.

In a large bowl mix together well all the ingredients except the salt pork or bacon. Spread the mixture in a flat, ovenproof dish. Top with the sliced salt pork or bacon and bake for 1 hour. Serve very hot.

Notes: *This recipe can be doubled or tripled easily. Take care when multiplying the amount of chili powder, tasting after every addition to be sure the mixture does not become too spicy. For outdoor barbecuing, spread the mixture in large baking pans, cover each with aluminum foil, and place on a grid over the coals for at least 1 hour.*

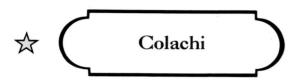

Colachi

(6–8 servings)

5 small summer squash
2 tablespoons butter
2 tablespoons olive oil
1 onion, chopped
1 clove garlic, minced
1 chilie pepper, minced
3 tomatoes, peeled, seeded, and chopped
½ cup corn, freshly cut from the cob
  Salt and freshly ground pepper to taste

Cut the squash in cubes or ½-inch slices. In a skillet melt the butter with the oil. Saute the onion until transparent. Add the garlic and chilie pepper and cook 2 minutes. Add the tomatoes, corn, and seasonings. Cover and simmer until tender, about 20 to 25 minutes.

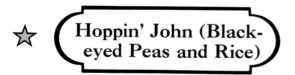

Hoppin' John (Black-eyed Peas and Rice)

(6 servings)

1 cup dried black-eyed peas, soaked overnight
4 cups water
2 teaspoons salt
4 slices bacon, cut in ½-inch strips

1 cup raw rice
1 medium onion, chopped
¼ pound well-cooked link sausage, cut up

Boil the peas in 4 cups water with the salt for 1 hour, or until tender. Fry the bacon in a skillet and remove with a slotted spoon. Saute the onion in 3 tablespoons of bacon grease. Add the rice, bacon, onion, and sausage to the black-eyed peas. Simmer 25 to 30 minutes. Remove from the heat. Cover the pot with a double thickness of absorbent paper and a lid. Allow to stand 15 minutes. Stir gently with a fork and serve hot.

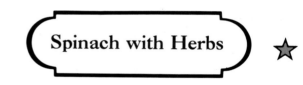

Spinach with Herbs

(6 servings)

2 pounds fresh spinach, washed thoroughly, stemmed and cooked just until wilted in the water that clings to the leaves
3 tablespoons butter
1 tablespoon finely chopped fresh basil
1 tablespoon finely chopped fresh parsley
  Salt and freshly ground black pepper

Thoroughly drain the cooked spinach. In a skillet melt the butter and add the spinach and herbs. Toss until thoroughly heated. Season to taste with salt and pepper.

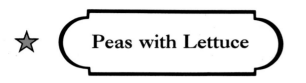

(6 servings)

6–8 lettuce leaves, washed and dried
  3 cups peas, fresh or frozen
  ½ cup water
  2 tablespoons butter
    Salt and freshly ground pepper
    Fresh mint

Shred the lettuce. In a saucepan simmer the peas with the lettuce in the water and butter. (The time will depend on the age and size of the peas. It could be as short as 6 to 8 minutes, or as long as 20 minutes. Do not overcook.) Season with salt and pepper. Garnish with fresh mint.

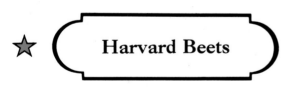

(6 servings)

  2 pounds fresh unpeeled beets, well washed
  ⅓ cup vinegar
  ⅓ cup sugar
  1 teaspoon cornstarch
  1 teaspoon mustard
    Salt and freshly ground pepper

Boil the beets until tender—at least 45 minutes, perhaps longer. Remove from the pan, cool, peel, and slice. In a bowl combine the vinegar, sugar, cornstarch, mustard, and seasonings. Simmer until thickened. Add the beets, cover, and cook over very low heat for 15 to 20 minutes.

Note: *Beets can also be baked, unpeeled, on a rack in a 375° oven for 3 hours or until tender. Peel and continue with the recipe.*

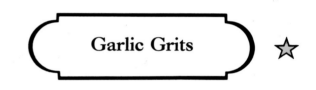

(6 servings)

  1 cup grits
  ¼ pound (1 stick) butter
1½ tablespoons Worcestershire sauce
  ¾ pound sharp cheddar cheese, grated
  ½ clove garlic, minced
    Red pepper sauce to taste
  2 egg whites

Cook the grits according to package directions. To the hot grits add all the remaining ingredients except the egg whites. Let cool. Preheat the oven to 400°.

Beat the egg whites until stiff. Fold into the cooked grits. Place in a casserole and bake for 20 minutes.

Baked Avocado

(4 servings)

  2 avocados, halved and pits removed
  1 tablespoon lemon juice
  1 tomato, peeled, seeded, and chopped
  ½ green pepper, seeded, and chopped
  ½ cup grated Monterey Jack cheese
  2 tablespoons chopped green chilies
  ½ cup homemade mayonnaise

  Preheat the oven to 375°.
  Brush the cut avocado halves with lemon juice. In a bowl toss together the tomato, green pepper, cheese, and green chilies. Pile into the avocado shells. Spread mayonnaise over the filling and bake for 10 to 15 minutes, or until mayonnaise is puffed and golden. Serve very hot.

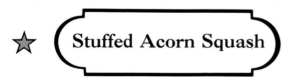

Stuffed Acorn Squash

(4 servings)

  ¼ pound pork sausage
  1 small onion, finely chopped
  ¼ green pepper, seeded and finely chopped
   Freshly ground pepper to taste
  ⅓ cup Italian-herbed bread crumbs
  2 whole acorn squash, split and cleaned

  Preheat the oven to 475°.
  In a large skillet saute the pork sausage, onion, and green pepper until sausage is lightly browned and vegetables are transparent. Season with pepper. Stir in the bread crumbs. Fill the centers of the squash. Arrange the stuffed squash in a baking dish and bake for 1 hour.

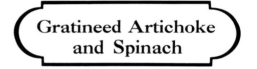

Gratineed Artichoke and Spinach

(6 servings)

  1 tablespoon butter
  6 artichoke hearts
  2 pounds fresh spinach, washed and
   stemmed
  1 egg, beaten
   Salt and freshly ground pepper
  ¼ cup dry white wine
  ½ cup heavy cream
  1 cup grated Gruyere cheese

  Preheat the oven to 350°.
  In a skillet melt the butter and saute the artichoke hearts. Arrange in an oven-proof dish. Set aside. In a saucepan wilt the spinach in the water that clings to its leaves after washing. In a bowl beat together the egg, salt, pepper, wine, and cream. Stir into the spinach. Arrange the spinach on top of the artichoke hearts. Sprinkle with the cheese. Bake for 20 minutes until brown and bubbling.

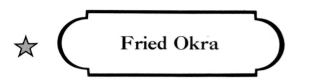

Fried Okra

(6 servings)

½ cup shortening
2 teaspoons bacon drippings
1 pound fresh okra, washed, sliced in rounds
   and drained on absorbent paper
   Salt and freshly ground pepper
   Cornmeal

In a large, heavy skillet heat the shortening and the bacon drippings. Season the okra rounds with salt and pepper and dredge in the cornmeal. Drop rounds a few at a time into the hot shortening and fry until golden brown. (Be careful not to overcrowd the pan.)

Gingered Carrot Soufflé

(6 servings)

2 tablespoons butter
2 tablespoons flour
½ cup hot milk
   Salt to taste
3 eggs, separated
1 cup minced boiled carrots
½ teaspoon ground ginger

Preheat the oven to 350°.

In a skillet melt the butter and stir in the flour. Cook gently for 1 minute, but do not brown. Add the milk all at once and whisk until the mixture is thick. Remove from the heat. Add the salt. Beat in the egg yolks one at a time. Let cool. In a mixing bowl beat the egg whites until stiff peaks form. Stir the carrots and ginger into the flour mixture. Fold in the egg whites gently. Butter a one-quart soufflé mold. Pour in the carrot mixture. Bake for 20 to 35 minutes. Serve at once.

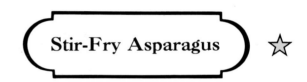

Stir-Fry Asparagus

(4 servings)

2 tablespoons oil
2 cloves garlic, minced
1 pound asparagus, trimmed and cut
   diagonally into 2-inch pieces
1 tablespoon sherry or sweet white wine
2 tablespoons soy sauce
   Salt and freshly ground pepper

In a wok or skillet heat the oil, add the garlic and asparagus, and saute for 1 minute. Add sherry, soy sauce, and seasonings. Cook 3 to 5 minutes, stirring, until the asparagus are tender.

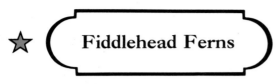

Fiddlehead Ferns

(6 servings)

1 pound fiddlehead ferns
2 tablespoons butter
   Salt and freshly ground black pepper

Drop the fern heads into rapidly boiling, salted water. Boil for 3 minutes. Drain and keep warm. In a skillet melt the butter and stir in the ferns. Season with salt and pepper.

Note: *Fiddlehead ferns are the tightly coiled shoots of young ferns—generally the Ostrich fern. If the fern has a fuzzy coating, scrape it off before cooking. Ostrich ferns have a delicate taste similar to asparagus. If using the ferns in a salad, simmer just until crisply tender.*

Sweet Potato Flans

(6 servings)

6 dariole molds, or small soufflé molds
½ cup sweet potato puree
⅛ teaspoon ground ginger
2 eggs, well beaten
1 tablespoon butter
¼ cup heavy cream
⅓ cup milk
   Salt and freshly ground white pepper

Spinach bed:
1 pound fresh spinach, washed thoroughly, and stemmed
   Salt and freshly ground black pepper
3 tablespoons butter, melted

Preheat the oven to 375°.

Generously butter and flour the molds. In a mixing bowl beat the puree, ginger, and eggs together well. Beat in the butter. Stir in the cream, milk, salt, and pepper. Fill each mold about ¾ full. Set the molds in a pan of boiling water and bake for 30 minutes. Allow to cool in the molds for about 15 minutes.

Cook the spinach in the water that clings to the leaves after washing. Drain well. Season with salt and pepper and toss in melted butter. Arrange the spinach on a serving platter. Invert the sweet potato flans onto the spinach-lined serving platter.

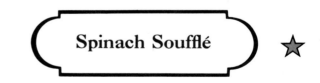

Spinach Soufflé

(6 servings)

3 tablespoons butter
2 tablespoons flour
   Salt and freshly ground pepper
1 cup milk
4 eggs, separated
½ teaspoon nutmeg
1½ pounds spinach, washed, stemmed, steamed and chopped

In a medium saucepan melt 2 tablespoons of the butter, add flour, and stir. Season with salt and pepper. Pour in milk all at once, whisking hard. Simmer until thickened. Remove from heat and beat in the egg yolks, one at a time. Beat in the remaining tablespoon of butter and the nutmeg. Cool to room temperature.

Beat the egg whites until stiff peaks form. Preheat the oven to 425°.

Stir the spinach into the egg mixture. Gently fold in the egg whites. Pour into a buttered soufflé dish. Bake 25 to 30 minutes. Serve very hot.

Fried Squash Flowers

(6 servings)

Fat for deep frying
1 can beer
1 cup flour
Cayenne pepper
Fresh squash flowers, washed and thoroughly dried

In a heavy pot or skillet heat enough fat for deep frying.

In a large bowl mix together the beer, flour and pepper. Dip the flowers in the beer batter. Shake off excess. Fry in deep, hot fat (375°) until golden. Drain on absorbent paper and serve at once.

Note: *These are delicious on a bed of mixed greens dressed with a tart vinaigrette.*

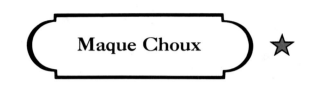

Maque Choux

(6 servings)

2 cups corn kernels
1 cup whole hominy, washed and drained
2 tablespoons butter
¼ cup chopped shallots
½ green pepper, diced
½ onion, chopped
¼ cup chopped celery
5 large tomatoes, peeled, seeded, and chopped
5 slices bacon, cut in ¼-inch strips and fried until crisp
1 teaspoon sugar
Salt and freshly ground pepper
Red pepper sauce to taste

In a bowl mix together the corn and hominy. In a heavy skillet melt the butter, add the shallots, green pepper, onion, and celery, and saute until tender. Stir in the tomatoes. Cook 10 minutes over low heat. Add the corn mixture, bacon, sugar, and seasonings. Simmer 15 minutes.

Notes: *Hominy is readily available in cans. This dish can also be served as a main course.*

Desserts

Carrot Cake

(8 servings)

1 teaspoon cinnamon
1 teaspoon mace
   Pinch of salt
1 cup butter, softened
2 cups sugar
4 large eggs
1½ cups grated carrots
⅔ cup pecans
2½ cups flour
3 teaspoons baking powder
⅓ cup hot water
   Cream Cheese Frosting

Preheat the oven to 375°.

In a large bowl beat together the spices, butter, and sugar. Beat in the eggs one at a time. Stir in the carrots and pecans. Stir together the flour and baking powder. Add to the carrot mixture alternately with the hot water. Beat the batter for at least 30 seconds. Grease and flour two 9-inch cake pans. Divide the batter between the pans. Bake for 35 minutes. Cool in the pans for 10 minutes. Turn out and cool completely. Frost with Cream Cheese Frosting.

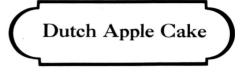

Dutch Apple Cake

(8–12 servings)

5 tablespoons butter, softened
¾ cup dark brown sugar
1 egg
1 tablespoon molasses
2 cups flour
   Pinch of salt
1 teaspoon baking soda
1 teaspoon cinnamon
1 teaspoon allspice
1¼ cups apple sauce
2 tablespoons calvados (optional)
   Confectioners' sugar

Preheat the oven to 350°. Butter and flour a tube pan and line the bottom with greased parchment paper.

In a mixing bowl cream together the butter and sugar until fluffy. Beat in the egg and molasses. In a separate bowl stir together the flour, salt, baking soda, and spices. Stir into the sugar mixture and beat 300 strokes or 2 minutes with an electric mixer. Beat in the apple sauce and calvados. Pour the batter into the prepared pan. Bake for 45 minutes or until done. Cool slightly and remove from pan. Dust the top with confectioners' sugar just before serving.

White Mousse with Raspberry Sauce

(6 servings)

White Chocolate Mousse:
  6 ounces white chocolate (appropriate for melting)
  1½ cups heavy cream, ice cold
  ¼ cup confectioners' sugar
  8 egg whites, room temperature
  ½ teaspoon cream of tartar
  ¼ cup granulated sugar
  2 tablespoons heavy cream
  Shaved semisweet dark chocolate

Raspberry Sauce:
  1 cup fresh raspberries
  ¼ cup sugar
  ¼ cup brandy

To prepare the mousse slowly melt the chocolate in a double boiler over very low heat. When melted, remove the chocolate from the heat. In a mixing bowl whip the cream until soft peaks form. Add the confectioners' sugar and whip until stiff peaks form. In another bowl whip the egg whites with the cream of tartar, gradually adding the granulated sugar until stiff peaks form. Do not overbeat. Cool the melted chocolate slightly. Add the 2 tablespoons of heavy cream to the chocolate to achieve a pouring consistency. Slowly add the chocolate to the whipped cream. Fold the egg whites and chocolate-cream mixture together gently.

To make the sauce, combine the raspberries and sugar in a saucepan. Bring to a boil, reduce to a simmer, and cook for 2 minutes. Flame with the brandy. Stir until the flame is extinguished.

To serve, spoon 2 tablespoons of raspberry sauce into the bottoms of six 1-cup wine glasses. Spoon the mousse over this sauce. Chill several hours before serving. Garnish with shaved, semisweet dark chocolate.

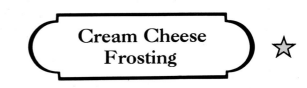

Cream Cheese Frosting

(Enough for 2-layer cake)

1 8-ounce package cream cheese, softened
1 cup confectioners' sugar
1 teaspoon lemon juice
2 tablespoons or more heavy cream

In a mixing bowl beat the cream cheese with an electric mixer until fluffy. Beat in the sugar and lemon juice. Beat in the cream until the frosting is of spreading consistency. Use this frosting for Carrot Cake or other spiced layer cake.

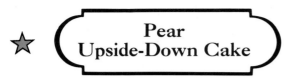

Pear Upside-Down Cake

(6–8 servings)

Topping:
⅛–¼ pound (½–1 stick) butter
  ½ cup brown sugar
  ⅓ cup white sugar
  1 teaspoon cinnamon
  ⅓ cup chopped pecans
  4 large pears, peeled, cored and sliced

Cake:
  1 cup flour
  1 teaspoon baking powder
  ½ teaspoon salt
  3 eggs, separated, whites stiffly beaten
  1 cup sugar
  ¼ cup milk
  ½ pint heavy cream whipped with 2 tablespoons amaretto liqueur (optional)

In an iron skillet or a 12″ × 8″ cake pan melt the butter and add the sugars and cinnamon. Heat over low flame until sugars are melted. Stir in the pecans. Arrange the sliced pears in a circular pattern in the melted sugar. Preheat the oven to 375°.

In a bowl combine the flour, baking powder, and salt and mix well. In a large bowl, beat the egg yolks until light and fluffy. Beat in the sugar a little at a time. Beat in the milk. Stir in the flour mixture, then gently fold in the beaten egg whites. Spread the batter over the pears and bake for 35 min-

utes. Cool cake slightly and invert onto a cake plate. Serve warm, but not hot. If desired, serve with cream whipped with 2 tablespoons amaretto liqueur.

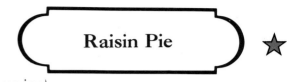

Raisin Pie

(6 servings)

  Pastry for 2-crust pie
1 cup raisins, plumped in 2 cups warm water
1 cup sugar
4 tablespoons flour
1 egg, beaten
3 tablespoons lemon juice
2 tablespoons grated lemon rind
  Pinch of salt
1 teaspoon cinnamon
1 tablespoon butter

Roll out half of the pastry and line a 9-inch pie plate. Heat the raisins and water in a heavy saucepan. Add the sugar, flour, egg, lemon juice, lemon rind, salt, and cinnamon. Simmer over low heat for 15 minutes. Cool. Preheat the oven to 400°.

Beat the butter into the filling. Pour into the pastry-lined plate. Roll out the remaining pastry and cut into 1-inch strips. Arrange in a lattice pattern on top of the filling. Bake for 30 minutes.

Notes: *An apple can be peeled, cored, sliced, and stirred into the filling before baking. One quarter cup rum may be added before cooking the filling.*

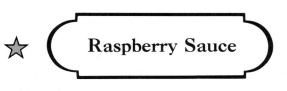

Raspberry Sauce

(2 cups)

2 cups fresh raspberries
⅓ cup sugar or more, to taste
¼ teaspoon vanilla
1 tablespoon cornstarch

In a saucepan combine all ingredients and bring to a boil, stirring constantly. Reduce heat and simmer about 7 minutes. Cool. Serve with Apple Cider Sherbet or another complementary dessert.

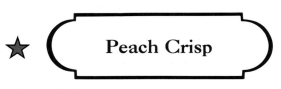

Peach Crisp

(6 servings)

6–8 ripe peaches, peeled and quartered
¾ cup dark brown sugar
½ cup flour
¼ cup oatmeal (uncooked)
   Pinch nutmeg or cinnamon
4 tablespoons butter
   Heavy cream

Preheat the oven to 375°. Lightly grease a flat baking dish.

Arrange the peaches in the bottom of the dish. In a bowl mix together the sugar, flour, oatmeal, and nutmeg. Cut the butter into the dry ingredients until the mixture resembles coarse meal. Spread over the peaches. Bake for 25 to 30 minutes. Serve with heavy cream.

Lemon Sponge Pudding

(4 servings)

⅔ cup sugar
3 tablespoons flour
3 tablespoons lemon juice
2 tablespoons grated lemon rind
2 egg yolks, beaten
1 tablespoon butter, softened
   Pinch of salt
1 cup milk
2 egg whites, beaten until stiff peaks form
   Confectioners' sugar

Preheat the oven to 350°.

In a bowl mix together the sugar and flour. Beat in the lemon juice, rind, egg yolks, butter, and salt. Beat in the milk. Gently fold in the beaten egg whites. Pour the mixture into a 1-quart Pyrex dish or mold. Set the mold into a pan of hot water and bake 45 minutes to 1 hour, or until set. Serve warm, sprinkled with confectioners' sugar.

Indian Pudding

(6–8 servings)

¼ cup cornmeal
5 cups milk
¼ cup molasses
Salt
½ teaspoon cinnamon
¼ teaspoon ginger
1 tablespoon butter
½ cup heavy cream or 1 pint vanilla ice cream

Preheat the oven to 275°.
    In a bowl mix the cornmeal with 1 cup cold milk. In a saucepan scald the other 4 cups milk. Add the cornmeal and cold milk, molasses, salt, spices, and butter. Pour into a well-buttered baking dish. Bake for 2½ to 3 hours, or until set. Serve warm with heavy cream or vanilla ice cream.

Guava Shells and Cream Cheese

(4–6 servings)

1 cup sugar
1 cup water
1 tablespoon lemon juice
1 pound guavas, stemmed, halved, and seeded
8 ounces cream cheese, softened

In a saucepan dissolve the sugar in the water. Stir in the lemon juice and boil for 5 minutes. Add the guava halves and simmer gently until the fruit is transparent and tender, but not too soft. Cool the fruit in the syrup. Drain the fruit and chill. Reserve the syrup. Whip the softened cream cheese until fluffy. Fill each guava shell with the cheese. Serve syrup on the side.

Note: *If fresh guavas are not available, canned guava shells may be substituted.*

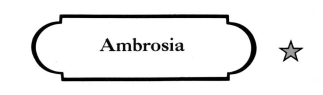

Ambrosia

(6 servings)

6 large oranges, peeled, seeded, and sectioned or thinly sliced
¼ cup sugar
⅔ cup grated coconut
½ cup sweet white wine
Grated coconut

In a large bowl toss the oranges with the sugar and half of the coconut. Arrange in a glass serving bowl. Pour the white wine over the fruit. Sprinkle the remaining coconut over all. Allow to sit for at least 1 hour. Garnish with more coconut just before serving.

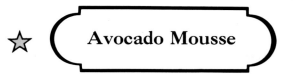

Avocado Mousse

(6 servings)

2 avocados
¼ cup lime juice
1 envelope gelatin
⅔ cup sugar
4 eggs, separated
¼ cup water
3 tablespoons rum
1 cup heavy cream, whipped
   Additional whipped cream

In a blender or food processor puree the avocados with the lime juice. Combine the gelatin with a ½ cup sugar in a double boiler over hot water. In a small bowl beat the egg yolks with the water. Turn into the gelatin mixture and stir over boiling water until the gelatin is completely dissolved. Remove from the heat. Stir in the avocado and rum. Cool until the mixture begins to thicken. In a separate bowl beat the egg whites with the remaining sugar until stiff peaks form. Fold into the gelatin mixture. Fold in the whipped cream. Turn the mixture into a soufflé dish or mold. Chill until firm. Serve garnished with more whipped cream.

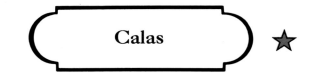

Calas

(6 servings)

1½ cups rice, cooked soft (use 3-to-1
   water-to- rice measure)
½ teaspoon dry yeast
2 tablespoons warm milk
3 eggs, beaten
¼ cup sugar
   Salt
   Nutmeg to taste
½–¾ cup flour
   Oil or fat for frying
   Finely granulated sugar or
   cinnamon sugar

Mash the hot rice. Cool. Dissolve the yeast in warm milk. Stir into the rice. Put the mixture aside and let rise for several hours or overnight.

Stir in the egg, sugar, salt, and nutmeg. Add the flour to make a thick, but not too firm, batter. Cover and let rise 15 to 20 minutes. In a heavy skillet heat the fat to 365°. Stir down the batter and drop by tablespoonfuls into hot fat. Brown on both sides. Drain on absorbent paper and roll in finely granulated sugar or cinnamon sugar. Serve very warm with hot black coffee.

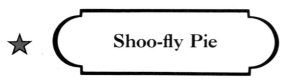

Shoo-fly Pie

(6–8 servings)

Pastry for 1-crust pie
1½ cups flour
1 cup brown sugar
¼ cup butter
½ teaspoon baking soda
½ cup hot water
1 egg
½ cup molasses

Preheat the oven to 350°. Line a pie tin with the pastry.

In a bowl combine the flour, brown sugar, and butter until the mixture resembles coarse meal. Dissolve the baking soda in the hot water. In a separate bowl beat the egg and stir in the molasses and the soda and water mixture. Alternate layers of liquid and crumb mixture in the lined pie tin, finishing with a layer of crumbs. Bake until firm, about 35 to 45 minutes.

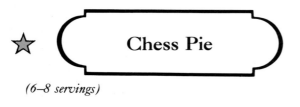

Chess Pie

(6–8 servings)

Pastry for 1-crust pie
3 cups sugar
4–5 tablespoons butter

⅔ cup milk
4 egg yolks
4 tablespoons lemon juice
2 tablespoons grated lemon rind
2 tablespoons flour
4 egg whites
Pinch of salt

Preheat the oven to 350°. Fit the pastry into a 9-inch pie plate.

In a large bowl cream the sugar and butter until light and creamy. Beat in the milk gradually. Beat in the egg yolks. Beat in the lemon juice, lemon rind and flour. In a separate bowl beat the egg whites with salt until stiff peaks form. Fold the egg whites into the lemon mixture. Pour into the pie shell and bake for 25 to 30 minutes until set.

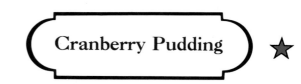

Cranberry Pudding

(6 servings)

1½ cups fresh cranberries, washed and well
   picked over
¼ cup brown sugar
1 teaspoon grated lemon rind
1 egg, beaten
½ cup sugar
½ cup flour
1 teaspoon vanilla
5 tablespoons butter, melted
Heavy cream

Preheat the oven to 325°. Butter a Pyrex pie plate or a 9-inch cake pan.

Toss the berries with the brown sugar and lemon rind. Pour into the prepared pan. In a bowl beat the egg and sugar until light and fluffy. Beat in the flour, vanilla and butter. Pour the egg mixture over the cranberries. Bake for 40 to 45 minutes. Serve warm with heavy cream.

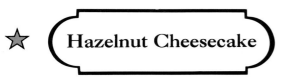

Hazelnut Cheesecake

(6–8 servings)

½ cup butter, melted
1½ cups chocolate wafer crumbs
5 8-oz packages cream cheese, softened
1⅔ cups light brown sugar, firmly packed
5 eggs
1 teaspoon vanilla
2 tablespoons coffee-flavored liqueur
1 cup finely chopped hazelnuts

In a bowl stir the butter into the chocolate crumbs. Press the buttered crumbs into the bottom of a 9-inch springform pan. Refrigerate for 2 hours. Preheat the oven to 325°.

Using an electric mixer, beat the cream cheese until fluffy. Beat in the brown sugar. Beat in the eggs, one at a time. Beat in the vanilla and coffee liqueur. Stir in the hazelnuts. Fill the prepared springform pan and bake for 1 hour. Turn off the oven and let

the cake cool for 30 minutes before opening the oven door. Cool completely and chill. Do not remove the form pan until ready to serve.

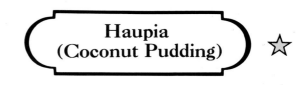

Haupia (Coconut Pudding)

(6 servings)

2 tablespoons cornstarch
3 tablespoons sugar
⅛ teaspoon salt
2 cups coconut milk (the coconut milk is
  imperative; no substitutions will do)

In a bowl make a smooth paste of the dry ingredients and ½ cup of the coconut milk. In a saucepan scald the remaining milk over low heat and add the paste, stirring rapidly. Cook over low heat to avoid curdling. When the pudding is clear and thick enough to coat a spoon, pour into a shallow pan and set in a cool place until firm.

Note: *For* Haupia *firm enough to cut into squares for serving, the usual Hawaiian method is to increase the cornstarch to 2½ tablespoons. See the Resource Guide for information on ordering prepared* Haupia.

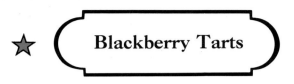

Blackberry Tarts

(6 servings)

Sweet pastry for a 2-crust pie
¾ cup sugar
2 tablespoons flour
¼ teaspoon cinnamon
Pinch of salt
3 cups blackberries
1 tablespoon butter

Preheat the oven to 350°. Line 6 tart pans with the pastry.

In a bowl combine the sugar, flour, cinnamon, and salt. Add the berries and toss lightly. Fill the lined tart shells with the berry mixture. Dot each tart with butter. Bake for 20 minutes. Cool. Serve topped with Lemon Curd.

Lemon Curd

¾ cup sugar
3 tablespoons cornstarch
¾ cup water
1 egg, lightly beaten
⅓ cup lemon juice
1 teaspoon lemon rind, grated
2 tablespoons butter

In the top of a double boiler stir together the sugar and cornstarch. Stir in the water. Beat in the egg, lemon juice, and lemon rind. Cook until thick. Remove from heat and stir in the butter. Cool.

Note: *Serve on Blackberry Tarts or other blackberry or blueberry desserts.*

Cider Baked Apples

(6 servings)

6 tablespoons raisins plumped in rum
1 teaspoon cinnamon
⅓ cup brown sugar
6 fresh apples, generously cored and peeled ⅓ of way down
¼ cup maple syrup
2 tablespoons butter
⅔ cup sweet cider
Heavy cream (optional)

Preheat the oven to 350°.

In a bowl mix together the raisins, cinnamon, and brown sugar. Stuff the apples. Boil remaining ingredients, except the cream, in a saucepan. Arrange the apples in a baking dish, pour syrup mixture over them, and bake for 1 hour, basting every 15 minutes.

Serve the apples warm with the syrup spooned over them. A pitcher of fresh heavy cream can be served with these.

Cider Baked Apples ▶

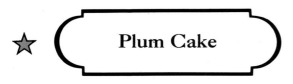

Plum Cake

(6 servings)

Dough:
 2 cups flour
   Pinch of salt
 ½ teaspoon baking powder
 3 teaspoons sugar
 ⅔ cup butter
 2 egg yolks
 ⅓ cup cold water
   Fresh dry bread crumbs

Filling:
 2 pounds fresh plums, halved and stoned,
   but not peeled
 1 cup light brown sugar
 2 eggs
 2 tablespoons sugar
 ¼ cup cream

In a mixing bowl stir together the flour, salt, baking powder, and sugar. Cut in the butter. Beat in the egg yolks and cold water. Turn the dough out on a floured board and knead for 2 minutes. Chill 1 hour. Preheat the oven to 350°.

Roll out the dough and line a jelly roll pan. Sprinkle the dough with bread crumbs. Dot with butter. Arrange the plums on top of the bread crumbs. Sprinkle sugar heavily over all. In a small bowl beat together the eggs, sugar, and cream. Pour carefully over the plums and bake for 45 minutes.

Schnecken

(6–8 servings)

Dough:
 1 envelope dry yeast
 3 cups warm milk
 ⅓ cup sugar
   Pinch of salt
 2 eggs, beaten
 8 tablespoons butter, melted
 6 cups flour (approximately)

Filling:
 ⅓ cup sugar
 2 teaspoons cinnamon
 5 tablespoons butter

Topping:
 ½ cup butter
 1 cup brown sugar
 ½ cup chopped nuts

In a bowl soften the yeast in 1 cup of warm milk and stir in the sugar and salt. Add the remaining 2 cups of milk, eggs, melted butter, and enough flour to make a soft dough. Cover and put in a warm place. Let rise until double in bulk. Punch down and roll out into a rectangle.

Mix the filling ingredients together in a bowl. Spread the filling on the dough and roll up like a jelly roll. Cut in 2-inch pieces.

To make the topping melt the butter in a jelly roll pan. Add the sugar and nuts. Place the rolls, cut side down, in the pan. Let rise until doubled. Preheat the oven to 400°.
Bake for 20 minutes.

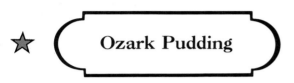

Ozark Pudding

(4–6 servings)

3 large apples, peeled, cored, and diced
½ cup chopped pecans
2 eggs, beaten
1¼ cups sugar
2 teaspoons vanilla
⅔ cup flour
3 teaspoons baking powder
Pinch of salt
3 tablespoons rum
Rum-flavored whipped cream or rum-raisin ice cream (optional)

Preheat the oven to 350°.
In a mixing bowl toss together the apples and pecans. In a separate bowl beat together the eggs, sugar, and vanilla until light and fluffy. In another bowl stir together the flour, baking powder, and salt. Beat into the sugar mixture. Stir in the apples and nuts along with the rum. Pour the mixture into a greased, rectangular baking dish. Bake for 25 to 30 minutes or until golden. Serve with rum flavored whipped cream or rum raisin ice cream, if desired.

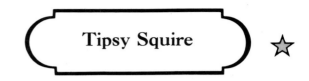

Tipsy Squire

(8 servings)

Creme Anglaise:
1 quart milk
6 eggs
1 cup sugar
1 teaspoon vanilla

2 round sponge cake layers
1 quart *Creme Anglaise*
1 cup sweet sherry
½ cup blanched almonds, toasted
1 cup heavy cream, whipped

To make the *Creme Anglaise* filling, heat the milk in a saucepan until scalding. Beat the eggs until light and creamy. Beat in the sugar. Whisk a little hot milk into the eggs and turn the mixture back into the hot milk. Cook over low heat, whisking constantly, until mixture thickens enough to coat the back of a spoon. Strain into a chilled bowl, add vanilla, stir to combine, and cool completely. Chill.
To make Tipsy Squire, place one layer of sponge cake in the bottom of a serving bowl. Pour 3 cups of *Creme Anglaise* over the cake. Top with the second cake layer. Pour the sherry evenly over the cake. Top with the remaining custard and sprinkle with the nuts. Decorate the dessert with the whipped cream and chill before serving.

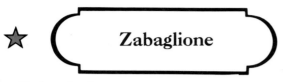

Zabaglione

(2–4 servings)

6 egg yolks
⅓ cup sugar
¼ teaspoon cinnamon
1 cup Marsala wine

In a bowl beat the egg yolks until light and fluffy. Beat in the sugar, cinnamon, and wine. Set the bowl over hot water and cook, beating with a whisk until the mixture is light and fluffy and there is no liquid left in the bottom of the bowl. Serve in wine glasses, or as a topping for berries or sliced peaches.

Piña Colada Ice Cream

(8 servings)

1 cup crushed pineapple, drained
⅔ cup sugar
1 cup coconut cream
2 cups half and half
¼ cup rum

In a bowl stir together all ingredients. Freeze in electric freezer, following manufacturer's instructions. (This takes 15 to 20 minutes in a Simac.)

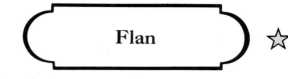

Flan

(8 servings)

¾ cup sugar
2½ cups milk
2 cups cream of coconut
6 eggs
5 egg yolks
2 teaspoons vanilla extract, Mexican if available
1 cup sliced almonds
Fresh berries or kiwifruit slices (optional)

Preheat the oven to 325°

Caramelize the sugar by melting in a saute pan or skillet over medium heat, watching constantly so that it does not burn. As the sugar bubbles, lift the pan off the heat, tilting to move caramel around the pan surface. When the sugar is caramelized, quickly pour into a 10-inch round cake pan or 8 individual flan molds, tilting to coat evenly. (If caramel hardens, return pan to heat to liquefy, then continue to coat pan or molds.) Place pan or molds in a larger pan filled with hot water.

In a mixing bowl beat the eggs and egg yolks lightly with a whisk. Add remaining ingredients, except almonds and fruit, whisking together to make a custard.

Pour the custard into the caramelized pan or molds and sprinkle the almonds evenly over the top. Cover all the pans with aluminum foil. Bake for 1 hour or until a knife inserted in the custard comes out clean. Remove flan from water bath and refrigerate. When ready to serve, invert pan or molds onto serving platter. Garnish with berries in season or kiwi slices, if desired.

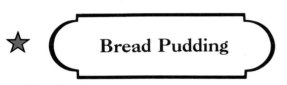

Bread Pudding

(6 servings)

> 3 cups milk
> 6 tablespoons sweet butter
> ½ cup raisins
> 3 large eggs
> 1¼ cups sugar
> ½ teaspoon grated fresh nutmeg
> ½ teaspoon cinnamon
> 1 teaspoon vanilla extract
>   Pinch salt
> 8–10 cups of French or Italian bread torn into 2-inch chunks (2 to 3 loaves)
>   Whisky Sauce

Preheat the oven to 350°.

In a saucepan, scald the milk and melt the butter. In another saucepan place the raisins with water to cover and bring to a boil to plump them. Drain well and set aside.

In a bowl, whisk together the eggs, sugar, nutmeg, cinnamon, vanilla, and salt. Add the milk in a slow, steady stream, whisking constantly so that the eggs will not curdle.

Add the raisins and the bread. Push down the bread to make sure it soaks up most of the custard mixture but is still very moist. Place in a well-buttered 2-quart baking dish or earthenware crock. Place baking dish in a larger baking pan half-filled with hot water. Cover it all with aluminum foil.

Bake the pudding for about 1 hour, remove foil, and bake another 15 minutes to brown. Serve hot with Whisky Sauce.

Whisky Sauce

(About 1 cup)

> 1 cup light brown sugar
> 2 ounces bourbon
> 6 tablespoons sweet butter
> ⅓ cup heavy cream
>   Pinch salt

Combine all ingredients in a saucepan, bring to a boil, and simmer until thickened, about 1 hour, whisking regularly. Serve hot over Bread Pudding.

Note: *This sauce is also excellent over other pudding and custard desserts.*

Chinese Chews

(Makes about 16 chews)

    1 cup sugar
    ¾ cup flour
    1 teaspoon baking powder
      Pinch of salt
    1 cup chopped dates
    1 cup chopped pecans
    2 eggs, beaten
      Confectioners' sugar

Preheat the oven to 375°.

In a bowl stir together the sugar, flour, baking powder, and salt. Add the dates and pecans and stir. Beat in the eggs. Grease a jelly roll pan. Spread the dough in the prepared pan. Bake for 20 minutes. Cut into bars while warm. Cool. Sprinkle with confectioners' sugar before serving.

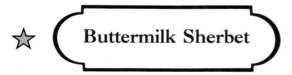

Buttermilk Sherbet

(8 servings)

    ⅔ cup sugar
      Pinch of salt
    1 8¼-ounce can crushed pineapple in natural
      juice
    2 cups buttermilk
    1 teaspoon vanilla extract

In a saucepan combine the sugar, salt, and pineapple. Heat just until the sugar and salt dissolve. Remove from heat, add buttermilk and vanilla, and mix well. Cool. Pour into the container of an ice cream freezer and freeze according to manufacturer's directions.

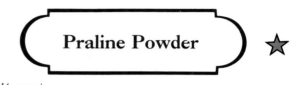

Praline Powder

(1½ cups)

    2 cups granulated sugar
    ¼ cup water
    1 tablespoon vanilla
    2½ cups pecans, toasted

In a heavy skillet or saucepan melt the sugar in the water. Cook to a golden-brown, caramel color. Stir in vanilla. Add the hot nuts and stir. Pour candy onto a well-greased jelly roll pan or marble slab. Let cool. Break into pieces and then process in a food processor until pulverized.

Note: *Keeps well frozen.*

Rice Pudding

(4–6 servings)

    2 eggs, separated
    ½ cup sugar

Pinch of salt
2 cups milk
1 teaspoon vanilla
1 teaspoon cinnamon
¼ cup raisins, plumped in hot water and well drained
2 cups cooked rice

Preheat the oven to 350°.

In a mixing bowl beat the egg yolks until light. Beat in the sugar, salt, milk, vanilla, and cinnamon. Stir in the raisins and rice. In a separate bowl beat the egg whites until stiff peaks form. Fold gently into the rice mixture. Pour into a buttered baking dish and bake for 45 minutes or until set.

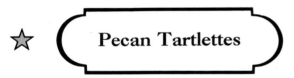

Pecan Tartlettes

(8–10 3-inch tartlettes)

Sweet pastry for 1-crust pie
2 small eggs
3 tablespoons sugar
2 tablespoons melted butter
⅓ cup light corn syrup
⅓ cup dark corn syrup
½ teaspoon vanilla
½ cup chopped pecan pieces

Preheat the oven to 350°. Press pastry into tart molds.

In a bowl beat together well the eggs and sugar. Stir in the remaining ingredients. Fill the tartlette shells. Bake for approximately 20 minutes. Cool and unmold tartlettes. Arrange on serving plate.

Note: *Also makes enough for one 8-inch pie. Bake at 350° for 35 to 40 minutes.*

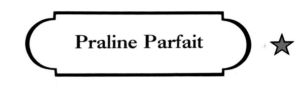

Praline Parfait

(8 servings)

6 eggs
1 cup sugar
Pinch of salt
4 cups half and half
3 tablespoons vanilla extract
Praline powder

In a bowl beat the eggs until light and fluffy. Beat in the sugar and salt. In a saucepan, bring the half and half to a boil. Pour a little hot cream into the egg mixture, whisking constantly. Pour the eggs into the rest of the hot cream. Cook over low heat, stirring constantly, until custard coats the back of a spoon—2 to 3 minutes. Strain custard into a clean bowl, stir in the vanilla, and chill. Pour cold mixture into the container of an ice cream freezer and freeze according to manufacturer's instructions.

To make the parfait, alternate layers of this rich ice cream with Praline Powder in tall parfait glasses. Freeze 30 minutes and serve.

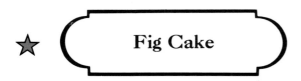

Fig Cake

(12 servings)

> 4 cups fresh figs
> 1½ cups sugar
>   Water
> 2 tablespoons flour
> ¼ pound (1 stick) butter, softened
> 3 eggs
> 2½ cups flour
> 1 teaspoon baking soda
> 1 teaspoon baking powder
> 1 teaspoon ground cinnamon
> 1 teaspoon allspice
> 1 tablespoon molasses
> 1 cup milk
>   Confectioner's sugar

Simmer the figs in a saucepan with ½ cup sugar and enough water to barely cover them. When the figs are beginning to turn translucent, drain and chop them into small pieces. Dry them on absorbent paper and toss with the 2 tablespoons flour (this will keep the pieces of fruit from sinking to the bottom of the cake). Preheat the oven to 375°. Generously butter a tube pan.

In a bowl cream the butter and 1 cup sugar until light and fluffy. Beat in the eggs. In a separate bowl sift together the flour, baking soda, baking powder, cinnamon, and allspice. Stir the molasses into the butter and sugar mixture. Add the dry ingredients, alternating with the milk. Stir in the figs. Pour the batter into the tube pan. Bake for 1 hour.

Cool the cake in the pan and then turn out onto a serving plate. Dust with confectioner's sugar just before serving.

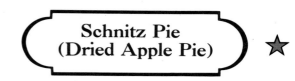

Schnitz Pie (Dried Apple Pie)

(6 servings)

> 1 pound dried apples
> 4 cups water
> ⅓ cup orange juice
>   Rind of one orange, cut in fine julienne
> 1 tablespoon cinnamon
> 1½ cups sugar
>   Pinch of salt
>   Pastry for 2-crust pie
>   Sugar

In a saucepan combine the dried apples with the water and simmer until very soft. Add the orange juice and orange rind. Stir in the cinnamon, sugar and salt. Cool. Preheat the oven to 375°.

Roll out half the pastry. Line a 9-inch pie plate. Pour in the cooled filling. Roll out the remaining pastry and cover the filling. Sprinkle the top crust with sugar. Bake for 35 minutes.

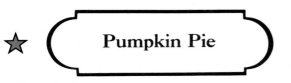

Pumpkin Pie

(8 servings)

Pastry for 1-crust pie
1½ cups pumpkin puree
⅔ cup brown sugar
½ teaspoon ginger
½ teaspoon cinnamon
½ teaspoon nutmeg
¼ teaspoon ground cloves
¼ cup molasses
3 whole eggs, lightly beaten
2 cups half and half or condensed milk

Preheat the oven to 400°.

In a mixing bowl beat together all the ingredients in the order listed. Pour into lined pie shell. Bake for 45 minutes until set. Cool.

Cherry Omelet

(2–3 servings)

6 eggs, separated
6 tablespoons milk
½ teaspoon salt
1 tablespoon butter
½ cup cherry preserves
Confectioners' sugar

In a bowl beat the egg yolks with the milk. In another bowl beat the egg whites with the salt until stiff peaks form. Fold the egg yolks into the egg whites. In a large heavy skillet melt the butter and pour in the egg mixture. Cook until the mixture begins to set. Run the pan under the broiler until the omelet is light and fluffy. Spread the cherry preserves over the omelet. Fold and turn out onto a serving plate. Dust with confectioners' sugar and serve.

Transparent Pie

(6 servings)

Pastry for a 1-crust pie
8 egg yolks
1 cup sugar
1 cup butter, cut into pieces
½ cup heavy cream
½ teaspoon lemon extract

Preheat the oven to 375°. Roll out the pastry and line a 9-inch pie plate, fluting the edges.

In a mixing bowl beat the egg yolks and sugar until light and fluffy. Pour into a saucepan and place over low heat. Beat in the butter, a little at a time, until the butter melts. Remove from the heat and beat in the cream and extract. Pour the filling into the pie shell. Bake for 30 minutes, or until fully set. Cool and serve.

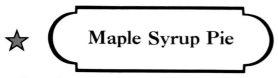

Maple Syrup Pie

(8 servings)

2 tablespoons butter
2 tablespoons flour
2 eggs
1 cup maple syrup
4 tablespoons water
½ cup chopped walnuts
1 pie shell, baked
1 cup whipped cream

Preheat oven to 325°.

In a saucepan melt the butter and stir in the flour. Take the pan off the heat. Beat the eggs into the mixture and stir in the maple syrup and water. Set over boiling water and cook, stirring constantly, until thick. Stir in the nuts and cool. Pour into a pie shell and bake for 15 minutes. Cool. Serve with whipped cream.

Heavenly Hash

(4–6 servings)

1 16-ounce package milk chocolate bits
2 cups mini-marshmallows
1 cup chopped pecans

Melt the chocolate in a double boiler. Pour half of the chocolate onto a tray lined with waxed paper. Top with the marshmallows and pecans. Cover with the rest of the chocolate. Cool. When cold, break into pieces.

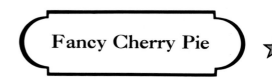

Fancy Cherry Pie

(6 servings)

Pastry for 2-crust pie
2 cups sour red cherries, stoned (fresh or canned), or 2 cups fresh Bing cherries, stoned
1 large apple, peeled, cored, and thinly sliced
2 tablespoons raisins, plumped in 3 tablespoons rum
2 tablespoons flour
⅔ cup sugar
½ teaspoon almond extract
2–3 tablespoons butter
3 tablespoons rum

Preheat the oven to 425°. Roll out half of the pastry and line a 9-inch pie pan.

In a bowl toss the cherries, apple, and raisins with the flour, sugar, and almond extract. Pile the mixture into the pie shell. Dot with butter and pour in the rum. Roll out the remaining pastry and cut into 1-inch strips. Weave the strips into a lattice crust. Crimp the edges. Bake for 35 minutes.

Fancy Cherry Pie ▶

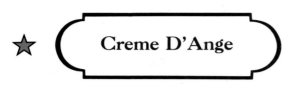

Creme D'Ange

(4 servings)

 1 can sweetened condensed milk
½ cup whipped cream
   Chopped pecans

Preheat the oven to 425°.

Pour the condensed milk into a pie plate or small glass soufflé dish and cover. Place the pie plate or soufflé dish in a pan. Pour water into the pan to a level of ¼ inch. Bake for 1½ hours, adding boiling water to the pan as needed. Cool the custard and chill several hours. Serve with whipped cream and chopped pecans.

Notes: *The name means Angel's Cream. This dessert is very similar to a Spanish favorite called* Dolce de Leche, *A Sweet Made From Milk.*

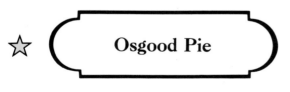

Osgood Pie

(6 servings)

   Pastry for 1-crust pie
3 eggs, separated
1 cup sugar
1 teaspoon pumpkin pie spice

½ cup raisins, plumped in hot water, drained
   and dried
½ cup chopped pecans
 1 tablespoon sugar

Preheat the oven to 350°. Roll out the pastry. Line a 9-inch pie plate and flute the edges.

In a mixing bowl beat the egg yolks and sugar until light and fluffy. Beat in the spice. Stir in the raisins and nuts. In a separate bowl beat the egg whites with 1 tablespoon sugar until stiff peaks form. Fold into the raisin mixture. Pour into the pie shell and bake for 30 to 35 minutes, or until set.

Stack Cake

(6–8 servings)

4½ cups cake flour
 4 teaspoons baking powder
 1 teaspoon salt
 1 cup butter
2½ cups sugar
 4 eggs, separated
1½ cups pineapple juice
 2 teaspoons vanilla
 3 cups applesauce
 1 cup whipped cream

Sift the flour, baking powder, and salt into a bowl. In another bowl cream the butter and sugar until light and fluffy. Add the egg yolks, one at a time, beating after each addition. Add the flour alternately with the pineapple juice. Beat in the vanilla. Preheat the oven to 375°.

Beat the egg whites until stiff peaks form. Grease and flour six 8-inch cake pans. Divide the batter between the six pans; the layers will be thin. Bake for 15 to 20 minutes. Cool. Spread applesauce between the layers and frost the top with whipped cream.

Bananas Foster

(6 servings)

4 tablespoons butter
½ cup brown sugar
1 teaspoon cinnamon
1 teaspoon nutmeg
6 bananas, ripe but not soft, peeled
¼ cup rum

Melt the butter in a heavy skillet. Add the sugar, cinnamon, and nutmeg. When dissolved, arrange the bananas in the syrup. Simmer, spooning syrup over bananas until they are browned and tender. Pour the rum over the bananas, heat, and ignite. Serve bananas very hot with syrup spooned over them.

Note: *Some aficionados like vanilla ice cream with these.*

Cranberry Apple Pie

(8 servings)

Pastry for 2-crust pie
1 cup thinly sliced apples
2 cups cranberries
½ cup cider
¾ cup sugar
  Pinch of salt
¼ teaspoon ground cinnamon
1 tablespoon butter

Preheat the oven to 375°.

Line a pie dish with the pastry. Roll out the second crust, cut a design—heart, diamond, apple, etc.—from the crust and lift onto a baking sheet with a spatula. Bake design for 8 to 10 minutes, until golden. Remove from the oven and cool. In a saucepan, simmer the apples, cranberries, and cider for 15 minutes or until tender. Stir in the sugar, salt, cinnamon, and butter. Pour into the pie shell. Increase oven temperature to 450°.

Bake the pie for 20 to 25 minutes. Cool slightly. Using a spatula, lift the decorative pastry from the baking sheet and place carefully on top of the cranberry filling. Serve warm.

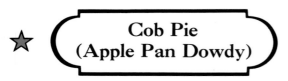

Cob Pie
(Apple Pan Dowdy)

(6 servings)

6 tart apples
⅔ cup maple syrup
½ teaspoon cinnamon
3 tablespoons butter
⅓ cup cider
1 recipe Buttermilk Baking Powder Biscuits
1 cup whipped cream

Preheat the oven to 375°.
Peel and slice the apples. Pile in a well-greased, flat baking dish. Pour maple syrup over all. Sprinkle with cinnamon and dot with butter. Pour in the cider. Roll out the biscuit dough until ¼-inch thick. Lay over apple mixture. Slash to allow steam to escape. Bake for 30 minutes, or until biscuit topping is well browned. Cut in squares. Spoon apples over biscuit and top with whipped cream.

Fig Ice Cream

(1½ quarts)

1 cup milk
3 cups heavy cream
¾ cup sugar
2 eggs, beaten

2 cups fig puree (about 6 cups fresh fruit)
1 tablespoon lemon juice
1 teaspoon vanilla

In a saucepan scald the milk and cream. Add the sugar and stir until dissolved. Stir ½ cup of hot cream into the beaten eggs. Pour back into the cream mixture, beating constantly. Simmer 3 to 5 minutes over low heat, stirring. Stir in the figs, lemon juice and vanilla. Cool completely. Pour into the freezer container of an ice cream maker and freeze according to manufacturer's directions.

Gratineed Oranges
à la Monte Carlo

(4 servings)

4 blood oranges or mandarin oranges, peeled and sliced
8 tablespoons clover honey
4 sprigs fresh mint

Preheat the broiler to 550°.
Brush the slices of each orange with 2 tablespoons honey. Arrange the slices of each orange in an overlapping pattern in a 4-inch souffle dish or shirred-egg dish.
Broil the oranges for 7 to 8 minutes, or until the surfaces are slightly caramelized. Place each dish on an attractive dinner plate and garnish the center of each orange with a sprig of fresh mint.

Orange Shortcake

(Serves 8)

2 cups flour
2 teaspoons baking powder
  Pinch of salt
9 tablespoons butter
½ cup cream
1 cup orange juice
1 cup sugar
⅓ cup Grand Marnier
  Grated peel of one orange
5 oranges, peeled and sectioned,
  membrane removed
½ cup heavy cream, whipped

Preheat the oven to 450°.

In a mixing bowl stir together the flour, baking powder, and salt. Cut in 5 tablespoons of the butter until the mixture resembles coarse meal. Stir in the cream. Blend just until the dough holds together. Pat the dough into two 8-inch cakes. Place one on top of the other. Bake the shortcake for 15 minutes, until golden brown.

In a saucepan combine the orange juice, sugar, Grand Marnier, remaining 4 tablespoons butter, and orange peel and simmer for 5 minutes. Cool.

Split the shortcake into 2 layers. Soak the bottom layer in two-thirds of the syrup. Arrange two-thirds of the orange sections on top. Top with the second layer. Pour the remaining syrup over the top layer. Arrange the remaining orange sections on top. Decorate with the whipped cream.

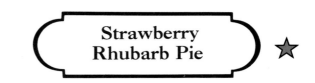

Strawberry Rhubarb Pie

Sweet pastry for 2-crust pie
1 pound rhubarb, leaves trimmed, stalks cut
  into ½-inch pieces
1 pint fresh strawberries, hulled and sliced
¾ cup sugar
2 tablespoons flour
1 teaspoon cinnamon
1 teaspoon lemon juice
  Sugar

Preheat the oven to 450°. Roll out half of the pastry and line a 9-inch pie plate.

In a large bowl, toss together the rhubarb, strawberries, sugar, flour, cinnamon, and lemon juice. Pile into the lined pie shell. Roll out remaining pastry and cut into 1-inch strips. Arrange strips in a lattice pattern on top of the filling and crimp the edges. Bake for 10 minutes, reduce heat to 350° and bake 30 to 45 minutes longer. Sprinkle the top of the pie with sugar as soon as it comes from the oven.

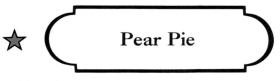

Pear Pie

(6 servings)

> Pastry for a 2-crust pie
> 6 large pears, peeled, cored, and sliced
> ⅔ cup sugar
> ¼ cup orange juice
> 2 tablespoons flour
> ¼ teaspoon nutmeg
> 2–3 tablespoons butter

Preheat the oven to 425°. Roll out half of the pastry and line a 9-inch pie pan.

Toss the pear slices with the sugar, orange juice, flour, and nutmeg. Fill the pastry with the pear mixture. Dot with butter. Roll out the remaining pastry and cover the filling. Seal and flute the edges. Bake for 40 minutes. Cool before serving.

Angel Food Cake

(8–10 servings)

> 10 large egg whites
> 1½ teaspoons cream of tartar
> Pinch of salt
> 2 teaspoons vanilla
> ½ teaspoon almond extract
> ⅔ cup sugar

> 1 cup sifted cake flour
> ¾ cup sugar

Preheat the oven to 350°.

With an electric mixer beat the egg whites with the cream of tartar until soft peaks form. Beat in the salt, vanilla, and almond extract. Beat in the ⅔ cup sugar a little at a time until the meringue is stiff and shiny. In a separate bowl stir together the flour and ¾ cup sugar. Fold into the egg whites a little at a time. Be careful not to over mix. Turn the batter into a ungreased tube pan and bake for 40 minutes. Invert the pan, hang it on a small bottle or funnel, and cool thoroughly before loosening the edges and removing from the pan.

Sour Cream Raisin Pie

(6 servings)

> 2 cups seedless raisins plumped in hot water and well drained
> ½ teaspoon cinnamon
> ⅛ teaspoon ground cloves
> 1 teaspoon grated lemon rind
> Pastry for 1-crust pie
> 1 egg
> ¼ cup sugar
> 3 tablespoons flour
> Pinch of salt
> ½ cup sour cream
> ½ cup honey

Preheat the oven to 425°.

Toss the raisins with the cinnamon, cloves, and lemon rind. Roll out the pastry. Line a 9-inch pie plate and crimp the edges. In a bowl beat together the egg and sugar. Beat in the flour and salt. Stir in the sour cream and honey. Fold in the raisins. Pile the filling in the pastry and bake for 30 minutes or until the center is completely set. Let cool. Chill before serving.

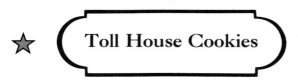

Toll House Cookies

(3 dozen cookies)

½ pound (2 sticks) butter, softened
¾ cup granulated sugar
¾ cup dark brown sugar
2 eggs
1 teaspoon vanilla
2¼ cups flour
½ teaspoon salt
1 teaspoon baking soda
12 ounces chocolate chips, or 12 ounces chopped dark chocolate

Preheat the oven to 375°.

In a mixing bowl cream the butter and sugars until light and fluffy. Beat in the eggs and vanilla. In a separate bowl stir together the flour, salt, and baking soda. Stir the flour into the butter mixture. Stir in the chips. Drop batter by spoonfuls onto ungreased cookie sheets. Bake 6 to 8 minutes. Cool on racks.

Sweet Potato Pie

(6 servings)

Sweet pastry for a 1-crust pie
½ cup sugar
¼ cup molasses
Pinch of salt
1 tablespoon lemon juice
3 eggs, separated
½ teaspoon cinnamon
¼ teaspoon ground cloves
¼ teaspoon allspice
2 cups pureed sweet potatoes
1 cup half and half
Rum-flavored whipped cream

Preheat the oven to 425°. Roll out the pastry and line an 8- or 9-inch pie plate.

In a mixing bowl beat the sugar, molasses, salt, lemon juice, egg yolks, and spices until smooth. Beat in the sweet potatoes and half and half. In a separate bowl beat the egg whites until stiff peaks form. Fold into the sweet potato mixture. Pour into the prepared pie shell. Bake for 10 minutes. Reduce heat to 350° and bake 35 to 40 minutes longer or until custard is set. Serve with rum-flavored whipped cream.

Strawberries and Meringues

(6 servings)

Meringues:
  6 egg whites
    Pinch of salt
¼ teaspoon cream of tartar
  1 cup sugar

  1 quart strawberries
½ cup sugar
  1 cup whipped cream

Preheat the oven to 200°.

To make the meringues, beat the egg whites, salt, and cream of tartar with an electric mixer until stiff. Beat in the sugar a little at a time until all sugar is incorporated and the mixture is smooth and shiny. Fill a pastry bag with the meringue. Pipe individual nest shapes about 4 inches in diameter onto a lightly oiled cookie sheet. Bake for 2 hours. Prop open the oven door and allow the meringues to cool in the oven for at least 2 or 3 hours.

Hull the strawberries and cut half of them in half. Sweeten the strawberries with the sugar. Fill the meringue shells with the sweetened berry halves and garnish with the whole berries. Pipe a small amount of whipped cream on top of each filled meringue. Serve quickly so that the meringues remain crisp.

Note: *Meringues quickly absorb moisture from the atmosphere. It is best to make them on a dry day and to store them in a metal tin with a tight-fitting lid.*

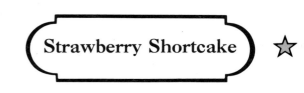

Strawberry Shortcake

(6 servings)

Shortcake:
2½ cups flour
    Pinch of salt
  3 teaspoons double-acting baking powder
  3 tablespoons sugar
⅓ cup butter
  1 whole egg
¾ cup milk
  2 tablespoons butter, softened

  1 quart strawberries
¾ cup sugar
  1 cup heavy cream, whipped

Preheat the oven to 375°.

In a bowl mix together the flour, salt, baking powder, and sugar. Cut in ⅓ cup butter until the mixture resembles coarse meal. In a separate bowl beat the egg with the milk. Stir into the flour mixture to form a stiff dough. Turn the dough onto a floured board and knead for 1 minute. Separate the dough into two parts. Roll out one half of the dough to fit an 8-inch cake pan. Generously flour the top of the layer. Roll out the second half of the dough and pat on top of the first layer. Bake for 25 minutes. Separate the layers and spread the bottom layer with the 2 tablespoons softened butter.

Stem and cut up half of the strawberries, and mix them with the sugar. Spread a little whipped cream on the bottom layer of the shortcake. Top with the sweetened berries. Place the second layer of the cake on top. Spread the second layer generously with whipped cream and arrange the reserved whole berries on top. Serve in wedges.

Apple Cider Sherbet

(8 servings)

   4 teaspoons grated lemon rind
   4 cups sugar
   8 cups unfiltered apple cider
   ½ teaspoon salt
   ½ cup lemon juice
   ¼ cup apple jack brandy

In a large saucepan, combine lemon rind, sugar, cider, and salt. Bring to a boil, stirring constantly. Reduce heat and simmer 5 minutes without stirring. Chill; add lemon juice and apple jack. Freeze according to ice cream freezer manufacturer's directions. Serve with Raspberry Sauce.

Fastnachts

(Makes 12–18 doughnuts)

   1 envelope dry yeast
   1 cup warm water
   6 cups flour, approximately
   2 cups milk
   ½ cup sugar
      Salt
   3 eggs, beaten
   4 tablespoons butter
      Pinch of nutmeg
      Fat for deep frying
      Granulated sugar

In a bowl dissolve the yeast in the water. Add a ½ cup of flour to the yeast and stir until smooth. Add the milk. Stir in 1 tablespoon sugar and half of the remaining flour. Put in a warm place and let rise. When the sponge is at least double in bulk, stir in the salt, eggs, butter, remaining sugar, nutmeg, and enough flour to make a firm dough. Let rise until double in bulk. Punch down and roll out on a floured board. Cut into squares or normal doughnut shapes. Set on a floured board and let rise. Fry in hot deep fat until light and golden. Drain on absorbent paper and roll in granulated sugar while still warm.

Note: *These are traditionally eaten on the day before Ash Wednesday.*

Sauces and Accompaniments

Creole Sauce

(1½ cups)

1 16-ounce can tomatoes, crushed
3 hot red chili peppers, finely chopped
1 cup minced onion
⅓ cup white vinegar
¼–½ teaspoon red pepper sauce
    Dash of sugar
    Salt to taste

In a medium saucepan combine all ingredients and bring to a boil. Lower the heat, cover, and simmer 30 minutes, stirring often to prevent sticking. Refrigerate.

Note: *This flavorful sauce is a welcome accompaniment for meat loaf, hot dogs, ham, sausage, eggs, and sandwiches.*

Celery Sauce

(About 4 cups)

1 large bell pepper, chopped
4 cups coarsely chopped celery
2 medium onions, chopped
1 small clove garlic, minced
1 cup vinegar

½ cup sugar
1 tablespoon salt
½ teaspoon chili powder
¼ teaspoon pepper
¼ teaspoon cinnamon
1 16-ounce can tomatoes
1 jalapeño pepper, minced

In a saucepan combine all ingredients. Cook slowly for 2 hours or longer.

Note: *This sauce can be served over rice or noodles, or as an accompaniment to grilled meats.*

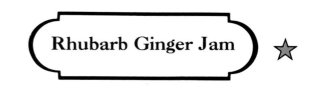

Rhubarb Ginger Jam

(About 6 cups)

2½ pounds rhubarb, trimmed, leaves removed
4 cups sugar
½ cup water
2 oranges
2 ounces fresh ginger, cut in fine julienne

Cut the rhubarb into small pieces, and place in a saucepan. Add the sugar and water. Grate the rind from the oranges and add to the rhubarb. Squeeze the oranges and add the juice to the rhubarb. Add the ginger. Simmer 30 minutes. Fill hot, sterilized jars and seal.

Green Goddess Dressing

(1½ cups)

1½ teaspoons minced fresh tarragon
1 tablespoon tarragon vinegar
1 clove garlic, minced
2 anchovy filets, minced
¼ cup finely minced parsley
2 scallions, minced
1 cup homemade mayonnaise
⅓ cup sour cream

In a mixing bowl soak the tarragon in the vinegar. Add the garlic and anchovy. Beat in the parsley and scallions. In another bowl stir together the mayonnaise and sour cream. Beat in the anchovy mixture. Serve this dressing over salad greens or raw vegetables.

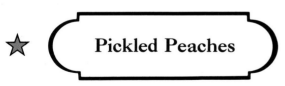

Pickled Peaches

(3–4 pints)

3 cups dark brown sugar
6 cinnamon sticks, broken into pieces
1 teaspoon mace
2 tablespoons whole cloves
1 tablespoon allspice
4 cups cider vinegar
5 pounds clingstone peaches, peeled

In a heavy saucepan bring the sugar, spices, and vinegar to a boil. Add the peeled peaches. Simmer gently, until they are tender, but not falling apart. Carefully pack the peaches in hot, sterilized jars. Reduce syrup by one quarter of its original volume and pour over the peaches. Run a table knife carefully through each jar to eliminate air bubbles. Seal.

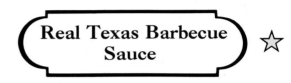

Real Texas Barbecue Sauce

(4 cups)

¼ cup Worcestershire sauce
½ cup chopped onions
1 cup butter, melted
¼ cup brown sugar
1 cup catsup
1 teaspoon dry mustard
2 teaspoons red pepper
1 tablespoon freshly ground black pepper
3 cloves garlic, finely chopped
2 teaspoons chili powder
1 cup oil
   Juice of 3 lemons
   Red pepper sauce to taste
2 teaspoons salt

In a saucepan combine all the ingredients. Bring to a boil, reduce heat, and simmer for 15 minutes.

Note: *This sauce will keep for several weeks in the refrigerator.*

Creole Vinaigrette

(1 cup)

3 tablespoons red wine vinegar
2 tablespoons flavored vinegar
   (tarragon, etc.)
1 tablespoon hot mustard
   Salt and freshly ground pepper
   Red pepper sauce to taste
½ cup oil
1 hard cooked egg, chopped
½ bunch scallions, thinly sliced
1 tablespoon pimiento or red pepper, minced
2 tablespoons chopped fresh basil

In a bowl beat together the vinegars, mustard, and salt, pepper, and red pepper sauce to taste. Beat in the oil. Stir in the egg, scallions, pimiento and basil. Cover and refrigerate for several hours to bring out the flavors.

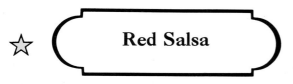

Red Salsa

(About 1½ cups)

4 tomatoes, peeled, seeded, and chopped
1 large onion, chopped
1 large red bell pepper, seeded and chopped
1 small red chili pepper, seeded and minced
   Salt and freshly ground pepper to taste
3 tablespoons vinegar

In a bowl stir together all the ingredients. Chill several hours.

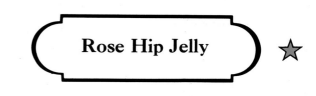

Rose Hip Jelly

(About 3 pints)

8 cups rose hips, very ripe
   Water to cover
1 cup sugar for each cup of juice

Wash the rose hips well. Split with a sharp knife and remove the pips and fibers. Place the prepared hips in a heavy kettle and cover with water. Boil gently until the fruit is very soft. Pour the juice and fruit into a jelly bag. Allow all the juice to drip into a container without squeezing the bag. Discard the fruit. Measure the juice. Make jelly using no more than 4 cups of juice at a time. Bring 4 cups juice to a boil. Add 4 cups sugar and boil gently until the juice "sheets" when poured from a spoon. (Dip a cold spoon into the hot juice. Pour out juice. If two drops run together in a sheet as they pour out, the jelly stage has been reached.) This could take 20 minutes or more. Pour into hot, sterilized jars or glasses and seal.

Notes: *Rose hips are the hips or fruit from either the* Rosa Canina *or* Rosa Rugosa. *They are a rich source of vitamin C. See the Resource Guide for information on ordering rose hips.*

Fried Apples

(6 servings)

3 large apples, washed and cored but
   not peeled
3 tablespoons butter
3 tablespoons sugar
¼ teaspoon cinnamon

Slice the apples into thin rounds. In a
large skillet melt the butter and arrange the
apple slices in one layer. Sprinkle with sugar
and cinnamon. Saute until golden. Turn once
and brown the other side. Serve very hot.

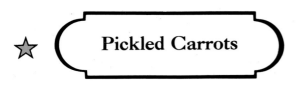

Pickled Carrots

(About 3 pints)

2 pounds carrots, cut in 1-inch pieces or 2
   pounds tiny carrots
1 tablespoon cinnamon
1 teaspoon whole cloves
1 teaspoon whole allspice
2 pounds sugar
2 cups vinegar
2 cups water
1 lemon, thinly sliced

Soak the carrots in a brine mixture to
cover of ¼ cup salt to 1 quart water for 6
hours. Drain off the brine. Cook the carrots
in clear water until tender. Drain. Tie the
spices in cheesecloth. In a large saucepan
bring the spice bag, sugar, vinegar, water,
and sliced lemon to a boil. Add the carrots
and boil until the carrots become just barely
transparent. Remove the spice bag. Fill hot,
sterilized jars and seal.

Green Tomato Pickle

(About 5 cups)

4 cups thinly sliced green tomatoes
2 onions, sliced
¼ cup salt
½ teaspoon black pepper
1 teaspoon dry mustard
¼ teaspoon whole cloves
½ teaspoon mustard seed
2 cups vinegar
1 cup sugar

In a bowl mix the tomatoes and onions
with the salt. Let stand overnight.
   Drain the vegetables. Tie the spices in a
bag and put the vegetables and spices in a
kettle with the vinegar and sugar. Bring to a
boil. Simmer slowly for 20 minutes. Skim.
Remove the spices. Pack the pickles into
hot, sterilized jars and seal.

Apple Butter

(About 6 cups)

6 cups sliced apples
6 cups apple cider
3 cups sugar
1 tablespoon cinnamon

In a saucepan simmer the apples in the cider until very soft. Place the mixture in a food processor and process just until smooth. Stir in the sugar and cinnamon. Spread in a flat enameled pan. Bake at 300° for 6 hours, stirring from time to time to prevent burning. Pour into sterilized jars and seal.

Horseradish Cream Sauce

1 cup sour cream
4 tablespoons freshly ground horseradish
Freshly ground white pepper

In a small bowl, mix together well all the ingredients.

Note: *This is the traditional accompaniment for Corned Beef or a Boiled Dinner.*

Plum Ketchup

(About 2 pints)

5 pounds fresh plums, halved and stones removed
½ cup sugar
½ cup water
1 teaspoon ginger
1 teaspoon cinnamon
1 teaspoon whole cloves
2 cups vinegar
1 teaspoon pepper
1 teaspoon mustard
2 teaspoons salt

In a large saucepan simmer the plums with the sugar and water until tender. Puree in a food grinder or food processor. Pour the puree into an enameled kettle, add the remaining ingredients and simmer until thick. Pour into hot, sterilized jars and seal.

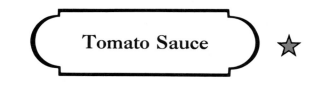

Tomato Sauce

(About 1½ cups)

3 tablespoons butter
1 bunch scallions, finely sliced
2 tablespoons chopped fresh parsley
2 cups canned Italian tomatoes, chopped

In a saucepan melt the butter and saute the scallions until transparent. Stir in the parsley and tomatoes. Simmer until slightly reduced.

☆ Hushpuppies

(8 servings)

   Fat for deep frying
2 cups white cornmeal
2 tablespoons baking powder
½ teaspoon salt
2 eggs, beaten
⅔ cup milk
1 onion, minced

Heat the oil for deep frying in a large pot or heavy skillet.

In a large bowl sift together the cornmeal, baking powder, and salt. In another bowl mix together the eggs and milk and stir into the dry ingredients. Add the minced onion and stir. Drop batter by teaspoonfuls into the hot fat and fry for 2 minutes.

Note: *If you are having the hushpuppies with fried fish, for better flavor fry them in the fat used for the fish.*

Green Salsa ☆

(About 1 cup)

1 small tomato, peeled, seeded, and chopped
6 green chilies, peeled, seeded, stemmed, and chopped
2 cloves garlic, minced
1 large onion, minced
   Salt to taste
2 tablespoons vinegar

In a bowl mash the tomato and mix with the remaining ingredients. Refrigerate for several hours.

Raspberry Vinegar Dressing for Asparagus ★

(½ cup)

4 tablespoons light safflower oil
4 tablespoons raspberry vinegar
1 teaspoon salt
1 tablespoon sugar
   Few grindings fresh white pepper
1 small clove garlic, peeled and minced
¼ teaspoon basil

In a cruet or a covered jar combine all the ingredients. Shake well. Let stand 1 hour before serving. Pour over asparagus.

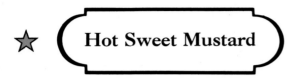

Hot Sweet Mustard

(About 1 cup)

¼ cup dry mustard
⅔ cup water
1¾ tablespoons cornstarch
½ teaspoon salt
¼ cup sugar
⅓ cup vinegar

In a small bowl mix the mustard well with half of the water. In the top of a double boiler combine the other ingredients. Bring to a boil and cook for 5 minutes. Cool and add mustard mixture. Beat well. Serve with cold meat or shellfish.

Easy Marchand de Vin Sauce

(About 1 cup)

4 tablespoons butter
¼ cup minced mushrooms
3 tablespoons finely chopped shallots
3 tablespoons finely chopped onion
3 cloves garlic, minced
3 tablespoons minced ham
1 tablespoon flour
   Salt and freshly ground pepper
1 cup reduced beef stock
½ cup hearty red wine

In a skillet melt the butter and "sweat" the vegetables and ham until the vegetables are transparent. Stir in the flour. Brown. Add salt and pepper to taste.

Stir in the stock and wine. Simmer until reduced by one third of its original volume. Strain before using.

Notes: *Use in preparing Eggs Hussarde. Can also be used for other hearty egg dishes.*

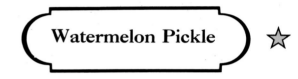

Watermelon Pickle

(7 pints)

6 cups watermelon rind
1 cup salt
6 cinnamon sticks, broken into pieces
1 teaspoon whole cloves
1 teaspoon whole allspice
3 cups sugar
2 cups cider vinegar
2 cups water
1 lemon, *very* thinly sliced

Cover the watermelon rind with water in which the 1 cup salt has been dissolved. Soak overnight.

Drain well and cut into bite-sized pieces. Simmer the rind in fresh water until just tender. Wrap the cinnamon, cloves, and allspice in cheesecloth. In a kettle combine the spice bag, sugar, vinegar, water, lemon and drained watermelon rind. Boil until the rind is clear. Remove the spice bag. Fill hot, sterilized jars and seal.

Pepper Relish

(Makes 3 pints)

6 green peppers, halved and seeded
6 red peppers, halved and seeded
6 large white onions
  Boiling water
1 cup sugar
2 tablespoons salt
2 cups cider vinegar

Finely chop the peppers and onions, place in a saucepan, and cover with boiling water. Drain after 30 minutes. In a kettle, bring the sugar, salt and vinegar to a boil. Add the peppers and onions. Simmer 15 minutes. Pack into hot, sterilized jars and seal.

Onion Sauce

(Makes about 4 cups)

½ pound (2 sticks) butter
3 cups thinly sliced onions
6 tablespoons flour
1 teaspoon salt
3 cups milk

In a heavy saucepan melt the butter and saute the onions until transparent. Stir in the flour and salt. Slowly add the milk and cook, stirring, until thick.

Note: *This sauce is traditionally served with Fried Herring.*

Green Tomato Pickle

(About 12 pints)

10 pounds green tomatoes, sliced
 4 pounds onions, peeled and sliced
 4 green peppers, seeded and chopped
 2 cups salt
 6 cups cider vinegar
 1 cup dark brown sugar
 6 cinnamon sticks, broken in two
 2 tablespoons mace
 1 teaspoon whole cloves
 1 teaspoon peppercorns

Layer the tomatoes, onions, green peppers, and salt in a large glass bowl. Let stand overnight.

Pour off the brine, pressing hard to get out as much as possible. Boil the tomatoes, onions, and pepper with the vinegar, sugar, and spices. Simmer 35 to 45 minutes. Ladle into hot, sterilized jars and seal. Allow to mellow for at least 2 weeks.

Note: *Some people like these sliced as thin as possible.*

Strawberry Sauce

(1 cup)

¼ pound (1 stick) butter, softened
1½ cups superfine granulated sugar
¼ cup brandy
1 cup crushed or pureed and strained
    strawberries

In a mixing bowl beat the butter, sugar, and brandy until smooth. Beat in the pureed berries. Cool to room temperature.

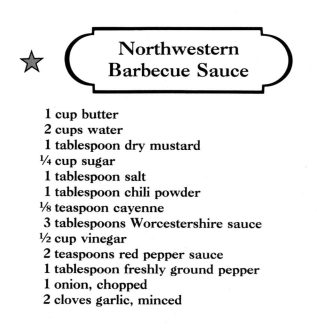

Northwestern Barbecue Sauce

1 cup butter
2 cups water
1 tablespoon dry mustard
¼ cup sugar
1 tablespoon salt
1 tablespoon chili powder
⅛ teaspoon cayenne
3 tablespoons Worcestershire sauce
½ cup vinegar
2 teaspoons red pepper sauce
1 tablespoon freshly ground pepper
1 onion, chopped
2 cloves garlic, minced

In a saucepan heat together all the ingredients and simmer for 30 to 45 minutes.

Note: *This sauce keeps well in the refrigerator. The quantity can be increased easily; simply multiply the amounts of ingredients.*

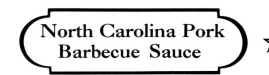

North Carolina Pork Barbecue Sauce

1½ quarts vinegar
    Red pepper pods, chopped

Season the vinegar with red pepper to taste.

Note: *Sufficient for a 65-pound pig cut in small pieces with a knife (not a food chopper).*

Green Mayonnaise

(1 cup)

1 cup homemade mayonnaise
3 tablespoons chopped parsley
1 tablespoon chopped chives
1 clove garlic, minced

In a bowl beat together all the ingredients. Refrigerate at least 2 hours.

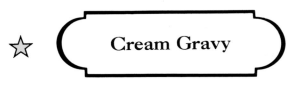

Cream Gravy

3 tablespoons pan drippings
3 tablespoons flour, seasoned with salt and
  pepper
  Salt and pepper
1 cup heavy cream

Pour off all cooking fat except 3 tablespoons. Add the 3 tablespoons seasoned flour and cook, stirring until the flour is lightly browned. Stir in the cream and simmer until thick. Check the seasonings before serving.

Note: *Cooks in some areas of the South and West like to add red pepper sauce to the gravy for zip. Cream Gravy is the traditional accompaniment to Chicken Fried Steak.*

Sauerkraut Relish

(4 cups)

1 pound sauerkraut, drained, rinsed, and
  chopped
½ green pepper, finely chopped
1 onion, thinly sliced
2 tablespoons finely chopped pimiento
⅓ cup finely chopped dill pickle
⅔ cup sugar
1 cup cider vinegar

In a bowl combine the sauerkraut with the green pepper, onion, pimiento and pickle. Stir in the sugar and vinegar. Toss well and refrigerate, tightly covered.

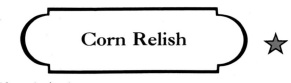

Corn Relish

(About 4 pints)

2 cups fresh corn
¼ head green cabbage, finely chopped
6 large green tomatoes, finely chopped
3 carrots, finely chopped
3 onions, finely chopped
1 cucumber, washed and finely chopped
1 green pepper, seeded and finely chopped
½ cup celery, finely chopped
4 cups malt vinegar or cider vinegar
1 cup sugar
¼ cup salt
½ teaspoon dry mustard
¼ teaspoon turmeric
⅛ teaspoon cayenne

In an enamel kettle combine the vegetables and 2 cups vinegar. In a bowl beat together the remaining vinegar, sugar, salt, and spices. Stir into the vegetables. Simmer 40 to 45 minutes. Pack into hot, sterilized jars and seal.

Note: *Vegetables can be chopped in a food processor. Chop each one separately. Be careful not to puree them.*

Resource Guide

If a recipe calls for an ingredient that is not readily available in a local market, these mail order businesses will be glad to help you. We suggest that you write or call before ordering to determine current prices.

ANDOUILLE Bourgeois Meat Market, 519 Schriever Highway, Thibodaux, Louisiana 70121 Tel. 504-447-7128

CRAYFISH Battistella Seafood, 910 Touro Street, New Orleans, Louisiana 70116 Tel. 504-949-2724

FILÉ POWDER Creole Delicacies, 533 St. Ann's Street, Box 5102, New Orleans, Louisiana 70116 Tel. 504-525-9508

FRESH HERBS Taylor's Herb Garden, 1535 Lone Oak Road, Vista, California 92083 Tel. 619-727-3485

FRESH MEAT AND POULTRY Pfaelzer Brothers, 4501 West District Blvd., Chicago, Illinois 60632 Tel. 312-927-7100

FRESH TROUT AND SALMON Wisconsin Fishing Company, P.O. Box 965, Green Bay, Wisconsin 54305 Tel. 414-437-3582

GRAPE LEAVES H. Roth and Sons, 1577 First Avenue, New York, New York 10028 Tel. 212-734-1110

HAUPIA (prepared mix) Noh Foods, P.O. Box 8392, Honolulu, Hawaii 96815 Tel. 808-946-6549

HERB PLANTS Le Jardin du Gourmet, West Danville, Vermont 05873 (no phone) Taylor's Herb Garden, 1525 Lone Oak Road Vista, California 92083 Tel. 619-727-3485

HISPANIC FOODS Casa Moneo, 210 West 14th Street, New York, New York, 10011 Tel. 212-929-1644 Casa Lucas Market, 2934 24th Street, San Francisco, California 94110 Tel. 415-826-4334

OLD BAY SEASONINGS Baltimore Spice Company, P.O. Box 5858, Baltimore, Maryland 21208 Tel. 301-363-1700

OLYMPIA OYSTERS	Latta's Oregon Delicacies, P.O. Box 1377 Newport, Oregon 97365 Tel. 503-265-7675
ORIENTAL FOODS	Katagiri & Co., Inc., 224 East 59th Street New York, New York 10022 Tel. 212-755-3566 Chico San, 1264 Humboldt Avenue, P.O. Box 1004 Chico, California 95927 Tel. 916-891-6271
PENNSYLVANIA DUTCH DELICACIES (Sweets and Sours, etc.)	Pennsylvania Dutch Company, P.O. Box 128, Mount Holly Springs, Pennsylvania 17065 Tel. 717-486-3496
QUAIL	Manchester Farms, P.O. Box 97, Dalzell, South Carolina 29040 Tel. 803-469-2588
ROSE HIPS	Aphrodisia Products, 282 Bleecker Street, New York, New York 10014 Tel. 212-989-6440
SMALL ARTICHOKES	Boggiato Packing Co., 11000 Blackie Road, Castroville, California 95012 Tel. 408-633-2486
SMITHFIELD HAM	Smithfield Packing Company, Smithfield, Virginai 23430 Tel. 804-357-4321
SNAPPER SOUP	Bookbinder's Foods, P.O. Box 472, Narberth, Pennsylvania 19072 Tel. 215-642-5152
TRUFFLES	Le Jardin du Gourmet, West Danville, Vermont 05873 (no phone) Maison Glass, 52 East 58th Street, New York, New York 10022 Tel. 212-755-3316

The following mail order resources offer many fine regional specialty foods and ingredients as well as kitchen equipment and accessories.

Epicure, 65 East Southwater, Chicago, Illinois 60611
Lekvar by the Barrel, 1577 First Avenue, New York, New York 10028
The Silo, Upland Road, New Milford, Connecticut 06776
Williams-Sonoma, P.O. Box 3792, San Francisco, California 94119

Many fine specialty and department stores now carry regional cooking equipment and accessories such as spattered tinware, earthenware, and woodenware, including the stores listed below.

Bloomingdale's, 1000 Third Avenue, New York, New York 10022 (and branches)
Frederick & Nelson, 5th and Pine Streets, Seattle, Washington 98101 (and branches)

Macy's, and The Cellar at Macy's, Herald Square, New York, New York 10018 (and branches)
Nieman-Marcus Co., Commerce and Ervay Streets, Dallas, Texas 75201 (and branches)
Zabar's, 2245 Broadway, New York, New York 10024

Many state and local organizations and fine purveyors have from time to time issued attractive and interesting regional cookbooks. The following are among the many excellent ones available.

Maryland Seafood Cookbooks, I, II, *and* III, available by mail at a cost of $3.95 per volume from the Office of Seafood Marketing, Maryland Department of Economic and Community Development, 45 Calvert Street, Annapolis, Maryland 21401.

Philadelphia Main-Line Classics, available by mail at a cost of $12.50 plus $1.50 for postage and handling from Philadelphia Main-Line Classics, Box 521, Wayne, Pennsylvania 19087.

Colorado Cache, available by mail at a cost of $12.95 plus $1.30 for postage and handling from Colorado Cache, 3372 South Broadway, Englewood, Colorado 80110.

The Best from New Mexico Kitchens and More of the Best from New Mexico Kitchens, available by mail at a cost of $6.95 each postage-inclusive from New Mexico Magazine, Bataan Memorial Building, Santa Fe, New Mexico 87503.

Delectable Dishes from Termite Hall, available by mail at a cost of $9.80 postage-inclusive from The Madaloni Press, 355 Saint Michael Street, Mobile, Alabama 36602.

Winston-Salem's Heritage of Hospitality, available by mail at a cost of $6.25 plus $1.50 for postage and handling from Winston-Salem's Heritage of Hospitality, P.O. Box 10176, Winston-Salem, North Carolina 27108.

San Francisco a la Carte, available by mail at a cost of $19.95 plus $2.50 for postage and handling (plus tax in California) from The Junior League of San Francisco, Inc., 2226 Fillmore Street, San Francisco, California 94115.

Fresh, Fast, & Fabulous Cookbook, available by mail at a cost of $8.95 plus $1.50 for postage and handling from the Psychoanalytic Association of Seattle, 4029 East Madison, Seattle, Washington 98112.

The Secrets of Creole Cooking, available by mail from B. F. Trappey's Sons, Inc., P.O. Drawer 400, New Iberia, Louisiana 70560.

America's Country Inn Cookbook, available by mail from The R. T. French Company, Consumer Services Kitchens, 1 Mustard Street, Rochester, New York 14692.

From the Land of Tabasco Sauce, available by mail from McIlhenny Company, Avery Island, Louisiana 70513.

$\mathcal{I}$ndex

Numerals in italic refer to illustrations

Regional Recipe Index

Numerals in italic refer to illustrations

Acknowledgments

Principal photography by Dan Barba.
Principal food styling by Lloyd Davis, caterer.
Food styling for photographs on pages 47, 63, and 67 by Susan Trilling/Seasons of my Heart, caterer. Food styling for photograph on page 39 by Pat Benton of Old Edwards Inn, Highlands, North Carolina; for photographs on pages 31 and 197 by Herb Wilson of Jack's Restaurant, New York City. Floral arrangements on pages 33, 37, 47, 55, 57, 63, 65, 73, 77, 157, and 215 by Diana McDermott; floral arrangement on page 39 by Lulie and Galax Cocke.

The following have granted permission to reprint photographs in this volume: Maryland Office of Seafood Marketing, frontispiece, pages 25, 29, 98, 139, 166; Hawaii Visitors Bureau, pages 9, 69; David Witbeck, pages 10, 19; Pfaelzer Brothers, pages 15, 53, 61, 71; Mississippi Farm Catfish Growers Association, page 35; Adam Carter, page 39; McIlhenny Company, Makers of Tabasco® brand products, page 45; Courtesy B.F. Trappey and Sons/Greg Greer, pages 49, 256; Glade Bilby II, page 51; the R.T. French Company, pages 59, 75.

The following have granted permission to reproduce their recipes in this volume: Maryland Office of Seafood Marketing, Statehouse Oyster Chowder, Spicy Crab Soup, Dijon Crab Salad, Spring Crab Salad, Crab and Wild Rice Salad, Bluefish Alfredo, Bluefish Rollups, Baked Bluefish, Trout Crepes; the R.T. French Company, whose food products were used in the preparation of the following recipes from their publication, *America's Country Inns*, Buffalo Stew from Sylvan Lake Resort, South Dakota, and Nevada Beans from the Hearst Six Ranch, Wyoming; Susan Trilling of Seasons of my Heart, New York City, Peacemaker, Flan, Bread Pudding and Whisky Sauce; Jack's Restaurant, New York City, Quail Salad with Nasturtium Flowers, Duck Breast with Steamed Vegetables, Gratinéed Oranges à la Monte Carlo; *New Mexico* magazine, Navajo Fry Bread, Green Chili Stew, Colachi, Posole Ortiz; Hawaii Visitors

Bureau, Kalua Pig, Chicken Luau, Laulau, Haupia; Commander's Palace of New Orleans, Oysters Marinières, Black Forest Escargot Soup, Garlic Bread, Trout in Leek Sauce, White Mousse with Raspberry Sauce; B. F. Trappey and Sons, Creole Sauce, Celery Sauce; Cindy Porchier Catering of Charleston, South Carolina, Squash Medley.

We wish to thank the following individuals for their help and cooperation: Mr. and Mrs. John N. Wall of Highlands, North Carolina, at whose home we photographed the Smoky Mountain Luncheon on page 39; Mrs. Angela Weldon of New York City, at whose home we photographed the Kentucky Derby Brunch on page 41; Ms. Terry Eargle of the Seventeenth Street Gallery in New York City, who provided us with the splendid quilt shown on page 67, which was made by Ruby Gray; Mr. Tom Wicker, for his invaluable help with the research for the North Carolina Barbecue, and for sharing some of his own family's traditional recipes; Ms. Claire Sobel of CGS International, for her help in locating their spattered tinware in New York City.

Thanks also to the following individuals for their valuable cooperation at various stages in this endeavor: Ms. Clare Vanderbeek of the Maryland Office of Seafood Marketing; Mr. Walter S. McIlhenny and Mr. Paul C.P. McIlhenny of the McIlhenny Company; Mr. Donald Davidson of the Marketing Corporation of America; Mr. Eugene Walter of the Madaloni Press; Ms. Scottie King, Managing Editor of *New Mexico* magazine; Mr. Jerry Panzo and Mr. Jim Kinat of the Hawaii Visitors Bureau; Mr. John Frazier of Peter A. Mayer Advertising, Inc., in New Orleans; Ann W. Sinatra of the Junior League of Philadelphia; Patricia J. Long of the Junior League of Denver; Vicki P. Hunt of the Junior League of Winston-Salem; Sue Koffel of the Junior League of San Francisco.

The staff of Media Projects would like to acknowledge the help, support, and cooperation of Joan Nagy, Ian Gonzalez, and Cheryl Asherman of William Morrow and Company. We wish also to convey our special thanks to Sonja and Richard Glassman of Blackbirch Graphics for their superlative contribution to this enterprise. And we would like to express our thanks to Frank Blume, Fran Harper, and the staff of Eastern Typesetting Company for fine work and extraordinary service.

I would like to thank Joan Nagy, Carter Smith, and Julie Colmore for their constant support and confidence in me. A special thank you to Ellen Coffey, whose indefatigable spirit has made *American Feasts* a reality. I would also like to thank my family, who continued to consume every recipe test and re-test with good humor and constructive comments.